THE FIRST INTERVIEW

THE FIRST INTERVIEW
A Guide for Clinicians

James Morrison, M.D.

THE GUILFORD PRESS
New York   London

To Dorothy Morrison, writer,
and to the memory of Carl Morrison, psychiatrist

©1993 **The Guilford Press**
A Division of Guilford Publications, Inc.
72 Spring Street, New York, NY 10012

Printed in the United States of America

This book is printed on acid-free paper.

Last digit is print number: 9 8 7 6 5 4 3 2 1

Library of Congress Cataloging-in-Publication Data

Morrison, James R., 1940–
    The First interview: a guide for clinicians / James Morrison.
      p. cm.
    Includes bibliographical references and index.
    ISBN 0-89862-992-6
    1. Interviewing in psychiatry—technique.   I. Title.
    [DNLM: 1. Interview, Psychological.   2. Mental Disorders—
diagnosis.   WM 141 M879f]
RC480.7.M67   1993
616.89'075—dc20
DNLM/DLC
for Library of Congress   92-48703
                                   CIP

Acknowledgments

Any book of this sort is really the work of more than one person. This book owes much to many—too many to name them all. But there are several people to whom I owe a special debt of gratitude.

For taking the time to read the manuscript in one or more of its various stages, thanks to Matt Blusewicz, PhD, Rebecca Dominy, LCSW, Nicholas Rosenlicht, MD, Mark Servis, MD, and Kathleen Toms, RN, MSEd, MSN. As always, Mary Morrison provided especially insightful and relevant comments at various stages of the preparation of this manuscript. I also want to thank my editor, Kitty Moore, for her sound, patient suggestions. Any factual errors or infelicities of expression that remain are my own responsibility.

James Morrison, MD
San Rafael, CA

Contents

Introduction: What Is Interviewing?

My first interviewing experience was no disaster, but I felt uncomfortable, just the same. The patient was a young woman with a thought disorder (who I later determined had early schizophrenia). Her speech was vague and she often wandered off the topic or made sexual references in a manner that I, in that more innocent era, had never before encountered. I wasn't sure what to talk about, and it seemed that I spent more time thinking about what I would ask next than I did considering what the previous answer meant. For some reason this patient seemed to like me, which was a good thing; I had to make three more trips to the ward that weekend just to get the entire history.

I now realize that my early experience was about par for the course. No one had told me that most novice interviewers have trouble thinking up questions to ask, that many feel acutely uncomfortable with their first few patients. I later wished that someone had pointed out to me what I now know: that mental health interviewing is usually easy and almost always quite a lot of fun.

It should be easy. After all, successful clinical interviewing is little more than helping people talk about themselves, which is something most people love to do. In the field of mental health we ask patients to reveal something of their emotions and their personal lives. With practice, you learn what to ask and how to direct the conversation so that you can obtain the information you need to help your patient best. Developing this ability is important: In a survey of practicing and teaching clinicians, comprehensive interviewing was ranked the highest of 32 skills needed by mental health practitioners.

If interviewing only involved getting patients to answer questions, clinicians could assign the task to computers and spend their time doing other things. But a good interviewer must know how to work with a range of different personalities and problems: to give free rein to the informative patient, to guide the rambling one, to encourage the silent one, and to mollify the hostile one. Nearly anyone can learn these skills. There is no single kind of interviewing personality; you can succeed with a variety of interviewing styles. Still, you will need guidance and practice to develop a style that works well for you.

Clinical interviews are used to accomplish a variety of goals, of course, and professionals from diverse fields have different agendas. But all interviewers—psychiatrists, psychologists, family practitioners, social workers, nurses, occupational therapists, physicians' assistants, pastoral counselors, and drug rehabilitation specialists—must first obtain basic information from each patient they see. The similarities in the sort of data they need far outweigh any differences that might be expected from their different kinds of training and perspectives.

Good interviewers share three features. They

1. obtain the greatest amount of accurate information relevant to diagnosis and management
2. in the shortest period of time
3. consistent with creating and maintaining a good working relationship with the patient.

Of these three components, (1) the data base and (3) rapport are crucial. If you ignored time constraints, you could provide good care, although you might have difficulty coping with more than a very few patients at one time.

Your first contact with any patient could be for a variety of reasons—a brief screening, an outpatient diagnostic intake, an emergency room visit, a hospital intake, or a consultation for medication or psychotherapy. A nurse clinician might need to develop a nursing treatment plan based on each of several initial behavioral diagnoses. Each of these is a specialized form of the basic, comprehensive initial interview. Whatever your interview goals, this book aims to present a complete outline of the information you should try to obtain for all patients and to recommend techniques that will help you during different stages of your interview.

The First Interview grew out of a manual written to help psychiatrists prepare for their oral board exams. While doing research for it, I was impressed by how much we have learned in recent years about the interview process. In my everyday evaluations of student mental health professionals, I have been equally impressed by how little this knowledge is being used in the training process. In short, much of what we know is being wasted.

The First Interview attempts to remedy this deficit. Addressed primarily to students, it emphasizes the basic material novice interviewers of all mental health disciplines will need to know. Because it incorporates most of the findings of numerous recent studies of interviewing, more practiced clinicians may also find it helpful for review.

THE NEED FOR COMPREHENSIVE INFORMATION

Clinicians can view a patient in an astonishing variety of ways. Indeed, all clinicians should be able to view each patient from biological, dynamic, social, and behavioral perspectives, because a single patient may need the treatment implied by any or even all of these theoretical perspectives. For example, the problems of a young married woman who drinks too much alcohol might be determined by a combination of these factors:

Dynamic. Her overbearing husband reminds her of her father, who also drinks.
Behavioral. She associates drinking with relief from the tensions induced by these two relationships.
Social. Several girlfriends drink; drinking is accepted, even encouraged, in her social milieu.
Medical. The genetic contribution from her alcoholic father needs to be considered.

A comprehensive evaluation brings out the contributions of each of these points of view. Each is folded into the treatment plan.

Throughout the book I emphasize the need to hold all perspectives when conducting a comprehensive interview. Unless you do a complete evaluation, you are likely to miss vital data. You might not learn, for example, that a patient who seeks help for a "problem of living" actually has an underlying psychosis, a depression, or substance abuse. Even if your patient turns out to have no actual mental disorder, you need to learn how past experiences contribute to the current problems. Only a complete interview can satisfactorily give you this information.

Needless to say, you will obtain much more additional information as treatment progresses. You may even find that you must revise certain of the opinions you formed during your first meeting. But you can plan rationally for management only if you first carefully elicit the relevant data during the initial interview.

Your skill as a mental health interviewer will hinge on several different points. How well can you elicit the entire story? Can you probe deeply enough to obtain all the relevant information? How quickly can you teach your patient to tell you accurate, pertinent facts? How adequately do you evaluate and respond to your patient's feelings? Can you, when necessary, stimulate your patient's motivation to reveal embarrassing experiences?

All of these skills are needed by anyone who must obtain mental health histories. The time to learn these skills is early in your training, before ineffective interviewing habits become a fixed part of your style. The benefits of early training should persist for a lifetime. They will probably also enhance your ability to obtain histories from other patients, even those without mental health problems.

Forty years ago two volumes set the tone for interviewing style: *The Initial Interview in Psychiatric Practice* by Gill, Newman, and Redlich, and *The Psychiatric Interview* by Harry Stack Sullivan. Although a number of other books on interviewing have appeared over the years, most have followed the models established by the two works cited. But taste and needs have changed over the decades, and such venerable works no longer adequately serve the mental health interviewer. Over the past two decades a number of research papers, most notably those by Cox and associates, have provided a scientific basis for modern interviewing practice. I have based much of this book on these sources. I have also consulted nearly every available relevant monograph and research article on interviewing published during the past 40 years. Citations for the more important of these are in the reference list in Appendix F.

In their monograph, Cannell and Kahn (1968) stated, "The people who write instructions and books for interviewers are not themselves given much to interviewing." At least in the case of *The Fisrt Interview,* that assertion is wrong. A significant part of what has gone into this volume comes from my own interviews over the years with more than 15,000 psychiatric patients. Thus, the interviewing method and style I recommend is an amalgam of research, the experience of others, and my own perception of what works.

I admit that the method I present here is somewhat formulaic, but it works well. Once you have learned the basics, you can adapt and expand this formula to create your own interviewing style.

IMPORTANCE OF PRACTICE

When I was in training, my professors often said that a student's best textbook is the patient. Nowhere is this more true than in learning to do a mental health interview. Indeed, no textbook can be more than a supplement—a guide to the real learning that comes through experience. I therefore urge you to practice early and often.

First, read quickly Chapters 1 through 5. Don't try to memorize this material; the amount may be daunting, but it is presented in sequence to help you learn it a bit at a time. (Appendix A provides a concise outline of the information you need and strategies you can use at each stage of the typical initial interview.) Then find a patient who will help you learn.

For the beginning interviewer, patients hospitalized in a mental health unit are an excellent resource. Many of them have been interviewed before (some are highly experienced in this regard), so they have a good idea of what you expect of them. Even in modern hospitals with many scheduled activities, they usually have time available. Many patients appreciate the chance to ventilate, and most enjoy the feeling that from their own difficulties some good can come — in this case, the training of a mental health professional. Sometimes an interview by a fresh observer, even a trainee, reveals new insights that can help redirect therapy.

So, enlist the aid of a cooperative patient and start to work. Don't worry about trying to find a "good teaching patient"; for your purposes, any cooperative patient will do. And all lives are inherently interesting. Don't try to follow an outline too closely, especially in the early going. Relax and try to help both yourself and the patient enjoy the experience.

After an hour or so — a longer session will be too tiring for both of you — break it off with the promise that later you'll come back for more. Return to *The First Interview* to read about any areas of interview management that gave you trouble.

Carefully compare the personal and social information you have obtained with the outline recommended in Chapter 8 (also outlined in Appendix A). Finally, how complete is your mental status exam? Compare your observations with the suggestions in Chapters 11 and 12.

A student might reasonably ask, How can I interview about mental disorders when I know so little? Doing a complete interview does imply knowing the symptoms, signs, and course typical of various mental disorders, but you can study these while you learn interview technique. In fact, learning about disorders from patients who have experienced them will fix these diagnoses in your mind forever. In Chapter 13 you will find listed the features that you should cover in your interview, broken down by the areas of clinical interest your patient presents.

Armed with a list of the questions you forgot to ask the first time through, return for another session with your patient. There is no better way to learn what to ask than by going back to correct your own omissions. The more patients you interview, the less you will forget.

When you have completed your interview, any of several standard textbooks (see Appendix F for an annotated list) can help you with the differential diagnosis of your patient's disorder. Abbreviated descriptions of the better-studied disorders are provided in Appendix B, which also lists diagnostic criteria in somewhat simplified form.

You will become skilled faster if you have feedback from an experienced interviewer. It could be direct, as when an instructor sits with you while you interview your patient. Numerous studies have demonstrated the effectiveness of videotape or audiotape recordings, which can be played back while you and your instructor discuss the facts you have omitted and the interview techniques you could have used to better effect. You will probably find that you can learn a lot just by listening in private to audiotapes of your own early interviews. In Appendix E is a score sheet to help you evaluate the content and process issues of your interviews.

1 Openings and Introductions

By the time you have completed an initial interview, you should have (1) obtained information from your patient and (2) established the basis for a good working relationship. The information includes various types of history (everything that bears on your patient's life and mental health problems) and a mental status examination, which is the evaluation of your patient's thinking and behavior.

In the course of this book, I will take you through each section of the history and mental status exam, in more or less the chronological order you would use when talking with your patient. In separate chapters I will discuss the content of the information you should expect to obtain and the interview techniques that are most appropriate to that content. Where it seems appropriate, I will also discuss issues of rapport.

TIME FACTORS

In the first few moments of an initial interview you will need to accomplish several tasks.

- You should indicate what the interview will be like—how much time it will take, what sort of questions you will ask, and the like.
- You should convey some idea about the sort of information you expect your patient (or other informant) to give you.
- You need to create a comfortable and secure environment that will allow your patient as much control as possible, under the circumstances.

Table 1 lists the basic material that should be covered by the time you complete your interview. To examine the average patient should

TABLE 1. Outline of the Initial Interview

Chief complaint
History of present illness
  Stressors
  Onset
  Symptoms
  Previous episodes
    Treatment
    Consequences
  Course
  Treatment so far
  Hospitalizations?
  Effects on patient, others
Personal and social
  Childhood and growing up
    Where born
    Number of siblings and
      position
    Reared by one or both
      parents
    Relationship with parents
    If adopted
      What circumstances?
      Extrafamilial?
  Health as child
  Problems with puberty
  Abuse (physical or sexual)
  Education
    Last grade completed
    Scholastic problems
    Overly active
    School refusal
    Behavior problems
    Suspension or explusion
  Sociable as child?
  Hobbies?
Life as an adult
  Current living situation
  Lives with whom?
  Where?
  Ever homeless?
  Support network
  Mobility
  Finances
  Marital
    Age
    Number of marriages
    Number, age, and sex
      of children
    Stepchildren?
    Marital problems?
  Sexual preference, adjustment
  Problems with intercourse
  Birth control methods
  Extramarital partners
  Physical, sexual abuse?
  Work history
    Current occupation
    Number of jobs
    Reason for job changes
    Ever fired?
  Leisure activities
    Clubs, organizations
    Interests, hobbies

Life as an adult (cont.)
  Military
    Branch, rank
    Years served
    Disciplinary problems?
    Combat?
  Legal problems ever?
    Criminal
    Litigation
  Religion
    Denomination
    Interest
Past medical history
  Major illnesses
    Operations
    Nonpsychiatric
      medications
    Allergies
      Environmental
      Food
      Medications
  Nonmental hospitalizations
  Physical impairments
  Risk factors for AIDS?
  Adult physical or sexual
    abuse?
Review of systems
  Disorders of appetite
  Head injury
  Seizures
  Chronic pain
  Unconsciousness
  Premenstrual syndrome
  Review for somatization
    disorder
Family history
  Describe relatives
  Mental disorder in relatives
Substance abuse
  Type of substance
  Duration of use
  Quantity
  Consequences
    Medical problems
    Loss of control
    Personal and interpersonal
    Job
    Legal
    Financial
  Abuse of medicines
    Prescriptions
    Over-the-counter
Personality traits
  Lifelong behavior patterns
  Violence
  Arrests
Suicide attempts
  Methods
  Consequences
  Drugs or alcohol associated
  Seriousness
    Psychological
    Physical

Mental status exam
  Appearance
    Apparent age
    Race
    Posture
    Nutrition
    Hygiene
    Hairstyle
    Clothing
      Neat?
      Clean?
      Fashion
  Behavior
    Activity level
    Tremors?
    Mannerisms and
      stereotypies
    Smiles?
    Eye contact
    Speaks with accent?
  Mood
    Type
    Lability
    Appropriateness
  Flow of thought
    Word associations
    Rate and rhythm of
      speech
  Content of thought
    Phobias
    Anxiety
    Obsessions and
      compulsions
    Thoughts of suicide
    Delusions
    Hallucinations
  Language
    Comprehension
    Fluency
    Naming
    Repetition
    Reading
    Writing
  Cognitive
    Orientation
      Person
      Place
      Time
    Memory
      Immediate
      Recent
      Remote
    Attention and con-
      centration
      Serial sevens
      Count backwards
    Cultural information
      Five presidents
    Abstract thinking
      Similarities
      Differences
    Insight and judgment

take an experienced clinician about an hour. A student will probably require several hours to obtain all the relevant information. Regardless of your level of experience, your emphasis should be on collecting the most information possible.

Even a seasoned interviewer may occasionally require more than one session for an initial evaluation. You will need more time for a patient who is unusually talkative, vague, hostile, suspicious, or hard to understand, or for one who has a complicated story to tell. Some patients simply cannot tolerate a lengthy interview; even those who are hospitalized may have other appointments to keep. There are also advantages to multiple interviews: The patient has time to reflect and to recall material that might have been initially forgotten. Of course, if you interview relatives or other informants, you will also need additional sessions, plus time to integrate the information from all of your sources.

Here are the approximate percentages of time you will probably devote to the various portions of an average initial interview:

15%: Chief complaint and free speech
30%: Pursue specific diagnoses; ask about suicide, history of violence, and substance abuse
15%: Medical history, review of systems, family history
25%: Personal and social history; evaluate character pathology
10%: Mental status evaluation
 5%: Discuss diagnosis and treatment with patient; plan next meeting

Depending on your professional needs, you may want to change the focus somewhat. For example, social workers may need to spend additional time on the personal and social history. (Some institutions and agencies assign social workers responsibility for obtaining the entire social history. Most authorities would hold that all aspects of the entire history should be gathered by at least one clinician, who can then synthesize this information into a coherent clinical picture.)

Regardless of your profession, I recommend that you try to get the whole story early in the relationship with your patient. After the first few sessions, even experienced clinicians sometimes assume that they know a patient well and ignore the fact that certain vital information may have escaped them.

Of course, no one has unlimited time, and no evaluation can ever be considered complete. As long as you continue to care for your patient, you will be adding new facts and observations to your original data base. But if you have done your job well, these will largely be matters of corroborative detail that won't substantially affect diagnosis or treatment.

Patients seek help for serious problems that may seem frightening, overwhelming, or even life-threatening to them. They should be encouraged to tell their stories in such a way that they feel they have received a complete, fair, professional evaluation. If your patient is unusually dramatic, slow, or discursive, try to understand this behavior in the light of the stresses and anxieties any mental patient faces, and allow additional time.

SETTINGS

If you have your own private office, you can decorate it as nicely as you choose, but institutional offices are often less than regal. Fortunately, the effectiveness of the interview is not related to the elegance of the surroundings. I have seen excellent interviews done at the bedside, or even in a corner of a busy hospital day room. What is paramount is your concern for the patient's comfort and privacy.

Make the best of what you have available. Sitting across a desk from the patient, as is traditional in so many offices, creates an inflexible barrier between the two of you. Try instead to arrange your chairs so you can face the patient across the corner of a desk or table. That way, you will be able to increase or decrease the distance between the two of you, as the need of the moment indicates. If you are right-handed, seat the patient to your left so you can more comfortably take notes.

Regardless of where you interview, your own appearance can affect the relationship you have with your patient. What is considered professional may depend somewhat upon the region of the country and the customs of the particular clinic or hospital where you work. This observation may seem obvious, but it bears repeating: You will be perceived as more professional if you pay attention to your dress, grooming, and manner.

In general, conservative clothing and hair styles are more readily accepted by most patients. Whereas teenagers and children may be significant exceptions, their parents may not. Limit your jewelry to something modest; don't antagonize someone whose cooperation you want with adornments that suggest wealth or status beyond what that person could hope to achieve.

However, excessively casual dress or manners may suggest nonchalance about the importance of your meeting. Observe how other professionals in your setting dress and behave. Let their examples guide your judgment as to what is appropriate.

BEGINNING THE RELATIONSHIP

Introduce yourself, offer to shake hands, and indicate the seating ar-
rangement you prefer. (At the bedside always sit down, even if you intend to stay with the patient for only a few minutes. Even if you have
a plane to catch, you don't want to appear too hurried to take time with
the patient.) If you happen to be late for the interview, acknowledge
it with an apology. Is your patient's name an uncommon one? Be sure
that you have pronounced it correctly. If this is the first time you have
met, explain your status (student? intern?) and the purpose of this interview. What do you hope to learn? What information do you have already? Give your patient an estimate of how much time you expect to
spend together.

Often you will already know something about the patient from case
notes of previous workers, from a hospital chart or from a physician's
referral note. To save time and increase the accuracy of your assessment, try to review this material before you begin. However, for the purposes of this book, we'll assume that you have no access to such information.

Although some interviewers try to ease into a relationship with
small talk, I recommend against it. In most cases your patient has come
for treatment because of troubling problems. Comments about the
weather or baseball may seem a distraction, or at worst an expression
of unconcern on your part. It is usually better to go right to the heart
of the matter.

Should you feel that you *must* start with small talk, ask a question
that demands more than a yes–no response. For example:

"How was the traffic coming here?"

"How have you been enjoying the summer months?"

If nothing else, such a question establishes your expectation of the patient's active participation. Especially during the early part of your interview, you want to encourage the patient to elaborate, not to answer
with "yes" and "no" while you do most of the work. (This and other
aspects of control of the interview will be considered further in Chapters 4 and 10.)

TAKING NOTES

In most cases you will want to take notes. Few of us can remember even
briefly all the material we hear, and you may not have the opportunity
to write up your interview right away. So point out that you will be taking notes, and make sure that this is all right with the patient.

Nonetheless, you should try to keep note-taking to a minimum. This will allow you to spend more time observing your patient's behavior and facial expressions for clues to feelings. You won't be able to get everything down on paper or to write complete sentences (other than the chief complaint, which we will discuss in the next chapter). Instead, jot down key words that can indicate which issues to explore later or serve as reminders when you write up your report. Try to keep your pen in hand; this avoids the distraction of repeatedly picking it up. The only time you should lay it aside is when you discuss especially sensitive topics that the patient might not care to have recorded.

Sometimes a patient asks that certain material be kept "off the record." When this request comes early in your relationship, it is usually better to comply, especially if it applies to a limited portion of the interview. If the patient seems extremely uncomfortable with any note-taking, you can explain that you will need some notes for later review to help make sense of it all. In the rare event that the patient insists, give in, put down your pen, and later transcribe all that you can remember. What you want most of all is to complete an informative interview, not to win a contest of wills.

Reviewing a tape recording of a session can help you spot difficulties in your interview style. You can often uncover deficiencies that you would have missed with a less complete record of your conversation. As an everyday practice, however, it has drawbacks: Reviewing a tape takes time, and patients are far more likely to feel uncomfortable with tape-recording than note-taking. If you do decide to tape-record, begin only after you have explained its educational purpose and obtained permission.

It may also be necessary to explain that state laws and professional ethics could require you to report certain information that has a bearing on the safety of others. This principle, formalized in 1974 by the Tarasoff decision in California, clearly states that health care personnel have a duty to protect identifiable persons against whom threats have been made. Although this decision has not been emulated in all states, clinicians everywhere are advised to behave as if it has been. Of course, as a student you should never take such action on your own; discuss at once any threats or other concerns you have with a supervisor, who should then take the lead in discharging the duty to protect.

SAMPLE OPENINGS

Effective openings have many possible variations. Here is one that works well.

INTERVIEWER: Good morning, Mr. Dean. I'm Ms. Watts, a third-year medical student. I'd like to talk with you for about an hour to learn as much as I can about people with problems like yours. Do you have the time to spend with me now?

PATIENT: Yes, that will be fine.

INTERVIEWER: Why don't you sit right here (*motions toward a chair*)? Do you mind if I take some notes?

PATIENT: No, everyone else seems to.

This opening works well because it quickly conveys information that is important to the patient: the interviewer's name and position, the purpose of the interview, and the time that will be required. The interviewer also manages the business of seating arrangements and obtaining permission for note-taking.

Here's another opening that works well:

PATIENT: Are you the student they told me about?

INTERVIEWER: No, I'm Dr. Holden, a psychology intern. I spoke with your therapist earlier this afternoon, and I'd like to spend some time with you to see what we can do to help you out. We can use this little room.

PATIENT: (*Nods*)

INTERVIEWER: To help you best, I'm going to need all the information I can get. I'd like to jot down a few notes, if that's all right with you.

PATIENT: No problem.

SUMMING UP

The first moments any professional person spends with a new patient set the stage for all subsequent interactions. Careful consideration of such simple matters as introductions and the patient's comfort and sense of control helps establish a relationship well grounded in respect and cooperation.

2 Chief Complaint and Free Speech

The words you use to open your interview can greatly affect your subsequent interactions. There are two general styles, and they mirror the two principal overall styles of interviewing: directive and nondirective.

DIRECTIVE VERSUS NONDIRECTIVE INTERVIEWS

By asking many specific questions, a directive interviewer explicitly provides the structure that tells the patient what sort of information is wanted. The nondirective interviewer more passively absorbs whatever information the patient chooses to present. A nondirective style usually yields better rapport and facts that are more reliable. An exclusively nondirective style also produces less information, however, for example, the patient doesn't realize that family history is important or feels too embarrassed to volunteer highly personal information. To be maximally effective, your initial interview should use both nondirective and directive questions.

Most of the early portion should be nondirective. This helps you establish rapport and learn what sort of problems and feelings are uppermost in your patient's mind. But your opening request for information should clearly state what you expect of your patient.

THE OPENING QUESTION

When you ask your first question, be specific. Let your patient know exactly what you want to hear about. If, like some nondirective interviewers, you leave matters completely up to the patient ("What would you like to talk about?"), you could end up with quite a lot of information about last Sunday's football game. Eventually you would get the interview back on track, but at the cost of time and perhaps rapport from a patient who might wonder whether you knew what you really wanted.

You can avoid these difficulties by asking the right sort of question in the first place:

"Please tell me what problems made you come for treatment."

Notice that this request has two qualities that affect the type of information you will obtain:

- It tells the patient just what sort of information you seek.
- It is also open-ended. Open-ended inquiries are questions or statements that cannot readily be answered in a word or two. Because they invite patients to talk for a while about what seems important to them, they promote a relaxed interview style early in the interview that helps build rapport.

Open-ended questions and statements can serve two functions. Some simply request more information about a point:

"I'd like to hear some more about that."

"Could you expand on that?"

"What else happened?"

Others also move the story along toward the present:

"What happened after that?"

"What did you do next?"

Open-ended requests broaden the scope of information that you might obtain; with more freedom to respond, patients tell you what is important to them. They let patients know that their stories are important to you. They also allow you to spend less time talking and more time observing. The importance of this will become more evident in Chapter 11 on the mental status examination.

Closed-ended questions direct the sort of answer desired and can be answered in a few words. They can be "yes or no" or limited-choice questions ("Where were you born?" as opposed to "Tell me about your childhood"). They, too, are useful; they are sometimes necessary to obtain the most information in the least time. But in early parts of the interview, use open-ended questions that will encourage your patient to tell a story that touches on as many aspects of the case history as are relevant.

THE CHIEF COMPLAINT

The chief complaint is the patient's stated reason for seeking help. It is usually the first full sentence or two of reply to your opening question,

"Tell me about the problem that brought you here."

Importance

The chief complaint is important for either of two reasons.

1. Because it is usually the problem uppermost in the patient's mind, it tells you what area you should explore first. Most patients have some sort of a specific problem or request. Here are some samples:

"I can't reach my goals."
"I have trouble forming relationships with women."
"I hear voices."
"I'm so depressed I feel that I can't go on."

Each of these typical examples expresses some discomfort, life problem, or fear that the patient wants help with.

2. By contrast, sometimes the chief complaint is a flat denial that anything is wrong. When this is the case, it tips you off about your patient's insight, intelligence, or cooperation. For example,

"There's nothing wrong with me. I'm only here because the judge ordered it."
"I don't remember anything about it."
"Absolute zero is coming, and when it gets here my brain is going to turn to bread."

Chief complaints like these three indicate serious pathology or resistance that requires special handling. Chapter 16 discusses patients who resist efforts at being interviewed.

Responding

Some chief complaints suggest that your patient doesn't quite understand the purpose of the interview. You will sometimes encounter this sort of vague or slightly quarrelsome chief complaint, so you should be prepared with some good responses.

INTERVIEWER: Why did you come here for treatment?

PATIENT: You can read all about it in my record.

INTERVIEWER: I could, but it would help me learn more about you if you'd tell me in your own words.

Here's how one interviewer reacted to a patient who, instead of a complaint, gave a prescription:

PATIENT: I think I just need some vitamins.

INTERVIEWER: Perhaps, but let's decide that after you tell me what's been bothering you.

Another patient made a plea for help in getting started:

PATIENT: I really don't know where to begin.

INTERVIEWER: Why don't you start with when your most recent trouble began?

Try to Learn the Real Reason for Coming

What patients first say doesn't always express their real reasons for seeking help. Some patients don't recognize the real reason; others may feel ashamed or fearful of what they'll be told. In either case, the stated chief complaint may be only a "ticket of admission" to the help a mental health professional can provide:

"I've been in such pain." (But the real pain is emotional.)

"I feel anxious nearly every moment I'm awake." (Heavy drinking isn't mentioned.)

"I'd like to discuss some of my relationships." (The patient is afraid to discuss AIDS.)

"I want some advice about my mother — I wonder if she's becoming senile." (The patient really wonders, "Am I going crazy?")

Each of these superficial complaints masks a deeper, less obvious reason for seeking help. Often you can ferret out the real problem later in the interview by asking:

"Is anything else bothering you?"

Sometimes you will be able to determine your patient's underlying motivation only after you have completed your initial evaluation.

Regardless of what chief complaint is presented, you should write it down in your patient's exact words. Later, you will want to contrast it with what *you* believe prompted the patient to seek help.

FREE SPEECH

During the few minutes following the chief complaint, your patient should have the chance to discuss freely the reasons for seeking treatment. To encourage the widest possible range of information, the story should be allowed to emerge with little detailed probing or other interruption from you. We may call this nondirected flow of information "free speech" to distinguish it from the relatively constrained question–answer format of the later clinical interview.

What Is Free Speech?

Experienced interviewers recommend this period (as much as 8 or 10 minutes in an hour-long session) of free speech for several reasons. Some of them are the reasons for asking any open-ended question:

- Free speech establishes you as someone who cares enough to listen to your patient's concerns.
- It provides the patient an opportunity to organize and explore the reasons for seeking treatment.
- You have the opportunity to learn what is uppermost in your patient's mind.
- It gives you the flavor of the patient's personality.
- Unhampered by any need to direct the conversation, you can start making observations about mood, behavior, and thought processes.
- Character traits may be more likely to emerge in a person who is speaking spontaneously than in one who is answering a stream of questions.
- When you share control during this portion of the conversation, you establish early the expectation that your patient will be an active partner throughout therapy.
- You can devote close attention to the content of your patient's speech. One study showed that as much as half the total symptoms reported by patients are mentioned in the first 3 minutes of an initial interview.
- It provides your patient an opportunity to bring up other concerns that weren't mentioned in the chief complaint.

Most patients will respond quickly and appropriately to your request that they talk about their problems. Getting them to tell you all you need to know will take little redirection on your part. Some have had so much experience telling their stories that they give you complete, chronological accounts of their illnesses.

The opposite may be true of others. They have experienced too many interviewers who want only specific answers to closed-ended questions. You may have to teach these patients to give you an expanded version of their feelings and experiences. If your patient persistently makes brief statements, then waits for more questions from you, you should explicitly state what you expect. For example:

"What I'd really like is for you to tell me in your own words about your problem. Later on I'll ask some specific questions that you can answer briefly."

In fact, few histories unfold like a textbook account of a classical mental health problem. Patients have their own ideas about what is important, and, regardless of the apparent value of their information, it is important that you let them make a stab at telling their stories. An occasional patient who is mentally retarded or severely psychotic might not be able to give you a satisfactory narration. Then you might have to fall back on a much more structured, question-and-answer strategy to obtain any history. But these will be uncommon, and every patient who speaks at all will at least give you information in the form of the mental status observations you can make.

AREAS OF CLINICAL INTEREST

During free speech your patient will probably mention one or more problems. These concerns can be emotional, physical, or social; most will fall into one of several major areas of clinical interest. When people become mental health patients, it is usually because of problems covered by these seven areas:

Difficulty thinking (cognitive disorders)
Substance use
Psychosis
Mood disturbance (depression or mania)
Anxiety, avoidance behavior, and arousal
Physical complaints
Social and personality problems

Each area of clinical interest comprises a number of diagnoses that have symptoms in common. Later, when you obtain the history of the present illness, you will systematically ask about the symptoms usually associated with whichever of these areas you have identified. This information will allow you to determine which of the associated diagnoses seems appropriate for your patient. But for now, during free speech, just make a note (mentally or on paper) about any subject that seems worth exploring later.

Signaling Areas of Clinical Interest

A number of symptoms and items of historical information specific to each area of clinical interest signal the need for further exploration. When you encounter one in your interview, consider an intensive review of that area (discussed in Chapter 13). These "red flag" symptoms are summarized in Table 2.

TABLE 2. Problems That Signal Areas of Clinical Interest

Difficulty thinking (cognitive
disorders)
Affect fluctuates
Bizarre behavior
Confusion
Decreased judgment
Delusions
Hallucinations
Memory defects
Toxin ingestion
Substance use
Alcohol use heavier than one or
two drinks per day
Arrests or other legal problems
Financial: spends money needed
for other items
Health: blackouts, cirrhosis,
abdominal pain, vomiting
Illegal substance use
Job loss, tardiness, demotions
Memory impairment
Social problems: fights, loss
of friends
Psychosis
Affect that is flat or inappropriate
Bizarre behavior
Confusion
Delusions
Fantasies or illogical ideas
Hallucinations (of any of the senses)
Insight or judgment that is disturbed
Muteness
Perceptual distortions (illusions,
misinterpretations)
Social withdrawal
Speech that is hard to follow
or incoherent
Mood disturbance: depression
Abuse of drugs or alcohol
Activity level that is either markedly
increased or decreased
Anxiety symptoms
Appetite changes
Concentration poor
Death wishes
Depressed mood
Feelings of worthlessness
Interest decreased for usual
activities (including sex)
Sleeplessness or excessive sleepiness
Suicidal ideas
Tearfulness
Weight loss or gain

Mood disturbance: mania
Activity level increased
Distractibility
Grandiose sense of self-worth
Judgment deteriorates
Mood that is euphoric or irritable
Plans many activities
Sleep decreased (reduced need
for sleep)
Speech rapid, loud, hard to interrupt
Substance abuse recently increased
Thoughts move rapidly from one idea
to another
Anxiety disorders
Anxiety
Chest pain
Compulsive behavior
Dizziness
Fear of going crazy
Fear of dying or impending doom
Fears of objects or situations
Heaviness in the chest
Irregular heart beat
Nervousness
Obsessional ideas
Palpitations
Panic
Shortness of breath
Sweating
Trauma: history of severe emotional
or physical
Trembling
Worries
Physical complaints
Appetite disturbance
Convulsions
Depression, chronic
Headache
History that is complicated
Multiple complaints
Neurological complaints
Sexual or physical abuse during
childhood
Substance abuse in a woman
Treatment failure
Vague history
Weakness
Weight changes (up or down)
Social and personality problems
Anxiety
Behaviors that seem odd or bizarre
Dramatic presentation
Drug or alcohol abuse
Job problems
Legal difficulties
Marital conflicts

20

HOW MUCH TIME?

Unless your patient's speech is unusually vague or rambling, the chief complaint usually takes only a few seconds. However, the time you devote to free speech can vary tremendously. In the rare event that your patient is incoherent or nearly mute, you might decide after a few moments to adopt a more directive interview style. But if your patient is well-organized, experienced, and motivated to tell all, you could conceivably spend the entire interview in free speech, listening to a history that is presented just the way you would read it in a textbook.

Most patients will be neither of the above. On average you can probably listen without much interruption for the first 5 or 10 minutes. But don't try to stick to this recommendation too strictly—what you allot to free speech will depend on the total time you can spend interviewing and on what you already know about the history. As a rule, you should allow your patient to speak freely as long as the information you obtain seems important and relevant.

MOVING ON

The free speech portion will draw to a close as you sense that you have obtained a broad outline of the problems that are uppermost in your patient's mind. Before proceeding to the next section of your interview, you should ask whether there are problems other than those already mentioned. This decreases the risk that you will overlook vital problem areas. (Even if you missed something big, it would probably show up later. Yet the whole point of the initial interview is to try to get *all* relevant information up front.)

This is also a good time to check on your understanding of all problems. Briefly summarize each, and invite your patient's assessment of your analysis.

INTERVIEWER: Let's see if I have this right. You felt just fine until about 2 weeks ago when you proposed to your girlfriend, and she accepted you. Since then you've had increasing attacks of anxiety, you've felt depressed, and you can't concentrate on your studies. Now you're afraid you might have heart disease because your pulse races. Is that about right?

PATIENT: That's pretty much it.

INTERVIEWER: I want to learn more about that, but first, is there anything else that's been bothering you?

SUMMING UP

The chief complaint elicits the patient's stated reason for seeking treatment. Free speech, which immediately follows, encourages the patient to talk about all the reasons for seeking treatment. Throughout this early portion of the initial interview the clinician should use a nondirective interview style to develop rapport and encourage the expression of reliable diagnostic information.

3 Developing Rapport

A few minutes into your initial interview session, your patient should be relaxed and giving you the information you need. This will be the case for most patient interviews. If this does not describe yours, you should spend some time with Chapters 16 and 17, which deal with problem behaviors.

Rapport is the feeling of harmony and confidence that should exist between patient and clinician. As one of the goals of a good interview, good rapport has practical consequences. This is most obvious when you will be responsible for future treatment of the patient. The trust and confidence you begin to develop even in the first session or two can greatly enhance your ability to manage a course of therapy. In fact, how well you convey your interest is the factor most likely to keep your patient in treatment.

But rapport is also a principal method for obtaining good information. Even during the evaluation phase of your relationship, a positive rapport will help motivate your patient to talk spontaneously and to reveal important personal data.

The foundation for rapport is usually ready-made. Most patients come looking for help and expect that they will get it from you, the clinician. You can build on this expectation by your actions and words. Although it is possible that you could say something that might be upsetting, there is little you are likely to say or do that cannot be retrieved if you remain caring and sensitive to what your patient is experiencing.

ESTABLISHING RAPPORT

Right from the start, most patients expect to like their mental health professional. But real rapport between two individuals doesn't usually spring up over night. It develops gradually, with long acquaintance. Still, you can use certain behaviors to speed its development.

Your demeanor is key. Remember that professionalism doesn't demand stiff formality. In fact, you should take care to avoid the image of the stone-faced therapist that has been popularized in the movies and in fiction. If you appear relaxed, interested, and sympathetic, your patient is more likely to feel safe and comfortable. Carefully monitor your facial expression: Don't frown, grimace, or show other signs that might be interpreted as disapproval. Avoid fixed stares, which make you appear cold and critical. Make eye contact frequently, even if you are taking notes. Smiles and nods, when appropriate to the content of the discussion, will make it clear that you are attentive and sympathetic. (Be judicious in your use of praise this early in your relationship. Used as a reinforcer, praise can powerfully shape behavior. But early in your relationship you don't know enough to be sure what behavior you will be reinforcing. For example, you wouldn't want to praise apparent openness if your patient hasn't told you the whole truth.)

The patient's own demeanor will probably shape your interaction more than any other factor. Body language — drooping shoulders, a clenched fist, tears — provide one sort of obvious indicator of how your patient feels. Observe tone of voice for other clues to feelings. Suppose you have asked your patient, Mr. Kimble, how he and his wife get along and he responds, "Just fine." If his tone is warm and light, the couple probably has relatively few interpersonal problems. If his "Just fine" is delivered between clenched teeth, in a dull monotone or with a sigh, Mr. Kimble may harbor feelings of hopelessness or anger that he can't put into words just yet.

If your patient is depressed, you will probably feel like drawing a little closer to show your concern. You can follow that natural inclination. If you sense hostility, you may feel like withdrawing physically, even if only a few inches. Doing so will help relax the tension by giving both of you more elbow room. Similarly, you may laugh when your patient makes a joke and show concern and support during a panic attack. If you have arranged the furniture so you don't have a desk or table between you, you can easily and naturally adjust even to minor shifts in your patient's affect. By the time you have interviewed your first dozen patients you will do these things automatically in response to the clues each patient unconsciously gives.

At the same time you should carefully maintain a certain neutrality to what you are told. If your patient criticizes relatives, you would, of course, be unlikely to defend them. But joining in the criticism risks offending someone whose feelings are really ambivalent. A safe response is an empathic comment that doesn't take sides.

PATIENT: My mother is a real bitch! She keeps trying to interfere between me and my husband.

INTERVIEWER *(leans slightly forward):* That must be a real problem for you.

This interviewer's attitude—sympathetic, nonjudgmental, and respectful of patient and relatives alike—is likely to foster a good working relationship.

ASSESS YOUR OWN FEELINGS

How you feel about the patient can have important consequences. If your feelings are positive—here is the sort of person you would choose as a friend, for example—you will probably come across as warm and caring. Your attitude may serve as an encouragement to reveal additional sensitive information.

Heavily influenced by your own background and upbringing, your feelings could in turn affect your ability to obtain an accurate picture of the patient. Throughout the interview you need to be aware of the nature and the sources of your feelings, especially when something about the patient distresses you. It could be a problem with personal hygiene or of using coarse language or expressing ethnic prejudice. You must carefully monitor how you respond to this sort of patient. If you frown or otherwise appear uncomfortable, your patient may sense your disapproval and frustrate your efforts to gather accurate information.

Your goal is to show *empathy,* which means that on some level you can feel as your patient feels, that you can put yourself in the patient's place. You will probably convey your empathic feelings best if you keep in mind this thought: "What would it be like to be this patient talking with me now?"

Throughout your professional life you will have to work with all sorts of people. Some of them will seem less agreeable than others, but you will find that there is something in nearly every patient to which you can relate. If you cannot respond positively to the content of what you are being told, perhaps you can sympathize with some of the feelings behind it. For example, a moderately antisocial patient was speaking about his former therapist:

PATIENT: I had no use for that guy. Once or twice I even thought about blowing him away!

INTERVIEWER: Sounds as if you were feeling really angry.

Trying to deal directly with the content of this patient's comment would force the interviewer to choose whether to agree with or to confront a potentially violent patient. By keying into the patient's anger, this interviewer said something that both parties could feel comfortable with.

Every professional person has personal problems; we must all be constantly alert to prevent them from impairing our effectiveness with patients. Consider the effect of so ordinary an event as a clinician's divorce:

> One such clinician found that she was so upset during the time she was separating from her husband that she could not effectively manage a patient who was having similar problems.
>
> Another clinician, after a bruising telephone call from his ex-wife, decided to postpone his next interview while he cooled off enough to focus on the patient's problems.

Your own temperament and experience will determine how you deal with your personal Achilles' heel. Whatever it is, your effectiveness with patients will increase if you remain aware of your own limitations.

YOUR MANNER OF SPEAKING

To establish rapport, you must let the patient know that you understand. It is tempting to approach this directly by saying, "I know how you must feel about. . . ." Unhappily, this statement has a hollow ring to it. By the time they reach your office, most patients have heard it all too often from people who don't really understand, or who may understand quite well but do nothing to help. Some patients with severe problems, real or perceived, feel that nobody could possibly appreciate what they are going through. You will probably be better off using some other response to suggest your compassion and interest:

"You must have felt terribly upset."

"I've never been in that position before, so I can only imagine how you felt."

"That was a terrible experience. I can see that it upset you a great deal."

Sometimes you may find that you need to overemphasize your feelings a little. This suggestion might sound deceitful, but it isn't meant that way. Actors, for example, know that their recorded voices tend to flatten out and that they must overact to get across the feelings they intend to portray. In similar fashion you may need to amplify your own emotional output to impress upon some patients how deeply you sympathize with them. You can accomplish this with your facial expressions or with your voice by varying its volume, pitch, and emphasis. Even brief exclamations can do the job. An "oh, wow!" that is suitably timed and intoned may convey understanding and compassion more effectively than a more elegant speech of condolence. This reassurance of your emotional involvement can be vital to your patient.

Consider the use of humor in your interactions with patients. Humor can be a great facilitator of communication: It helps people to relax and feel that they are among friends. But all clinicians must take care to judge their use of humor carefully, even with patients they know well. With any recent acquaintance it is easy to misjudge and say something in jest that can be taken amiss; mental health patients are especially vulnerable to this sort of slip. (As always, put yourself in the patient's place: Consider how you might feel if you thought that your clinician was laughing at you.)

In general, it is safe to laugh with, but never at, the patient. During your first few sessions, any use of humor should be gentle, and only when it is clear that the patient is in a frame of mind to appreciate it. Beware of making jokes (they might be misinterpreted as hostile or demeaning). Whenever the patient jests, be sure to evaluate whether or not this is a subconscious attempt to sidetrack both of you from a discussion of important material.

Experienced interviewers sometimes find that their personalities seem almost to change as they move from one patient to the next. They might settle into a folksy persona with one patient and adopt a more formal manner with another. One interviewer persistently, and quite unconsciously, dropped his *g*'s when talking with a patient from a rural background who spoke that way. Within limits these behaviors are probably acceptable, although you should be careful not to overdo it to the point of mimicry.

TALK THE PATIENT'S LANGUAGE

Take pains to speak in terms your patient can understand. Your poorly educated patient may understand "polite" terms for sexual or excretory functions, but the relationship you develop might be better if you use plain language. Listen to your patient's language and use it, as long as you feel comfortable doing so. Because teenagers and young adults often distrust older people, they may respond more positively if you use language that is current for their generation. But be sure that your "cool" expression is still "in," or you risk being considered merely "square." (There is another point of view on this issue. Some adolescent patients may resent it enormously if you try to adopt their speech patterns; they become even more distrustful.) How you speak to any patient should be guided by the need for clarity and rapport, so monitor your patient's reactions and adjust your manner of speaking accordingly.

Certain terms may serve as red flags for many patients. These loaded words carry a message of illness, failure, or poor character, and you should generally avoid them. Here is a brief sample: abortion, bad, brain damage, cancer, crazy, defective, fantasy, frigidity, hysterical, impotence, neurotic, obscene, perversion. You will encounter many more during your interviewing career. Be ready with neutral synonyms for such words, or, better, pick up on terms your patient already has used.

Avoid psychological jargon. Even simple terms like *psychosis* may be misunderstood, and your patient could think that you seem insensitive towards someone who has less education than you do. Yet be sure that you understand your patient's own use of language; don't assume it is the same as yours. For example, to you "an occasional drink" may mean once a month, but to your patient it could mean "intermittently throughout the day." What does your teenaged patient mean by *coke*—does he drink it or snort it? In the language of the street, "I was really paranoid" doesn't mean that the speaker felt psychotically persecuted, but merely frightened.

If your patient is foreign-born or was reared in another part of your own country, you may have trouble understanding one another. Don't let your manner imply that it is the patient who "talks funny." Rather, acknowledge that you have different accents and that at times you may have to ask one another for repetition.

MAINTAINING BOUNDARIES

How clinicians should relate to their patients has been a moving target in recent years. The traditional image of an authoritarian lawgiver who decides *for* the patient has in many quarters been supplanted by that of a less formal collaborator who explores problems and their solutions *with* the patient. I strongly prefer the latter style. To me it feels more comfortable (it is less arrogant), and it encourages patients to participate in treatment decisions. This style in effect puts two minds to work, rather than loading all the responsibility on the clinician. When patients discuss and contribute to their own management plans, they are more likely to comply with treatment and less likely to complain if the course of improvement is bumpy.

Yet even clinicians who encourage friendly collaboration need to maintain boundaries. Especially in California, where I practice, it has become a custom to call patients by their first names. For adolescents this is fine. But even old men and women find themselves addressed in this overly familiar manner by mental health professionals young enough to be their grandchildren. I feel uncomfortable with this practice. It further tends to infantilize patients, who, if they are hospital inpatients, have already lost considerable autonomy. It also increases the professional's tendency to become parentalistic, that is, to make health care decisions that patients should be making for themselves.

Instead of using first names, I recommend that in most cases you call patients by last name and title (Miss, Ms., Mrs., Mr. Green). This practice maximizes personal dignity and reinforces a sense of adulthood, even at a time when there may be loss of autonomy. It also encourages patients to keep a certain distance from the caregiver. This distance is sometimes useful in staving off inappropriate attempts at amorous and other nonprofessional relationships.

Some patients will appear offended if you don't agree to use their first names. You can respond that it is your habit always to use last names and titles, and that it would be hard to change. If you are still a student, your excuse might be that this is what your institution requires of trainees, if this is the case. Rarely I have encountered patients who doggedly insist that I use their first names. If I judge that sticking to my "habit" will result in harm to our relationship, I will use *two* names *plus* title. For example, when calling such a patient from the waiting room, I will announce, "Mrs. Joanne Cremier," and say it with a big, friendly smile. So far, this compromise has always proven satisfactory.

In general, it is a good idea not to reveal too much about yourself to your patients. This is especially true during the initial interview, when you really don't know one another very well.

A beginning psychiatry resident confided to his new patient that he was a reserve peace officer. He learned to his chagrin that the patient had both a severe personality disorder and an abiding hatred of the police.

If you are having difficulty getting information from a patient, you might be able to encourage greater cooperation by identifying something that the two of you share. For example, you might remark that, just like the patient, you enjoy sailboating or were born in Indiana. Your status as fellow sailors or Hoosiers might nudge you a bit closer to the rapport you seek. This technique should be used sparingly, seldom more than once with a given patient, lest you begin to sound too familiar. You should also be careful not to let any resulting small talk distract you for long from the real purpose of your interview.

When a patient asks a personal question, try first to understand what prompted the request. Some questions stem from simple curiosity; others may cloak concern about your training or ability to help. To provide reassurance about training and competence is one reason that clinicians in practice display a wall full of diplomas, licenses, and other certificates. Trainees often have the benefit of neither wall nor certificate. Still, to whatever degree possible you should verbally provide this information when it is requested. Don't hesitate to invoke the names and positions of your supervisors if this is needed to reassure an especially anxious patient.

Some requests for personal information may be prompted by a largely unconscious desire to achieve a sense of equality between interviewer and patient; others may be an attempt to avoid discussing sensitive material. Such requests should be handled firmly, but with tact:

PATIENT: How old are you, anyway?

INTERVIEWER: Why do you want to know?

PATIENT: You seem so young to be doing this kind of work.

INTERVIEWER: Well, thank you for the compliment, but I don't think my age is especially relevant to our discussion. Now, to get back to the question I asked. . . .

In some circumstances personal information may seem relevant to your interview. If you decide this is the case, you should usually reveal something of yourself:

PATIENT: Were you raised in this city?

INTERVIEWER: What makes you ask that?

PATIENT: My mother told me to be sure to get a therapist who grew up here. She says no one else could really understand what it was like, growing up in a ghetto, and all.

INTERVIEWER: I see. Actually, I didn't grow up here, but this is where I took most of my training. I've lived in town for nearly 8 years, so I think I have a pretty good idea of what some of your experiences must have been. But I have the feeling you'll be able to tell me a whole lot more.

SUMMING UP

Achieving good rapport requires the cooperation of clinician and patient. It also takes time, but the interviewer can unilaterally take immediate steps to help the process along. Words and body language should express real interest in the patient. Perhaps most important of all, clinicians should be as aware as possible of their own feelings and attitudes that might affect the image they project.

4 Managing the Early Patient Interview

During the first part of the initial interview, much of your task is simply to keep your patient talking. Most patients feel highly motivated to talk, and you usually need only choose the device that will best encourage them to do so.

To keep speech flowing freely, try to intrude as little as you can. Anything you say—questions, comments, even clearing your throat—can prove distracting. So as long as you are finding out why your patient came for treatment, you should keep out of the way. (If your patient persistently avoids discussing any presenting problem, you will need some of the advice in Chapter 16.) In practical terms, you will usually just listen for only the first couple of minutes or so. Then the flow of information will slow down or take a wrong turn, and you will have to intervene. Your choice of interventions can help determine the overall success of your interview.

NONVERBAL ENCOURAGEMENTS

Your most frequent challenge during free speech may be to deal with silence. Beginners often find silence hard to tolerate. They feel that every hole in the conversation, no matter how small, must be filled up with words. It is true that pauses greater than 10 or 15 seconds can make the interviewer seem cold, and this discourages some patients. Briefer pauses often mean only that your patient is trying to organize some thoughts for further discussion. Don't let anxiety cause you to derail a train of thought that has only paused to gather steam.

You must learn to walk the line between allowing brief pauses to let your patient think and such long gaps that you seem unfeeling or uninterested. A glance should tell you whether the narrative is still under way. Watch for the patient to draw another breath or to show other signs of activity, such as the moistening of lips.

You can encourage further speech by using nonverbal cues of your own. Be careful not to break eye contact; a smile or nod will say, "It's all right to proceed at your own pace." Another technique experienced interviewers sometimes use almost without thinking is to lean a little closer to show interest in what the patient is saying. Nonverbal cues of this sort are the simplest and often the most useful encouragements you can use. Without interrupting, they clearly signal that you are attentive and interested; they are part of a universal body language that asks the patient to continue. But don't overemphasize any of these gestures: A clinician who nods too vigorously or smiles too broadly may distract the patient, who wonders what these antics mean.

VERBAL ENCOURAGEMENTS

Body language helps, but you will also have to talk some. Your choice of words is important: You want to facilitate, not distract. Therefore, speak as briefly as you can while still conveying your meaning.

A syllable or two is usually all it takes. "Yes" or "Mm-hmm" clearly indicates that the material is registering with you. Without being directive, brief interjections and phrases ask the patient to keep on talking. Use them frequently, perhaps interspersing them randomly with nonverbal encouragements. One such encouragement every minute or two should help keep your patient talking.

There are several other verbal techniques you can use to request additional information. These are more intrusive than those just mentioned, so you should use them sparingly. I will illustrate each—some of them have been termed "reflective listening"—with a brief example.

- Repeat your patient's own last word or two with a rising inflection in your voice to make a question of it.

PATIENT: I was so upset that for hours I seemed to be hearing voices. *(Pauses)*

INTERVIEWER: "Voices?"

PATIENT: In my head. I thought I heard the voice of my mother calling my name.

- Elaborate on a word the patient used earlier. This technique allows you to reach back to an idea that was *not* the last thought spoken.

PATIENT: I know I overreacted, but I was feeling desperate. I couldn't sleep or eat, and I screamed at my kids.

INTERVIEWER: You said you felt desperate. *(Pauses)*

PATIENT: Yes, I even considered suicide.

- Directly request more information.
  "Tell me more about that."
  "How do you mean?"
- Re-request information when the patient seems to have misinterpreted your original question.

INTERVIEWER: What kind of work do you do?

PATIENT: It's at the foundry on Elm Street.

INTERVIEWER: And what kind of work do you do there?

- Offer brief summaries. These will often begin with "So you feel that. . ." or "Do you mean that. . ."

INTERVIEWER: So for about 6 months now you've been feeling depressed and anxious.

PATIENT: That's right. Lately I've even started to think terrible thoughts, thoughts about killing myself.

OFFERING REASSURANCE

Reassurance is anything you do to increase a patient's sense of confidence or well-being. Because it shows that you like or are interested in a person, it can also foster rapport. Used sparingly during the initial interview, supportive statements say, "I'm on your side. We'll get this job done."

Any interview can be therapeutic. Studies have shown that the mere act of sharing problems with another human being (even, in some cases, with a computer!) can give a new slant to old issues or put ideas together in novel ways. But the initial interview is not primarily intended to be therapeutic. Your purpose is to obtain the information you need to plan treatment; you can't just jump in and start giving advice, making interpretations, or otherwise "doing therapy." Then again, you shouldn't pass up an opportunity to provide reassurance, as long as it doesn't interfere with the main goal of your interview. You might even raise the confidence of some patients enough that they will reveal especially sensitive material you would not otherwise have obtained.

Body language (smiles and nods) can be reassuring, but mostly we reassure with speech. To be truly reassuring, what you say must be based in fact. You wouldn't get far saying, "You have a good head for finances" to a patient who in 45 years hasn't saved a nickel toward retirement. And choose your words carefully. Avoid clichés and other stereotyped expressions, which will make you sound as if you are responding only by rote, not from the heart.

Your reassurance should be factual, heartfelt, and believable. Here are two examples:

PATIENT: I did manage to get two promotions last year.

INTERVIEWER: So, you've really done well with that job!

PATIENT: When he came at me with a knife I jumped right through a second story window onto a garage roof. It made me feel dumb. I thought I'd just saved him the work of cutting me to ribbons.

INTERVIEWER: It may have saved your life! Perhaps it was the only thing you could have done.

Avoid the false generality that comes too early in the interview or is based on too little fact. "I'm sure it will all work out" or "Those fears seem groundless" will probably ring false to most patients, especially to those who are paranoid or severely depressed; they *know* things won't turn out all right! Even those who are less severely ill might begin to question your knowledge if you leap in too quickly with bland reassurances.

Occasionally a patient will express concern based on a misconception about mental or physical phenomena. Then you can use your expertise to set the record straight without interfering with the history-taking.

PATIENT: I'd never even been to California before, but I suddenly thought, I've been on this same San Francisco street before. I wondered if I was losing my mind.

INTERVIEWER: That feeling is called déjà vu. It's very common, and doesn't mean anything at all is wrong. Now, tell me what happened next.

Notice, however, that this interviewer did make the mistake of providing *unconditional* reassurance. Although déjà vu is nearly always a benign phenomenon, it is sometimes associated with neurological conditions such as temporal lobe epilepsy. But without more substantiating evidence, to suggest that there could be any pathological significance would also be a serious mistake. Here is a reasonable compromise: "It doesn't *usually* mean that anything is wrong."

Be careful to avoid offhand comments that may prove disquieting. One patient described a sexual encounter with her cousin, then said that she didn't know if that would be considered molestation. "It sure sounds like molestation to me," responded the young interviewer. This response had the potential for raising anxieties that the patient was not ready to deal with.

Mostly, your efforts at reassurance and encouragement will meet with success. Nevertheless, any of these techniques can sometimes backfire. A patient with persecutory delusions might interpret even a friendly nod or smile as mockery. If you lean toward someone who is feeling angry, you might be rewarded not with more information but with increasing silence or hostility. Judging when a patient will not be receptive can be tricky. Your best bet is to start slowly. Be friendly and pleasant, but not aggressively so.

Watch for cues. If you are being too aggressively forward, your patient may exhibit some of these behaviors:

Loss of eye contact
Frozen expression
Decreased speech output
Nervous shifting of position

If you spot any of these telltale signs, quickly change to a more reserved manner.

SUMMING UP

During free speech, the interviewer should keep the information flowing by using nonverbal encouragements such as nods, smiles, and eye contact, as well as verbal encouragements that do not cause diversion of the patient's train of thought. Although the initial interview is not primarily intended to be therapeutic, simple reassurance may relieve anxiety and facilitate the flow of information.

5 History of the Present Illness

Once you determine that there are no additional major problem areas to discover, close the period of free speech and move smoothly into the history of the present illness. Now you will explore more thoroughly the problems that have brought the patient into treatment. Considering the areas of clinical interest that you identified during free speech aids this process. (These areas were first mentioned in Chapter 2; because they include material from the mental status examination, they will not be considered fully until Chapter 13.)

In some cases there may be no illness as such, but it is a convention to label as "illness" whatever brings anyone in for evaluation, whether or not any actual disorder exists. In this broad sense, then, marital disagreements and other problems of living, even the desire to understand oneself better, may constitute a present "illness" that no one, least of all the patient, would recognize as disease. But all of these problems do have precipitants, symptoms, course, and other features that will allow you to suggest an effective plan of action.

THE PRESENT EPISODE

Although you will eventually want to learn about present *and* previous episodes, concentrate first on the current episode of illness. Your patient will be most concerned about it, and its details will be freshest in the minds of all your informants.

DESCRIBING SYMPTOMS

Learn as much as you can about each symptom your patient reports. (Remember that a symptom is any subjective sensation that makes the

patient think that something is wrong. A symptom could be a pain, hallucination, feeling of anxiety, or any of many other thoughts, feelings,
or behaviors.) Clarify any descriptive terms that are used: For example,
what does *nervous* mean to the patient?

Characterize each symptom as fully as you can. Is it always present
or does it come and go (episodic)? If episodic (as is the case with anxiety attacks), how often does it occur? How intense is it? Is it always the
same, or does it vary? Remember that symptoms can wax and wane with
time or with changes in the environment. Has the patient noticed any
factors (such as activity or time of day) that seem to be associated with
the symptom? Has the intensity or frequency of the symptom been increasing, staying the same, or decreasing? When your patient has the
symptom, how long does it last? What is the context in which it occurs?
(Only at night? Only when alone? Or at any time at all?)

How does the patient describe the symptom? Pain can feel cutting,
burning, crushing, sharp, or dull. Auditory hallucinations can be
described as to their content (noises, mumbles, isolated words, complete
sentences), location (inside the patient's head, in the air, out in the hall),
and intensity (ranging from loud screams to faraway whispers). Other
sorts of hallucination—of vision, touch, smell, or taste—can be
described similarly.

VEGETATIVE SYMPTOMS

Many patients with serious problems such as anxiety attacks, depressions and psychoses have experienced vegetative symptoms. This old
term refers to body functions that are concerned with maintaining
health and vigor. Vegetative symptoms include problems with sleep,
appetite, weight change, energy level, and sexual interest.

Not every patient will spontaneously report these symptoms, but
they are found in so many of the more serious mental disorders that
they serve as a useful screening tool. You should ask about them routinely. Look especially for evidence of *change* from previous normal functioning. You may find one or more of the following responses:

• *Sleep.* Your patient may complain of either excessive sleepiness
(hypersomnia) or inability to sleep (insomnia). If the latter, find out
what portion of the normal sleep period is affected—early (initial insomnia), middle (interval insomnia), or late (terminal insomnia). Terminal insomnia is usually associated with more severe mental problems
such as depression with melancholia. Initial insomnia is much more
common; many normal adults experience this from time to time when

of interest in sex is often an early casualty of mental distress. Also learn how these aspects of the patient's sex life have changed: frequency, ability, and enjoyment. The direction of change could be either up or down, depending on the specific mental health problem. Number (and choice) of partners can also be affected if judgment is impaired. A more detailed description of sexual symptoms and patterns will be given in Chapter 9.

CONSEQUENCES OF ILLNESS

Mental disorder can interfere with the entire range of human interaction. It is important to learn how your patient's illness has affected specific relationships for several reasons.

1. It may provide your most reliable index of severity. So far, most of the history you have heard is highly subjective: You depend on your patient's ability to sort out facts from opinion. Perhaps because it can be verified by talking with informants, the fact that a patient has not gone to work for a week may be subject to less distortion than, say, how much vodka this same patient has consumed.

2. The diagnosis of some disorders depends heavily on social consequences. Examples include various substance abuse disorders and antisocial personality disorder, which can lead to legal, financial, health, and interpersonal problems.

3. You may learn that relatives blame the patient for being fired, getting divorced, and separating from family. Yet these and various other ruptured human relationships are really *effects* of mental disorder. This view may prove useful to patient and relatives alike: Teaching family and friends about the consequences of illness can help get your patient off the hook.

To learn what consequences of illness your patient's illness has caused, start with an open-ended question that doesn't limit the information you might obtain. If your patient asks what your question means, respond with some examples of the sort of facts that would interest you.

INTERVIEWER: What sort of difficulties has this problem caused you?

PATIENT: What do you mean, difficulties?

INTERVIEWER: For example, it would help to know whether your problem has changed the way you get along with your family, your friends, the job, hobbies—that sort of thing.

they have problems of living. Here is how you might inqu
problems with sleep:

INTERVIEWER: Have you had any problems with your sleepin

PATIENT: Yeah, it's been murder.

INTERVIEWER: What sort of trouble have you had?

PATIENT: What do you mean?

INTERVIEWER: Well, what part of the night do you not sleep

PATIENT: Oh. Mostly, it's trouble getting to sleep.

INTERVIEWER: Do you ever wake up early in the morning, before
to get up, and then you can't get back to sleep?

PATIENT: Yeah, that, too. I do that a lot.

INTERVIEWER: How long do you usually sleep?

PATIENT: Lately, I guess . . . probably only 4 or 5 hours.

INTERVIEWER: And do you feel rested when you wake up?

PATIENT: Yeah, rested like I've been hauling bricks all night!

INTERVIEWER: How much of a change is this for you?

- *Appetite and weight.* These, too, can either increase or d
with an episode of illness. You should also learn how signific
change has been (how much weight has the patient gained or lc
over what period of time?) Also ask whether this weight change
tentional or not. Some patients will tell you that they have not w
themselves recently; asking whether clothing no longer fits (toc
or too tight) may help you judge.
- *Energy level.* Does the patient complain of feeling con
tired? Is this a change from normal? Has it interfered in some wa
performance at work or school or with getting jobs done aroun
house? You may also hear complaints of change in other body
tions, such as bowel habits. For example, some severely depresse
tients experience constipation.
- *Diurnal variation of mood.* This phrase refers to the tender
some patients to feel better at a certain time of day. Patients wi
vere depression often feel worse upon arising and better as the day
on. By bedtime they may feel nearly normal. Those who are less sev
ill are more likely to report feeling pretty well early in the day
depressed, sluggish, and weary by nightfall.
- *Sexual interest and performance.* Sexual functioning usually
pends strongly upon the individual's sense of well-being. Therefore

Be sure to obtain complete details about any positive answers. The areas to explore include:

- *Marital.* Patients who are even moderately ill commonly experience discord in their marriages and other love relationships. All too often mental disorder can lead to divorce.
- *Social.* Has your patient felt estranged from relatives or shunned by friends? Can you tell whether this is only a perceived problem, or has behavior been so difficult for so long that others really do avoid the patient?
- *Legal.* Have there been legal difficulties? They are especially likely when the history is complicated by alcohol or other substance abuse. Ask:
  "Have you ever had any police or legal difficulties?"
  "Have you ever been arrested? How many times?"
  "Have you been in jail? For a total of how long?"
  "Have you ever been committed to an institution or placed under the control of a conservator, guardian, or fiduciary?"
These serious legal steps are usually taken only after a long siege of severe mental illness. Be sure to obtain complete details: events leading up to the legal action, duration, name and responsibilities of the legally responsible person, and the effect the action has had upon the course of the disorder.
- *Job.* As a result of emotional problems, has the patient ever missed work, quit work, or been fired? How often has this happened? Difficulties with job performance are sometimes noted by supervisors or co-workers even before families take much notice of the patient's difficulties. (For younger patients the questions to consider would be about school attendance and performance.)
- *Disability payments.* Have benefits been awarded from the Department of Veterans Affairs, Social Security Administration, State Compensation Board, or private insurance? For what disorder? What is the dollar amount? How long will the payments last?
- *Interests.* Has interest changed in hobbies, reading, or watching TV? What about chores at home? Has interest in sex either increased or decreased? What about sexual performance? Have there been complaints of impotence, painful intercourse, or inability to have climax?
- *Symptoms.* How much discomfort do the symptoms cause? What fears does your patient have about the meanings of the symptoms? Do they seem to imply death or permanent disability? Insanity? This information will also help you evaluate depth of insight and soundness of judgment, which will be discussed in Chapter 12.

Onset and Sequence of Symptoms

In addition to a complete and accurate description of the symptoms, you should establish their timing and sequence. When did these problems begin? Sometimes the onset may be reported quite precisely: "I started drinking again last New Year's Eve," or "I woke up feeling depressed a week ago Thursday." But usually the answer will be less exact, either because the patient is vague or because that episode began so gradually that there doesn't seem to be a definite starting point.

Try to encourage greater precision about the onset of especially noticeable symptoms. Patients can often remember the first time they experienced such important problems as death wishes or loss of interest in sex. You might be able to relate onset to noteworthy dates or events.

INTERVIEWER: Had you started to feel depressed by the Fourth of July last year?

PATIENT: No, I don't think so.

INTERVIEWER: What about in the fall, around the time of your birthday?

No matter how much you prompt, some patients simply can't give a date or even an approximation: "I only know, it's been a long time. A very long time." Pressing further for a precise answer will probably only frustrate both of you. Try focusing instead on something the patient may have thought about many times:

"When did you last feel well?"

If even this effort fails, at least try to learn which of your patient's several problems started first. As we will note in Chapters 18 and 19, it is important for diagnosis and treatment to know, for example, whether an episode of depression or a bout of drinking began earlier. So ask:

"Which symptoms did you notice first, the drinking or the depression?"

"How long did it take before the other symptom developed?"
If symptoms fluctuate
"Do they do so together?"

Stressors

A stressor is any event that seems to cause, precipitate, or worsen a patient's mental health problems.

"My husband ran off with his secretary."

"I didn't want to be dependent on medicine any longer, so I stopped taking it."

"My cat died."

The variety of possible stressors is vast, and what might be mildly stressful for one person could seem catastrophic to another. Nonetheless, the revised third edition of the *Diagnostic and Statistical Manual of Mental Disorders* (DSM-III-R) has attempted to rate two classes of possible stressors: acute events and enduring circumstances. In Table 3 I have paraphrased the five principal categories for each type of stressor. See the discussion of Axis IV in DSM-III-R for more information.

Patients often mention stressors during free speech, or even when stating the chief complaint. If they don't, you will have to ask. A good time to do so is right after you have pinned down the approximate onset of the episode of illness. If you find a stressor, try to learn how it affected the course of your patient's difficulty. Ask:

"Was anything happening then that might have started your symptoms?"

"How did it affect you?"

If your patient comes up with no possible stressor, you should run through a list of possibilities, pausing briefly to allow thinking time:

"Could there have been anything that happened at home? At work? With friends? Any legal problems? Sickness? Problems with the kids? With your spouse?"

For some episodes of illness you'll find no stressors at all, but to

TABLE 3. Severity of Psychosocial Stressors Scale

Code	Term	Acute events	Enduring circumstances
1	None		
2	Mild	Broke up with boyfriend or girlfriend; started or graduated from school; child left home.	Family arguments; job dissatisfaction; lives in high-crime neighborhood
3	Moderate	Marriage; marital separation; loss of job; retirement; miscarriage	Marital discord; serious financial problems; trouble with boss, being a single parent
4	Severe	Divorce; birth of first child	Unemployment; poverty
5	Extreme	Death of spouse; serious physical illness diagnosed; victim of rape	Serious chronic illness in self or child; ongoing physical or sexual abuse
6	Catastrophic	Death of child; suicide of spouse; devastating natural disaster	Captivity as hostage; concentration camp experience

From *Diagnostic and Statistical Manual of Mental Disorders* (3rd ed., rev., p. 11) by the American Pyschiatric Association, 1987, Washington, DC: APA. Copyright 1987 by the American Psychiatric Association. Reprinted by permission.

a patient almost anything can seem a possible cause of emotional disorder. Therefore, events reported as stressors may include births, deaths, marriages, divorces, job loss, broken love affairs, health problems, and virtually any other emotional trauma you can think of, as well as many seemingly routine life experiences.

But just because your patient identifies something as a stressor doesn't mean that it actually caused the disorder to happen. The two events could have occurred by coincidence, which is often the case. It is simply a human tendency to blame any problem on whatever happened before it. For example, if you carefully checked the time course of Mrs. Albertson's depression, you might find that she had some symptoms, perhaps insomnia and some crying spells, even before her husband left her.

Another patient's "stressor" may seem an unlikely cause of illness — like the man whose overwhelming depression started, he said, when he learned his dog had ticks! Whether or not the stressor seems related to the disorder, note it down. You can evaluate it later in the light of everything else you learn about your patient.

Even though you might find nothing that has precipitated the episode of mental illness, try to answer this question: Why did your patient come for evaluation now? The answer may be obvious, but if it is not, the best approach is to ask:

"This problem has been bothering you for a long time. What made you decide to come for help now?"

You are likely to hear about the urging of concerned relatives, fear of losing a valued job, or the patient's own anxiety about worsening symptoms.

PREVIOUS EPISODES

Knowing about previous episodes of the same or a similar mental condition will help you determine diagnosis and prognosis for the future. By this time you may already have heard details about any prior episodes. If not, ask:

"When was the first time you felt like this?"

"Did you first seek treatment then or later?"

"Why did you delay?"

"What diagnosis was given?" (There may have been more than one.)

Since that first attack, has there ever been complete recovery, or has the patient continued to have some residual symptoms or a change of personality? This issue of complete recovery can be critically important. For example, it can help differentiate schizophrenia, from which most patients never totally recover, from mood disorder with psychosis, which usually resolves completely.

How has your patient reacted to previous symptoms or prior episodes of illness? Some patients may have simply ignored them; others might have tried to escape by quitting work, running away from home, attempting suicide, or abusing alcohol or other drugs. People who experience auditory hallucinations sometimes play the radio loudly to drown out the sound. A few will have talked with a friend or a religious counselor. Whatever coping behavior was used, this information may help you evaluate the severity of the present episode by comparing it with earlier episodes. It could also help you predict how your patient would behave if the illness continued untreated.

PREVIOUS TREATMENT

Has your patient received treatment before? Who provided it? (Try to learn the name, but certainly the profession, of the therapist.) How long did treatment last?

You should also learn how well the patient complied with treatment. If you ask it as a straight question, pride or guilt may cause some patients to have trouble answering this question fairly. Try instead:

"Were you usually able to follow your therapist's directions?"
If the answer to that question is "No,"

"What sort of trouble did you have?"

Were drugs prescribed? If so, what was the dose? Were there any side effects to drug therapy? If your patient doesn't know the names of previous medications, a physical description of the tablets or capsules may give you (or a pharmacist consultant) some clues. A list of side effects may also help you with drug identification. Find out whether injectable medications were ever used, especially the long-acting injectable neuroleptics such as fluphenazine (Prolixin) decanoate and haloperidol (Haldol) decanoate.

What has been the effect of previous treatment? Has anything helped? If so, try to get an opinion as to which treatment helped most (talking with a therapist? behavior therapy? electroconvulsive therapy? medications?). You could be surprised. Even though a neuroleptic might be the current medication, your patient might answer that lithium helped most, and ask for it again.

Was the patient ever hospitalized? If so, how many times? Where? If time is short and your patient is both knowledgeable and cooperative, you might instead ask for a written summary of previous hospitalizations and treatment to be given to you at your next interview.

SUMMING UP

The history of the present illness attempts to encompass the "meat" of the initial interview, including a description of symptoms, their timing, and possible stressors for each of the problem types that has been identified. This phase of history-taking also covers previous episodes and prior treatment of similar problems. Throughout, the clinician should be listening carefully for clues to symptoms and problems special to each patient. They might point the way for further explorations.

6 Getting the Facts about the Present Illness

Of all portions of the initial mental health interview, the history of the present illness is probably the most important. (It is also frequently neglected.) During this part you will develop most of the information and test the hypotheses that provide the basis for your diagnosis. This process requires that you obtain highly valid information; that is, it should reflect as closely as possible the true facts of your patient's history. You can take several steps to increase the validity of the information you record in your history of the present illness.

BE CLEAR ABOUT THE GOALS OF YOUR INTERVIEW

Ideally, your expectations for accuracy will be understood from the very beginning of your interview. Still, in the middle of an interview your apparently truthful patient may appear to be holding back on you. Something in that patient's manner may tell you: a hesitation of speech or an unwillingness to look you in the eye. Of course, your first task should be to try to understand any behavior; the reasons for patient resistance will be covered in greater detail in Chapter 16. For minor evasions and omissions it may be enough simply to restate the goal of your interview:

"I know some of these topics are difficult for you, but to help you most I need every scrap of information I can get."

If you are a student, you will have less authority to require cooperation, so you might try: "I'm sorry to be causing you distress with this line of questioning, but you've really been helping me with my studies. I know it's painful to talk about, but maybe getting in touch with some of these memories could help you understand your problems."

It can be especially hard to obtain good-quality facts from teenagers. Some teens worry a lot about what you might tell their parents; others may mistrust anyone more than 5 years older than they are. Whatever the cause, some teenagers have trouble telling the truth. It sometimes helps to repeat your reassurances about confidentiality. I say something like this:

"Of course, after we're finished I will have to talk with your parents. But anything I might tell them I will first discuss with you. And if you tell me anything that you don't want me to repeat, I'll respect that confidence."

Even without informing their parents, in some states you can counsel or treat teenagers for certain indications such as venereal disease and birth control. By assuring confidentiality when they might be afraid to tell their parents, these laws hope to encourage young patients to consult appropriate care-givers about important health care conditions. In such a case you might work with your patient to determine the best way of informing the parent, but you shouldn't take it upon yourself to volunteer this information. Of course, if a teenager is brought in by a parent, then you would usually consult the parent—after informing your patient what you plan to say.

Information that isn't valid can be confusing, especially in the initial interview, so some clinicians begin interviews with teenagers by indicating that they prefer silence to misinformation. Here's how they might put it:

"A lot of the questions I am going to ask you are personal. Some of them may be pretty embarrassing or even frightening. But if I'm to help you, it's important that I not get confused by information that isn't the truth. So if I ask you about something that you can't bear to discuss, please don't make up an answer. Just say that you don't want to talk about that now, and we'll go on to something else."

TRACK YOUR DISTRACTIONS

Hardly any interviewer proceeds smoothly and logically, covering one topic completely before moving on to another. In fact, experienced interviewers expect to be distracted from time to time by the unexpected. When new material interrupts the flow of your interview, you can either pursue it immediately or, if you feel the first topic is more important, make a note to come back to it later. If you choose the latter course, you should acknowledge that your patient has said something important and promise that you will return to it shortly.

PATIENT: Yesterday I felt so disgusted with myself that I got out my suit-case, just to see how it felt in my hand.

INTERVIEWER: You must have been feeling pretty bad, to think about run-ning away. I'll ask you more about those thoughts in a few minutes, after we've finished talking about your drinking.

USE OPEN-ENDED QUESTIONS

Above all else, you want information that is valid. Studies have shown that patients give the most valid information when they are allowed to answer freely, in their own words and as completely as they wish. So, whenever possible, phrase your question in an open-ended way that al-lows the widest possible scope of response. Here are some examples:

Instead of "Did you have insomnia when you were most depressed?" try "How was your sleep then?" (Your patient might have been sleeping too much, rather than too little.)

Instead of "How many times have you been hospitalized?" say, "Tell me about your previous hospitalizations." (The details could re-veal suicide attempts or bouts of drinking.)

Instead of "Did you lose your appetite?" ask, "To what extent did your appetite change?" (The phrase "to what extent" can change nearly any closed-ended question into an open-ended one.)

TALK THE PATIENT'S LANGUAGE

Even the most experienced interviewers must guard against using tech-nical words that patients might not understand. ("Has your libido re-mained healthy?" asked one professor of psychiatry during ward rounds. The patient, a burly high school dropout, looked perplexed.) Of course, if you use an unfamiliar word and are asked to define it, you won't lose anything but a little time.

Some patients think they understand when they don't. If they an-swer the question they *thought* you asked, the information you get might not be accurate. Others are reluctant to admit their ignorance and so say nothing. You will improve validity if you pitch your questions at a level the patient can understand. At the same time, be careful not to talk down to your patient. An interviewer asked one patient, a man with a master's degree in psychology, "How's your thinker?" The patient at first did not understand. When the clinician's meaning was finally ex-plained, the patient felt so insulted that he left the room without finish-ing the interview. Although most patients will not react so extremely, remember to approach all adults (and children, for that matter) with full regard for their intelligence and feelings.

In polite society everyone uses circumlocutions at one time or another. "Sleeping with" for having sexual relations is a common example. You should try to preserve amenities, of course, but your first obligation should be to communicate accurately. Asking whether your patient had "sex before getting married" is discreet, but inaccurate; nearly everybody has, even if it is only masturbation. If you really need to know about a history of sexual intercourse, ask that question in so many words. Some methods to help you approach sensitive subjects such as sex, suicide, and substance abuse will be discussed in Chapter 9.

You should work hard to be sure that you understand what your patient is trying to say. For example, what does "I was off the wall" mean? To find out, you could:

1. Restate the expression in your own words: "You mean, you felt very upset?"
2. Simply ask what was meant: "I don't understand how your statement relates to what we were talking about."

Ensuring good understanding requires your constant vigilance: It is all too easy to assume you know what your patient means when in fact the two of you are speaking in different idioms.

In the same vein, be careful not to judge other people's behavior by your own standards. A common example is duration of sleep. You might suppose that your patient, who sleeps only 6 hours each night, suffers from insomnia, but for some people that's plenty (Thomas Edison slept only 4). Keep in mind the almost endless variety of human standards and habits, and guard against the temptation to impose your standards on others.

CHOOSE THE RIGHT PROBING QUESTIONS

When you want to know about something, just ask. A simple request for information will often produce the information you need with a minimum of effort. Your patient will probably appreciate your directness; if you use an open-ended question, you'll probably get the details.

When it comes time to delve more deeply into your patient's presenting problems, choose your probing questions with two principles in mind: (1) Select probes that will resolve unanswered questions. It's more efficient to concentrate your efforts on areas your patient has not already covered. (2) If your questions show that you know a lot about the illness, you will be perceived as knowledgeable. The resulting dividend of rapport and trust should lead to increased sharing of information.

At this point in your interview you are interested in the facts, so questions that begin with *why* are often better avoided. This is especially true if the questions refer to the patient's opinions or to other people's behavior.

"Why do you think you're having these symptoms now?"

"Why did your boss say that?"

"Why did your son leave home?"

Each of these questions invites your patient to give an interpretation, rather than facts. Later you may want to hear interpretations, but for now you should try to avoid the opinions and concentrate on the data that will allow you to form your own conclusions.

Getting a good history depends in part on knowing what questions will help you better understand the facts about your patient's symptoms or problems. Of course, each symptom has its own unique set of details that must be explored. But for a full, rich exploration of any behavior or event, certain items of detailed information are always necessary. They include accurate details about these aspects of your patient's symptoms:

Type
Severity
Frequency
Duration
Context in which they occur

Because you will now be looking for specific details, you will be using more closed-ended questions: those that can be answered in a few words and *don't* invite further comment from your patient. You should still include some open-ended questions, which will stimulate your patient to relate additional material that you may not have thought to ask about. In the following example the clinician uses a mixture of closed- and open-ended questions to explore a patient's anxiety attacks:

INTERVIEWER: When did you first notice these episodes of anxiety? [Closed-ended]

PATIENT: I guess it must have been about 2 months ago—I had just started my new job with the county.

INTERVIEWER: Would you describe an episode for me? [Open-ended]

PATIENT: It's pretty much the same every time. For no reason I start to feel nervous, and then I'm afraid I won't be able to breathe. It's awfully scary.

INTERVIEWER: How often have they occurred? [Closed-ended]

PATIENT: It's been getting more frequent. I'm not sure I can say.

INTERVIEWER: Well, has it been several times a day, once a day, once a week? [Closed-ended, multiple-choice]

PATIENT: About once or twice a day now, I'd say.

INTERVIEWER: What do you do about it? [Open-ended]

PATIENT: Usually, I just sit down. I'm usually too shaky to stand, anyway. After about 15 minutes it starts to go away.

INTERVIEWER: What sort of help have you sought before? [Open-ended]

Some rules of interviewing seem obvious, but they should be mentioned for the sake of completeness.

- *Don't phrase questions in the negative.* ("You haven't been drinking heavily, have you?") The effect is to telegraph an expected answer, which, in this case, would be "Of course not."
- *Don't ask double questions.* ("Have you had trouble with your sleep or appetite?") Double questions may seem efficient, but they are often confusing. The patient may respond to one part of the question and ignore the other, without your realizing it.
- *Encourage precision.* Ask for dates, times, and numbers where appropriate.
- *Keep questions brief.* Long questions with much explanatory detail can confuse the patient; they also occupy time you could be using to obtain information.
- *Keep on the lookout for new leads.* Even when you are hot on the trail of vital information, be alert for hints of other directions to explore later.

PATIENT: ....That's about the story of my first suicide attempt. It really upset my mother, so bad she had a nervous breakdown. Now, did you want to hear about the other attempt?

INTERVIEWER: (*Noting on pad, "Mother's breakdown"*) Yes, please.

CONFRONTATIONS

Of course, confrontation does not mean coming to blows, or even showing anger. In the context of a mental health interview, it simply means pointing out something that the patient might not have noticed earlier that needs clarification. It could be an inconsistency between two points of the history or between the story and how the patient appears to feel about it. The purpose of the confrontation is to help you and the patient communicate better.

INTERVIEWER: I've noticed that whenever I ask about your father, you glance away. Did you realize that?

PATIENT: No, I didn't.

INTERVIEWER: What do you suppose it means?

In the usual initial interview you should try to avoid any confrontation more than the mild sort just mentioned. In the first visit or two, you don't know one another well at all; your patient could feel tricked or trapped by a relative stranger who points out inconsistencies. This may lead in turn to decreased cooperation with the history-taking or, in extreme cases, to a breakdown in communications. But if you seem to be getting contradictory information on an important point, try to enhance validity by asking for clarification.

When you do ask, be gentle. The experience of being interrogated is an unpleasant one; it makes the subject feel attacked and defensive. If instead your confrontations are made in a warm, empathic way, they are less likely to be rejected. If the patient sees you as interested and concerned, the confrontation should lead to an increase in self-exploration.

You can also make the confrontation seem less like a challenge by choosing your phrases carefully. You might express puzzlement and ask for help:

"Here's something I don't understand. You just said that your husband drove you to the hospital, but I thought that earlier you told me he had run off with his secretary."

Notice the "I thought." It implies that the interviewer might have been mistaken. The overall effect of the confrontation just quoted is to make interviewer and patient collaborators in the search for truth.

Suppose you observe that your patient's appearance and thought content do not jibe. A confrontation asks for clarification:

"What you told me about your mother-in-law is sad, but you seem to be smiling. There must be something else to this story."

Whatever the issue, try to restrict your confrontations to one or two essential issues. Otherwise, you do put rapport with your new patient at risk. To be sure that you reserve this treatment for only the most important issues, it may be better to save confrontation until close to the end of the interview. Your relationship should be stronger by then (risk will be lessened), and you will have already obtained most of your information (less to lose). What little risk you do take can be to resolve the most important issues.

SUMMING UP

Obtaining details of the present illness requires that the clinician carefully choose probing questions (both open- and closed-ended) phrased in language the patient can easily understand. Confrontations, if used, should be gentle and few. With expectations for truth clearly stated and new leads carefully followed, even a beginning interviewer can obtain valid details about the history of the present illness.

7 Interviewing about Feelings

Whatever the nature of the presenting problems, you need to know how your patient feels about the illness and about the interview itself. Feelings will probably turn out to be among the most important information you obtain during the entire interview. Yet studies have shown that, of all the topics that must be covered in an initial mental health interview, the one most often ignored by beginning interviewers is feelings.

NEGATIVE AND POSITIVE FEELINGS

People can experience an impressive range of feelings. In listing a few of them (Table 4), I have tried to be representative. Some are major moods or affects; others are variants or combinations. All are represented by commonly used English words. Although in nearly every case a noun form exists, I have listed the adjective forms, with occasional synonyms, because that is how people use these words in reference to themselves. For example, a patient would be more likely to say, "I feel anxious" than "I have anxiety."

In most cases I have paired feelings with their opposites. Note that the negative feelings considerably outnumber the positive ones. I have omitted most of the obvious antonyms (un- and in- words) and have not included some words that are too vague to be useful as descriptors, such as *bad, good, nervous,* and *uncomfortable.* I have listed no antonym for some words because I wanted to include only those terms that are used to describe how people feel. Thus, *innocent* is not listed as an antonym for *guilty* because people don't usually state that they *feel* innocent—"I *am* innocent" proclaims conviction, not emotion.

You can obtain information about feelings from most normally expressive patients just by careful watching and listening. But some patients are reluctant to share their feelings; even when they are willing

TABLE 4. Negative and Positive Feelings

Negative feelings	Positive feelings
Afraid, fearful, apprehensive	Confident
Angry	
Anxious	Contented, calm, peaceful
Apathetic, indifferent	Eager, enthusiastic, interested
Ashamed	Proud
Confused, perplexed, puzzled	Certain, sure
Desiring	
Disappointed	Fulfilled
Disgusted	Delighted
Dissatisfied	Satisfied
Embarrassed	
Envious	
Foolish	
Frustrated	Encouraged
Guilty	
Hateful	Affectionate, loving
Helpless, dependent	Independent
Hopeless, trapped	Hopeful
Humiliated	
Impatient	Patient
Indignant	Pleased
Inferior	Important
Jealous	
Lonely	Sociable
Pessimistic	Optimistic
Regretful	
Rejected	Accepted
Resentful	
Sad, unhappy, depressed	Cheerful, happy, euphoric
Shy, timid	Confident
Surprised, astonished, amazed	Prepared
Suspicious	Trusting
Tense	Relaxed
Uncertain	Determined
Useless, worthless	Useful, worthwhile
Vulnerable	Secure
Wary	
Worried	Carefree
	Appreciative, grateful
	Sympathetic

to talk, they hide their emotions deeply. Then you will have to go prospecting to elicit feelings.

ELICITING FEELINGS

Many patients—perhaps the majority—will express their feelings adequately if you just ask them to. Patients don't seem to mind this method. In fact, studies show that this direct style is even preferred by most patients and informants, as long as the interviewer has a warm and caring manner and is attentive, courteous, and responsive to cues.

Such examiners effectively use two techniques that are especially good at eliciting emotions. These are direct requests for feelings and open-ended questions.

Direct Requests for Feelings

Watch for the opportunity to ask about the feelings associated with any of the facts you have been discussing. Simply asking is probably the most effective method of eliciting emotions. For example,

"How did you feel when you found out that you would have to move?"

"What was your state of mind when you were served with that subpoena?"

Patients are used to answering questions and will usually give you information about nearly any feeling or fact that you seem interested enough to ask about.

Open-Ended Questions

Without specifically asking how the patient feels, open-ended questions encourage the free expression of feelings. This method is effective because its relative lack of direction encourages patients to speak at length. The more people talk the more likely they are to reveal emotion-laden information.

This technique, which is really just an extension of free speech, probably succeeds because, on one hand, it suggests that you care about how the patient perceives the situation as a whole. On the other hand, closed-ended, short-answer questions may suggest that you have already decided what is significant. This could reduce your patient's motivation to tell the entire story. Furthermore, it seems obvious that the less time you spend asking questions, the more time your patient will have to reveal feelings.

Open-ended questions can also help patients who have trouble sorting out or accepting emotions that are ambivalent. Ambivalent feelings are those that conflict with one another, and they are hard for most people to express in a few words. But a comparatively long run of uninterrupted talk may provide the time needed to think about and express feelings that are ambivalent. Here's an example of an open-ended question that revealed decidedly mixed feelings:

INTERVIEWER: A few minutes ago you said that your wife was talking about divorce. Could you tell me more about that?

PATIENT: It's been an awful time for me. . . I know that. . . well, I've always felt that if you've failed in your marriage, you've failed in life. At least, that's what my mother always said.

INTERVIEWER: *(Nods encouragement)*

PATIENT: But when I think about it. . .you know, there's so much trouble we've had getting along, almost since. . .well, since the kids were born. Maybe we haven't really had much of a marriage at all. Maybe there are some things worse than divorce.

OTHER TECHNIQUES

Several situations can make it hard to elicit emotions from patients. Here are a few of them:

- From childhood, some people are discouraged from revealing their feelings. Grown up, this "machismo" view of appropriate behavior can lead them to deny their feelings. The most obvious example is when the childhood admonition "boys don't cry" becomes "men should show that they don't care." The same fate can befall women, too.
- Some patients don't recognize their own feelings or have difficulty connecting their feelings to their experiences. Perhaps this, too, develops from childhood experiences. In extreme cases people grow up without language to express how they feel, a condition called *alexithymia.*
- Still others may be reluctant to express themselves, especially to someone they don't know well, because it makes them feel vulnerable. "If you show a hard exterior, no one can hurt you" is how they might put it. These people know how they feel and could find words to express their emotions, if only they didn't feel a stronger need to protect themselves.

To elicit feelings in one of these situations may require techniques such as expressions of concern, reflection of feelings, picking up on emotional cues, and interpretation.

Expressions of Concern or Sympathy

Controlled studies have shown that any expression of concern or sympathy by a clinician may encourage a patient to share feelings. This is especially likely to work if your patient has already begun to share some feelings. The sympathetic expression you use might be verbal or behavioral (facial expressions or other body language):

PATIENT: I've worked for that company for 15 years, but when a supervisory position opens up, the boss passes me over for his own nephew. It really burns me!

INTERVIEWER: *(Frowns sympathetically)* It makes me feel unhappy just hearing about it! I think that anyone in that situation would feel hurt and angry.

PATIENT: I was beyond that—I was totally blown away. I wanted to flush myself out of existence! I still feel that way, sometimes.

Reflection of Feelings

This means that you state explicitly the emotion you think the patient might have felt in a given situation:

PATIENT: My daughter has always been a little wild, but last night she didn't come home until nearly daybreak.

INTERVIEWER: I'll bet you were nearly frantic.

Of course, this technique runs the risk that your interpretation could be wrong. But if it is, and your patient says so, you have at least accomplished your goal of promoting a discussion of feelings.

Picking Up on Emotional Cues

This means that you are constantly alert for indications of high emotional concern. Often these will be nonverbal cues: a slight frown, moistening of the eyes, or any other idiom of body language. Your response might be verbal:

"I thought you looked a little sad when you were talking about your mother. What were you feeling?"

You might also indicate your interest and support with some quiet action of your own, such as passing a box of facial tissues to someone who has begun to cry.

Interpretation

In this technique the interviewer draws parallels between the emotional content of current and past situations.

PATIENT: My husband never listens to my opinion on things.

INTERVIEWER: From what you told me before, it sounds like the way your father treated you when you were a teenager.

The technique of interpretation can be tricky to use. The patient must be receptive, looking for explanations of behavior; ideally, the patient should be the one who suggests the connection. If not, the interpretation should be offered tentatively: It may be briskly rejected. Interpretations should generally not be offered during the initial interview; they are a technique best used in later therapy by experienced clinicians.

Studies show that each of these techniques can encourage a reticent patient or informant to relate more emotions and to examine their emotions at greater depth. At the same time, none of them will discourage a normally expressive person from revealing emotions. They also require less in the way of detailed, extensive probing than do techniques that are less responsive to the needs of patients.

Analogy

Finally, for the patient who absolutely cannot identify the feelings that accompany a given situation, you could ask about times when similar feelings might have been experienced.

"Did you feel anything like this when your mother died?"

"Did you feel this way that time your boss used you as a bad example in front of the entire staff?"

FOLLOW UP FOR DETAILS

Once you have uncovered some feelings, increase the depth of the interview by asking for more. Probe to elicit examples and to evaluate details.

INTERVIEWER: I'd like to hear some more about those rage attacks. When do you feel that way?

PATIENT: For one thing, it's whenever we go to visit my father-in-law.

INTERVIEWER: Have you had some previous unpleasant experiences with him?

PATIENT: I'll say! He almost ruined my marriage with some of his sly cracks.

INTERVIEWER: I'd like to hear an example of how you felt then.

Be sure to ask follow-up probing questions when your patient gives you the opportunity. Beginners sometimes uncover evidence of significant events or pathology, only to ignore it in the subsequent dialogue. An unfortunate example:

INTERVIEWER: Were you ever approached for sex in any way when you were a child?

PATIENT: Well, yes, I was.

INTERVIEWER: *(Writes down "Yes")* Where are you employed now?

Perhaps this interviewer felt uncomfortable at pressing ahead for the details, but the patient was left to deal with the frustration of pent-up information. Positive information should be followed up until you have learned who, what, when, where, why, and how.

DEFENSE MECHANISMS

When following up, you should also learn what your patient does to cope with feelings. These strategies for dealing with emotions and behaviors are called *defense mechanisms*. They may seem almost endless in their number and variety. Following are a few of the more common ones. Rather than just stating definitions, I will try to clarify what is meant with examples of a number of defense mechanisms that might be used by an aspiring politician who feels anxiety and anger about losing an election to city council.

Potentially Destructive Defense Mechanisms

Acting out. [The politician smashes the camera of a news photographer who is trying to take his picture in defeat.]

Denial. "The recount will show that I really won."

Displacement. [The politician goes home and kicks the cat.]

Dissociation. [The politician awakens one morning in Berkeley, unable to recall where he has been for 3 days.]

Fantasy. "Next year I'll run for Congress—and win!"

Intellectualization. "I look at this defeat only as an example of democracy in action."

Projection. [Unconscious thought: "I'd like to kill him."] "He's plotting to kill me."

Repression. [The politician "forgets" to attend a banquet in honor of the victor.]

Splitting. "Some politicians are good, some bad; he's one of the bad ones."

Reaction formation. [Thought: "He's a miserable low-life."] "I'm proud to support the honorable council member."

Somatization. [The candidate develops persistent chest pain of unexplained origin.] "I couldn't have served anyway."

Devaluation. "It's a lousy job anyway—the hours are murder, and nothing but complaints from the taxpayers."

Effective Defense Mechanisms

When stressed, most of us occasionally resort to such measures to shore up our egos. Better-integrated adults rely principally on some of the more mature defense mechanisms.

Altruism. "I'll support him; he has better qualifications than I do."
Humor. "In the campaign I said he was honorable; he said I was a jerk. Perhaps we were both wrong."
Sublimation. "I'll write a book about the campaign."
Suppression. "I'll put it to the back of my mind, and concentrate on the business at hand."

HANDLING EXCESSIVELY EMOTIONAL PATIENTS

Although you usually want to encourage the expression of emotions, some patients are so emotional that it impedes their communication with other people, including therapists. Excessive emotionality can have a variety of causes.

- They may be people who are angry, sometimes without knowing why.
- Others, such as those with somatization disorder or antisocial personality disorder, have learned that high-volume emotions help them get their way. Drama has therefore become a way of life.
- Even some people who don't have such severe underlying psychopathology use high emotional output to control their families or friends.
- Some people have been reared in families where feelings are expressed loudly and often. By their imitation of others, this behavior becomes habitual.
- Anxiety causes some to behave this way.
- A few cannot stand the loneliness of silence.
- Perhaps your patient, recalling experiences with other clinicians, fears that you won't be interested or that there won't be enough time to tell the whole story.

Whatever the cause, excessive emotionality can focus too much of your attention on feelings, leaving insufficient time for gathering facts.

In such a situation, try to adopt a brisk, controlling manner in which you firmly direct the course of the interview. Several techniques can help you accomplish this objective.

1. Acknowledge the emotion. You may be able to turn down the heat by just acknowledging the emotion. Then the patient sees that you recognize the feeling and no longer needs to attract your attention to it.

PATIENT: *(Shouting)* She's not going to jerk me around that way, not ever again!

INTERVIEWER: You really feel angry. Frustrated and angry.

PATIENT: *(More quietly)* Well, sure. Who wouldn't be? Wait'll you hear what she did last week.

This technique shows that you understand and accept how your patient feels, so it is probably the best one to use. Try it first.

2. Talk quietly. If your patient shouts, try *lowering* your own voice. It will be hard for most people to maintain high-volume output when you are speaking so softly that you can barely be heard.

3. Explain again what information you are trying to get:

"What I really want at this point is to learn about your family history. Perhaps later we can talk some more about your husband's girlfriend."

4. Redirect any of the patient's questions or comments that change the topic.

INTERVIEWER: Now I'd like to hear about your son. You said that he was living with his mother?

PATIENT: That's right, and she hasn't let me even talk to him on the phone for the past 3 months. Don't you think I should get a court order?

INTERVIEWER: We might be able to talk about that later. Right now I really need to know about your relationship with your son. Have you been close?

5. Switch to a closed-ended style. The opposite of open-ended requests, this style indicates what sort of specific answer you would like to hear. It also tends to discourage further comment by the patient.

INTERVIEWER: Could you tell me about your first marriage?

PATIENT: It was a disaster! I've never forgiven that man! He was a complete brute! One time I cried for a month without stopping. Why, I couldn't even . . .

INTERVIEWER: *(Interrupts, recognizing that open-ended questions aren't useful)* Was he a drinker?

PATIENT: Oh gosh, yes, he drank like a camel. He. . .

INTERVIEWER: *(Interrupts)* How long did the marriage last?

PATIENT: Until I was 26, about 4 years. He was never. . .

INTERVIEWER: Was the divorce your idea, or his?

This interviewer was prepared to go on interrupting until the patient learned to stick to the main topic.

6. If you are still having trouble, check to be sure that the patient understands what you want. Here is how you might phrase this confrontation:

"We seem to be having some trouble here with our communication. Have I made it clear what I need to know?"

The aim of each these techniques is to reduce the patient's scope for excessive verbal and behavioral output. They should help you obtain the diagnostic information you need without sacrificing rapport.

Occasionally, even these techniques are insufficient. If an outpouring of tears or other feelings prevents you from obtaining the information you need, you may have to break off the interview long enough for the patient to get a better grip. Say something like this:

"I can see you're too upset to continue today. Let's take a rest for now. I'll stop back and see you again in the morning, when you've had some sleep."

SUMMING UP

Most patients will reveal their feelings with open-ended direct requests from the interviewer. Clinicians can encourage others with a variety of techniques that express their concern and support. Excessively emotional patients may calm down when shown that the interviewer understands their distress. In the extreme, excessive emotional displays may require firm handling to ensure that other important topics are covered.

8 Personal and Social History

Health care professionals don't treat illnesses; they treat people. You therefore need to know the context in which your patient's complaints have occurred. This requires learning all you can about family background and other biographical data. This knowledge will not only help you get to know your patient, but may also reveal additional information about the present illness. Your patient has spent a lifetime accumulating these experiences, so there is almost no limit to the amount and variety of the information that you may find available. What you learn will be determined by the purpose of your present interview and the time you can devote to it.

While you are gathering biographical information, maintain a healthy skepticism about its validity. Human memory is fallible, especially when the human has an intense personal interest in what is being remembered. Accurate recall is more likely for major historical events such as births, deaths, and marriages, and for recent events that constitute the history of the present illness.

Some material is especially subject to distortion: early childhood events, everything reported secondhand, interpersonal disputes, and any other item that requires interpretation. You should be constantly evaluating the validity of all interview data against your own internal standards ("Does this story seem likely? Does it even seem possible?"). But you should also use external checks on accuracy such as previous medical records and interviews with relatives and friends (see Chapter 15).

In this and subsequent chapters I will use *italics* to point out some of the possible interpretations of the material that is discussed.

CHILDHOOD AND ADOLESCENCE

Childhood Nuclear Family

A logical starting place is with your patient's birth. Where did it occur? Was this an only child? If there were brothers and sisters, how many were there of each? What was your patient's position in the sibship (first, second, middle, youngest, or only child)? How well did your patient get along with siblings? Was one sibling favored over the others? *Older children in a sibship tend to receive more attention when they are young, whereas middle children may be relatively neglected; youngest children may be babied or spoiled. Genetic disorders that are obvious at birth (such as Down's syndrome) tend to occur late in a sibship.*

If your patient was one of twins, were they identical (one-egg) or fraternal (two-egg) twins? *Identical twins have inherited the same genetic material; fraternal twins are no more genetically alike than ordinary siblings. Some mental disorders, including schizophrenia and bipolar mood disorder, are much more likely if your patient is the identical co-twin of someone who also has that disorder.*

Did your patient feel wanted as a child? How close was the relationship with the parents? Did this change with adolescence? Was the patient reared by both parents? If not, was this due to death? Divorce? *Absence of a parent (especially the father) has been associated with antisocial personality disorder. In some studies, early death of a parent has been associated with adult-onset depression.*

Occasionally a patient will tell you, "I never knew my father." You should gently try to learn whether the parents were ever married. (Using "Is it possible that. . ." can soften this question considerably.) *Being born "illegitimate" is a lifelong source of discomfort and embarrassment for some people.*

Whatever the exact nature of your patient's nuclear family, you should try to learn something about how the parents (or surrogates) related to one another. Did they communicate well with one another? Show affection? Did they quarrel often? Fight? Did one physically abuse the other? How did their relationship affect the emotional climate in the home while your patient was growing up?

If your patient was adopted, at what age did this take place? Can you learn anything about the biological parents or about the circumstances leading to adoption? Was the adoption intrafamilial (the adoptive parents were blood relatives of the patient) or extrafamilial? *Many adopted people, especially adolescents and young adults, feel incomplete because they don't know their biological parents. This can result in a "quest for roots" that drives some to extraordinary lengths to discover (and in some cases become acquainted with) the "birth parents" who gave them up.*

Growing Up

What was the age of each parent when your patient was born? Were they mature enough to provide responsible care? Did both work regularly? What were their jobs? Were they good providers? Did they have enough time left over to spend with children? What sort of disciplinary techniques were used? Were these harsh, firm, relaxed, or inconsistent?

If either parent was gone from home for an extended period of time, find out why. (Illness? Jail? A job far from home? Was your patient a "military brat"?) Did the family live in one place, or were there frequent moves? Did the family ever really put down roots somewhere?

Find out about hobbies, clubs, and other extracurricular interests. Was your patient sociable? A loner? *Schizophrenics have often been isolated or loners for most of their lives.*

Try to obtain a general picture of the childhood environment and your patient's place in it. Here are some questions that might help you with this broad task:

"Could you tell me something about your childhood?"
"What was life like for you then?"
"Who were your childhood friends?"
"Did you feel different from other kids?"
"How did you spend your free time?"
"Did you belong to organizations such as the Scouts or the Y?"
"Did you participate in organized sports?"
"Where did your family go on vacations?"
"Did your family have pets?"
"What chores or other responsibilities did you have?"
"What summer or after-school jobs did you have?"
"What did you want to be when you grew up?"
"With whom did you identify?"
"Was sex discussed in the home?"
"What were your parents' attitudes toward sex?"
"When did you become interested in the opposite sex?"

Asking about Abuse

Many adults were physically abused as children, an experience that can significantly affect adult personality. This information can be extremely difficult to obtain; sometimes, these patients do not themselves realize the extent to which they were abused as children. You should nonetheless make an effort to learn whether your patient's childhood involved such experiences. You can lead into these sensitive topics gradually.

"How well do you feel your parents provided for you?"
"What methods of discipline did your parents use?"
"Did you ever feel that you were mistreated as a child?"
Positive replies to questions about abuse must be pursued thorough-

ly, if carefully. You will need to develop the following areas of information:

> How often did this abuse occur?
> Who administered it?
> Did both parents participate?
> If one of them tried to shield the child, who was it?
> What form did the abuse take? (Beatings? What with?)
> How often did it occur?
> What was the provocation, if any?
> At the time, did the patient feel that this abuse was deserved? What about now?
> What effect did these experiences have on the patient as a child?
> What does the adult patient feel about these experiences now?

Childhood Health

Early developmental milestones (such as the age at which a child learns to sit, stand, walk, speak words, speak sentences) are usually not worth asking about. Most of what your patient knows about milestones has probably been passed along as family mythology, which is highly subject to distortion. But if you suspect mental retardation or developmental difficulties such as a specific learning disorder, these milestones may be important enough to ask informants about them.

Try to learn something about overall childhood health. Were there frequent visits to doctors, hospitalizations, operations, or long absences from school for health reasons? How did the family regard illness? (Overprotect? Reject?) If your patient was a sickly child, did the parents and other relatives "reward" illness behavior with a great deal of attention? *Overprotection or rewards for illness may precede some somatoform disorders.*

What was your patient's temperament and activity level, especially around ages 5 to 10? Was this child quiet and withdrawn or outgoing and friendly? *Temperament characteristics appear in the first few months of life and tend to persist throughout childhood, even into the adult years. They may correlate with adult mental disorders.*

Does your patient report any of these relatively common childhood problems?

> Bed-wetting
> Tics
> Stuttering
> Obesity
> Nightmares
> Phobias

What treatment, if any, was attempted? Did it help? How did these problems affect relations with siblings or schoolmates? *Any of these conditions suggests that the patient was under stress as a child.*

Were there any concerns about masturbation? At what age did puberty begin? If female, was your patient prepared for the onset of menses? Who told her? At what age did they begin? Was she concerned or teased about breast development? *Teens of either sex can be exquisitely sensitive about being noticed. Developmental delay (or acceleration) may have caused your patient some degree of embarrassment.*

When did dating begin? What feelings were associated with this? Sexual history will be covered in Chapter 9.

Education

What was the last grade completed, and how well did your patient do academically? If there were academic problems, what subjects caused the most trouble? Were there any specific problems with reading (dyslexia)? Did your patient like school? Were there behavior problems in school? Truancy? What were the consequences? (Sent to principal? Paddling? Suspension or expulsion?)

Did your patient repeat grades or have difficulty concentrating on schoolwork? *Hyperactivity, short attention span, and low school performance suggest attention deficit disorder. Some patients with attention deficit disorder as children (little boys, especially) were markedly hyperactive as children, and may even have learned to walk early.*

Did your patient ever miss school for long periods of time? Why? Was there any history of school refusal? How old was your patient when it occurred? *School refusal (once known as "school phobia") is fairly common in young children and does not necessarily predict later pathology.*

Finally, at what age did your patient make the transition from a life of dependency on parents or others to one of self-sufficiency?

LIFE AS AN ADULT

Work History

Employment history can help you judge both your patient's underlying potential and the effect of recent illness on performance. This information is also relatively objective: Work histories seem to be distorted less than more personal, perhaps embarrassing portions of the social history. You should therefore spend some time inquiring into the details of your patient's job history.

What is your patient's current occupation? Is it stimulating, satis-fying? How does it match earlier ambitions? How long has your patient worked for the current employer? If unemployed, why and for how long? If employed only briefly, how many jobs have there been in the last 5 years? Has each job change been for a better one? How much time is spent working? Investigate any gap, change of direction, or lack of pro-motion.

If your patient was ever fired from a job, what were the circum-stances? If unemployed now, why? When did your patient last work regu-larly? If currently unemployed, what is the means of support? *Multiple jobs of brief duration is a history often found in antisocial personality disorder. No job at all or none for many years is commonplace among patients with chronic schizophrenia.*

While you are at it, find out about adult leisure activities. Does your patient have any hobbies? Belong to any clubs or other organizations? Have there been efforts at continuing education as an adult? What about talents? To find out more you can ask,

"What do you think you're good at?"

Military History

Has your patient served in the armed forces? (Don't omit this question for female patients.) If the answer is "Yes," ask:

"What branch?"

"Was this a volunteer enlistment or were you drafted?"

"How long did you serve?"

"What was your job in the military?"

"What was the highest rank you attained?"

"Did you have any disciplinary problems?" (These include courts martial, articles 15, captain's masts, and lower-grade punishments.)

"What kind of discharge did you receive?" (Honorable? General? Dishonorable? Medical?)

"Did you see combat? For how long? What was your role?"

"Were you wounded?"

"Do you have a service-connected disability?" (This is more likely to be the result of accident or illness than wounds.)

"Were you a prisoner of war?"

"As a result of your experiences, have you persistently relived your experiences or had bad dreams or anniversary reactions?" *(Symp-toms such as these that persist after any severe trauma can indicate post-traumatic stress disorder. This condition has been reported in 10% or more of Vietnam-era combat veterans, but it may also occur after civilian calamities [car wrecks, natural disasters].)*

Legal History

Ask about any legal problems. These might include litigation over insurance or disability (especially likely in the case of a chronic illness, injury, or pain), evictions, and feuds with neighbors. In these litigious times, nearly any sort of dispute seems possible. *Legal history can serve as a clue to personality disorders as well as highlight illnesses such as bipolar disorder and substance abuse.*

Has your patient ever been arrested? At what age? What were the circumstances? How many times did this occur? What was the outcome? (Probation? Time in prison?) Was this in local confinement or in a penitentiary? What was the total duration of time served?

Has there been a continuing pattern of illegal behavior from adolescence throughout adult life? Have these criminal activities always taken place in the context of substance abuse, or have they also occurred when clean and sober? Have there been other illegal activities for which your patient has never been caught? It might be worthwhile to ask specifically about shoplifting, which is a relatively common behavior, especially in children and young adults. *In antisocial personality disorder there is a continuing pattern of illegal acts from a young age (12 or earlier for males, 15 or earlier for females). Partly because it carries such a poor prognosis, antisocial personality disorder is a diagnosis you should not make in any patient whose illegal behavior occurred entirely while under the influence of drugs or alcohol.*

Religion

What religion is your patient? Is this different from any religious affiliation of childhood? How often does your patient attend services? *Religion is useful to know about for several reasons. It can provide clues to possible sources of support and comfort and may reveal something of your patient's values and system of ethics. It may also suggest to what degree there has been a break with parents. Some authorities increasingly advocate exploration of the patient's spirituality and belief in God.*

Current Living Situation

Where does your patient live now? (House? Apartment? Mobile home? Rented room? Board and care facility?) What is the neighborhood like?

Does your patient live alone or with someone? With whom? How well does your patient provide self-care? If there has been wandering or a recent onset of excessive orderliness, you might not learn this from the patient. This is material for which you may have to depend on informants. *Excessive orderliness and wandering are both commonly found in patients with organic mental disorders.*

From what your patient says, can you characterize the quality of the home? Is there privacy for each person who lives there? Are there pets? Are there sufficient means of communication—telephone? postal service?—and transportation—car? bus? train?

Has your patient ever been homeless? If so, for how long? What were the circumstances?

What is your patient's financial situation? What is the source of income? Is it steady? Be sure to include jobs, disability compensation, Social Security, annuities, alimony, and investments. Ask, "Has money been a problem for you?"

Social Network

You can begin to assess the quality of social relationships by asking:
"To whom do you feel close in your family?"
"What about among your friends?"
"How often to you see these people?"

Does your patient provide care for another adult, such as a parent, other relative, or friend? How does your patient feel about these duties? Can you tell how well this function is carried out?

How much of a social support network does your patient have? Try to find out about the quality of relationships with family, friends, and co-workers. Are there memberships in any clubs or support groups? Have any government or private agencies helped out? What about home food services like Meals On Wheels? If there are grown children, how close is their relationship?

How does your patient use leisure time? Ask about hobbies, reading, TV, movies. If the last two are mentioned, are they viewed alone or with other people? Have there been any changes in the type of preferred activity or in the patient's ability to concentrate while pursuing it?

Marital Status

It has become commonplace for couples to live together without being married. I will use the terms "spouse" and "partner" to include any relationship between two people, without regard to legal status.

You might start by asking:
"Tell me about your spouse." (How does what you hear from the patient square with what you observe?)

"What do you see as the strong points of your relationship?"
Like all open-ended questions, this one gives enough scope to discuss whatever seems important. The report, favorable or not, could indicate

the overall state of the relationship.

Here are some specific items of information you should learn about:

Is the patient currently married?

Have there been any common-law marriages or long-term relationships?

Are the patient and spouse currently living together?

What are the relative ages of spouse and patient?

How long have they been together?

How long did they know one another before getting married?

How many marriages have there been for each partner?

If there have been prior marriages, how old was the patient each time?

Why did prior marriages end?

How have emotional problems affected the patient's current marriage?

How well does the partner support the patient during periods of illness or disability?

Certain issues, including money, sex, and relatives, are commonly disputed in contemporary marriages. They can develop into mammoth feuds between patients and their families as the burden of mental disorder produces an uncommon number and variety of arguments, fights, affairs, separations, and divorces. Expect to invest considerable time in—and gain extensive information from—inquiries into the quality of your patient's marriage or other love relationship. Following are some of the questions you can ask to elicit routine problems that can produce friction in any relationship:

"How well do you and your spouse communicate?" (Some couples almost never have a serious discussion; successful couples take the time to air their grievances, preferences, and points of view.)

"Does each of you consider the other a best friend?"

"How do you argue?" (Are old issues constantly brought up, or do they get laid to rest? Do the partners commonly say things they later regret?)

"What do you argue about?"

If there are children, you should find out:

How many are there from each marriage?

Are there stepchildren?

What age and sex are all the children?

Were there ever any children conceived outside marriage?

What is the patient's relationship with each of the children?
Do patient and spouse agree about sharing responsibility for child
    care?

Questions about sexual adjustment and preference logically belong
here. Because these can be difficult to discuss, they will be addressed
in a separate chapter on sensitive subjects (Chapter 9).

PAST MEDICAL HISTORY

This section, along with the next one about review of systems, is *not* intended only for psychiatrists and other physicians. It is vital for any practitioner to know about the medical history: It has practical implications
for diagnosis, treatment, and prognosis. Of course, it is also crucial to
any decision regarding requests for medical consultation. The topics
to be covered in these two sections are no more difficult than any of
the other areas we have already discussed.

Has your patient had any previous major illnesses? What were they?
Did they result in hospitalization? Have there been any operations? What
were they? When did they occur? Did the patient ever receive a blood
transfusion? If so, is this patient at risk for AIDS? If serious medical
illness or operations occurred during childhood, how did the patient
perceive them at the time? What about allergies to pollen, dust, or
animals?

While you are taking this history, you might try to ascertain how
well your patient has complied with recommendations made by physicians and other therapists. Many people, especially those who don't know
you very well, may have trouble admitting to poor compliance. Try
asking:

"Has it always been easy for you to follow your doctor's advice?"
"When have you had difficulty?"
You will find more advice on dealing with difficult patient behaviors
in Chapters 16 and 17.

Ask about any obvious physical problems. Don't be shy about bring-
ing up stuttering, an eye patch, a missing limb, or a severe limp. Any
of these could have a bearing on the present problem. They may also
have prompted teasing during childhood. Even if physical defects are
not causing emotional problems now, they probably did at some time
in the past. You might say:

"I noticed that you stammered once or twice while we were talking. I wonder what sort of problems that might have caused when you
were a child."

"Children can be pretty cruel about birthmarks. Could you tell me about yours?"

Medications

In the history of the present illness, you have already learned about the medicines your patient takes for emotional disorders. Now ask whether any other medications are used regularly. This information is especially important when your patient's problems include depression, psychosis, or anxiety. Any of these can be either caused or made worse by commonly prescribed medications. Pay special attention to birth control pills, other hormones (such as thyroid or steroids), pain pills, and drugs for blood pressure. For each medicine, try to learn dose, frequency, and how long your patient has been taking it.

Side Effects

Have there been side effects (unwanted effects) or drug reactions? This topic is often ignored by beginning interviewers, but it can influence the choice of therapies. Try to get a description of the side effect or drug reaction:

> What happened?
> How long after the first dose did it occur?
> Was treatment needed?

If the patient ever tried the drug again, did it produce the same reaction? *Often, patients assume that a drug has caused physical or mental symptoms when the two events were only coincidental. The question of cause and effect is sometimes settled when the drug is started again, and the symptoms either reappear or do not.*

You are most likely to hear complaints about rashes developing from sulfa or penicillin, but it is more important to learn about untoward reactions to psychotropic medications. True allergies to these drugs are rare, but side effects are not. Here are some of the more common ones:

> Antidepressants: drowsiness, dry mouth, skin rash, dizziness, nausea, weight gain, blurred vision, constipation
> Antianxiety agents: drowsiness, forgetfulness or confusion, dizziness
> Lithium: skin rash, tremor, excessive urination, thirst
> Neuroleptics: low blood pressure, extrapyramidal side effects

Extrapyramidal side effects are neurological symptoms that can be caused by taking neuroleptic (antipsychotic) medication. The four types are common enough that every mental health professional can expect to encounter each of them from time to time. The first three occur soon after starting medication and can be treated with antiparkinson drugs such as trihexyphenidyl (Artane) or diphenhydramine (Benadryl).

1. *Acute dystonia* develops within a few hours of the first dose of a neuroleptic. It is characterized by a sharp, cramping pain of the neck that may cause the head to turn to the side. Sometimes the gaze rolls upward. This side effect can be painful and frightening and may constitute a real emergency.

2. *Akathisia* usually begins within a few days of starting neuroleptics. Patients experience it as a profound restlessness, often with an inability to sit still that results in pacing.

3. *Pseudoparkinsonism* also occurs soon after starting medication. The patient experiences a decreased mobility of facial expression (masked facies); a tendency to walk with short, shuffling steps; and a back-and-forth tremor of the hands when they are relaxed, as when resting on a table. This tremor resembles the motions that old-time druggists would use to form drugs into pills, hence the term *pill-rolling tremor*.

4. *Tardive dyskinesia* usually does not begin until the patient has been using neuroleptics for months or years. Someone with tardive dyskinesia typically has uncontrollable motions of the tongue, jaw, and lips that result in persistent pursing, chewing, or licking movements. Patients themselves are often almost entirely unaware that they are doing this; it is not a debilitating disorder, but it is unsightly. *Tardive dyskinesia is all the more important because it has no specific treatment. Unless the neuroleptic is discontinued quickly, tardive dyskinesia can become permanent, persisting even after the medication is eventually stopped.*

REVIEW OF SYSTEMS

In the review of systems you ask patients to identify any symptoms they have had from a list that you recite. That list comprises symptoms from all the different organ systems of the body. The rationale for using it is that patients will recognize more symptoms by passive identification than if you depend upon their spontaneous, active recall.

A complete medical review of systems is long and not especially relevant to the initial mental health examination. However, you should ask about:

Disturbance of appetite *(found in severe depression, anorexia nervosa, and bulimia; over- or under-eating may begin as early as childhood).*

Head injury *(characteristic of organic mental states).*

History of unconsciousness, dizziness, or fainting spells *(suggests organic mental states, somatization disorder).*

Convulsions (seizures). These may be either organic or psychogenic in nature. Ask about these symptoms: loss of consciousness, loss of control of bowels or bladder, tongue biting, any premonition or sensation that warns the patient that a seizure is about to begin.

Symptoms of premenstrual syndrome. Before menses there may be persistent anger, labile mood, trouble with sleep, fatigue, tension, trouble concentrating, and physical symptoms such as weight gain. *Premenstrual syndrome is easy to ignore, especially if you are a male interviewer. But it is fairly common among women of childbearing age and can cause symptoms of depression. (In DSM-III-R it has been renamed late luteal phase disorder.)*

Somatization Disorder

In addition to these general-purpose questions, there is a specialized review of systems you can use to diagnose somatization disorder, a chronic illness that usually begins in the teens or early twenties and is seen in perhaps 8% of female mental health patients. Although this review is somewhat cumbersome to use (another long list), it remains the only reliable way to diagnose somatization disorder. The patient must respond positively to at least 13 symptoms from the list in Appendix B. To count as significant any symptom must

1. Not be accounted for by organic pathology
2. Not occur *only* during a panic attack
3. Have caused the person to take medicine (other than over-the-counter pain medication), see a doctor, or alter life-style

Note that you do not need to review the entire list of symptoms with every patient; a screening test of seven symptoms has been devised by Othmer and DeSouza (1985). Any patient who responds positively to two or more of these symptoms is likely to have somatization disorder. Any patient who gives seven negative responses is unlikely to have somatization disorder, and you don't need to complete the full review of systems. The seven symptoms are:

Vomiting (other than during pregnancy)
Pain in the extremities

Shortness of breath when not exerting
Amnesia
Difficulty swallowing
Burning in the sexual organs or rectum (other than during
      intercourse)
Painful menstruation

FAMILY HISTORY

In the family history you have the opportunity to accomplish three tasks:
(1) develop a brief biographical sketch of parents, siblings, spouse (or
significant other), and children; (2) learn about the relationships between patient and relatives, both childhood and current; and (3) learn
whether mental disorders run in your patient's family, including distant relatives. (Remember that the transmission of a familial disorder
could be either genetic or environmental.)

      You might start with an open-ended request for information about
your patient's current family at home.

      "Tell me how you get along with your (spouse, children)."

      "What sort of people are (were) your parents?"

A few additional probing questions along these lines should help you
answer the first two questions about family history. Keep in mind that
you should obtain your patient's assessment of childhood *and* adult families.

      By this time you have probably already learned such basics as par-
ents' occupations and ages of siblings, but you might not know how much
contact your patient has had with them as an adult. If there has been
a rupture of these relationships, find out why. The answer could tell
you something about the personalities of patient *and* relatives.

      To learn what sort of mental disorders may run in your patient's
family, you should be quite explicit. Carefully define the disorders and
the relatives you are inquiring about:

      "I'd like to know whether any of your blood relatives ever had any
nervous or mental disorders. By 'blood relatives' I mean your parents,
brothers and sisters, children, grandparents, uncles, aunts, cousins,
nieces, and nephews. Has any of these people ever had nervousness, nervous breakdown, psychosis or schizophrenia, depression, problems from
drug or alcohol abuse, suicide or suicide attempts, delinquency,
hypochondriasis (define this term if you think the patient won't understand), mental hospitalization, or arrests or incarcerations?"

      This is a long speech, but it tells the patient exactly what you want
to know and which relatives to consider.

Move through the list of disorders slowly enough to give your patient time to think. Explore the meaning of any positive answer. Just because someone (even a mental health professional) diagnosed Cousin Louise as having schizophrenia doesn't guarantee that she did. The relative could have misunderstood the diagnosis, or the clinician could have been wrong. Try to find out how old she was when she fell ill, what sort of treatment was given and how she responded. What was the ultimate outcome—chronic illness or complete recovery? Did she ever have another episode?

PERSONALITY TRAITS

We may define *personality* as the combination of all the mental, emotional, behavioral, and social aspects that make someone an individual human being. The term *character* is often used synonymously with personality.

Personality traits tend to be formed early and retained throughout adult life. With an episode of acute mental disorder, personality traits may become accentuated; sometimes they change dramatically. With complete remission of the acute episode, former personality characteristics will usually be reassumed.

Much of one's personality is under the surface, not readily apparent to the individual or to others. Psychological testing can help reveal aspects of your patient's personality, but you probably won't have this sort of material available. Your own impression will often depend upon several sources of information:

Your patient's self-assessment
Interviews with people who know the patient well (covered in Chapter 15)
Information about relationships, attitudes, and behaviors with other people
Behavior you observe during your interview session

Self-Assessment

Try to learn what characterized your patient's personality prior to the first episode. This is often referred to as the *premorbid personality*. Some of the following open-ended questions may help you evaluate premorbid personality:

"Describe yourself for me." (This is intended as an invitation. If the response is "What do you mean?" you could prompt for such physical, mental, or emotional characteristics that the patient thinks might be relevant.)

"What sort of a person are you normally?" Watch especially for answers indicating self-esteem that is either low or inflated or for responses that contradict facts you already know.

"What do you like best about yourself?"

"What is your mood normally?"

"What were you like as a teenager?"

You should be especially alert for evidence of lifelong behavior patterns. Your patient may use certain phrases that will tip you off:

"For as long as I can remember, I've made friends easily."

"All my life I've been an 'up' sort of person—until my illness."

The two examples just given suggest behaviors and attitudes that generally work well for the patient. Following is a list of personality characteristics that are generally considered positive:

Charming	Optimistic
Cheerful	Outgoing
Confident	Punctual
Dependable	Steady
Independent	

In the initial mental health interview, you'll often encounter lifelong patterns of maladjustment or interpersonal conflicts. Here are some typical self-evaluations from patients:

"I've always been an anxious, tense person. Kinda depressed."

"I've been a loner all my life."

"People are no damn' good. I don't like them, they don't like me."

"I've never felt comfortable around people—not unless I was drinking."

"I've never been successful the way I'd hoped."

A list of some of these negative personality traits would include:

Changeable	Quarrelsome
Compulsive	Resentful
Controlling	Rigid
Fussy	Self-centered
Histrionic	Suspicious
Irritable	Shy
Jealous	Volatile
Passive	Worrisome

A few other traits could be read as either positive, negative, or neither.

Demonstrative   Reserved
Meticulous   Sensitive

Relationships with Others

During a single interview with any patient, you may have trouble assessing past (or present) personality. Some mental health patients give
distorted assessments: The picture you obtain may be either too gloomy
or overly optimistic. Still, you might obtain valuable information by trying to learn how others view your patient — from the patient's own perspective.

"What sort of situations do people think you have trouble
handling?"

"How well do you control your temper?"

"Does anyone in your family think you have a problem with (alcohol, drugs, your temper, etc.)?"

What can you learn about your patient's prejudices and regard for
other people? Ask,

"How do you feel about your boss?"

"Is your spouse always as supportive as you'd like?"

"Is there anyone—any type of person—you can't stand?"

Questions beginning with *why* may help you sort out your patient's
motivations and style of relating to other people.

"Why do you think your brother wants your mother to move in with
him?"

"You said you can't work well with one of your partners. Why is that?"

Rather than taking what you see or hear at face value, try to evaluate all of this information against behavior you already know about.
For example, suppose you have already been told that a sibling was favored by their father, and that because of ethnicity a co-worker has an
inside track to promotion. How do these opinions square with your patient's claim to being an open and trusting person?

Observed Behaviors

Some of the behaviors you observe during the interview may reveal important character traits. Watch for actions or comments that seem to
go beyond what you would expect during an interview situation. For
example, your patient:

Yawns, slouches, gazes about the room, and otherwise appears
   uninterested
Asks for time out to smoke a cigarette
Questions your credentials as a therapist
Criticizes your clothing or hairstyle
Uses strong words to express prejudice against some ethnic or re-
   ligious group
Tries to argue about something you have said
Brags about qualities that others might seek to conceal, such as sex-
   ual liaisons, physical aggression, illegal activities, or substance
   abuse

   None of these behaviors is diagnostic of character pathology. Combined with the historical information you have obtained, however, they
may suggest style of personality or even a personality disorder.

SUMMING UP

The personal and social history provides a valuable record of a patient's
life. The process of obtaining this history may reveal material that il-
luminates and extends a clinician's knowledge about the cause and context of mental disorder.

9 Sensitive Subjects

Some subjects are hard to discuss. For the patient, they may raise feelings of guilt or shame. For the beginning interviewer, some subjects can be embarrassing. But exploring these sensitive topics—which include sex, substance abuse, and suicidal behavior—is critically important to your interview. In the event that your patient does not mention them spontaneously, you must at some point bring them up yourself. You may delay until later in the interview, after you know the patient a little better, but don't wait until the very end: You could run out of time and still have important material yet to cover. Any interviewer who ignores these topics risks committing serious errors of diagnosis and treatment.

SUICIDAL BEHAVIOR

To ask about suicidal behavior is an absolute must. This rule holds even if there has been no hint of death wishes or suicidal ideas during any portion of the previous interview time. If you violate the rule, you risk ignoring potentially life-threatening ideas and behaviors in a patient who may be too ashamed or too embarrassed to mention them spontaneously. Although the vast majority of mental health patients do not kill themselves, nearly every diagnostic category that has been studied carries some risk of suicide greater than that found in the general population.

When asking about suicidal behavior, you may feel some discomfort of your own. Beginning interviewers sometimes worry that mentioning this topic may plant the idea in a patient's mind. The truth is that any patient with a serious risk of suicide will have considered it long before anyone asks. The real risk is not asking soon enough. Then you might not learn until too late how gravely ill your patient really was.

You'll probably feel more comfortable if your patient is the one who raises the topic. If you aren't given such an opportunity, it is vitally important that you raise the question yourself. Unless your patient seems unusually uncomfortable, you don't need to precede these questions with apologies or explanations. Most patients will feel about as comfortable as you appear to feel.

In the context of the mental health interview it is perfectly all right simply to ask:

"Have you ever had any thoughts of hurting or killing yourself?" If the answer is "No," and this seems to jibe with the patient's mood and recent behavior, you can accept it as simple fact and move on to another topic. If the response is indefinite or delivered in a hesitating manner or with poor eye contact, you must pursue with further questioning.

Of course, you must also be careful not to damage rapport. Should your questioning seem to cause increasing discomfort (hesitation, tears), you may need to comment on the distress:

"You look so sad that I hate to pursue this subject, but I really feel that I must."

To someone who has attempted suicide or has been otherwise violent, you might ask,

"Your recent behavior makes me worry that you might try it again. What do you feel has changed?"

If you wish, you can gradually work toward your goal with a series of increasingly explicit questions:

1. "Have you been having any disturbing or gloomy thoughts?"
2. "Have any of these thoughts been desperate ones?"
3. "Have you ever wished you were dead?"
4. "Have you thought about harming yourself?"
5. "Have you actually made plans to take your own life?"
6. "Have you ever made any suicide attempts?"

It is important to expand upon a "Yes" answer to any of the above questions by asking a suitable, open-ended follow-up question:

"Could you tell me some more about that?"

"What happened then?"

Most of the actual attempts will have occurred prior to this episode—sometimes in the distant past—so memories may be dim. But you should learn as much as you can about previous attempts. The information will help you (1) predict what your patient might do next, and (2) assess what actions you should take. So, get answers to these questions:

- How many previous attempts have there been?
- When did they occur?
- Where was the patient at the time?
- What was the patient's mood at the time?
- What methods were used for the attempts?
- Was the attempt made under the influence of drugs or alcohol? (If so, had there been other attempts when the patient was straight and sober?)
- Did the patient have other mental disorders at the time? (In addition to substance abuse, you especially should learn about depression and psychosis.)
- What were the stressors that preceded the suicidal behavior? (Look especially for losses such as separation or divorce, death of a loved one, job loss, or retirement. However, any upsetting event in the life of the patient or of a friend or relative could serve as a precipitant.)
- How serious were the attempts?

Physical and Psychological Seriousness

The seriousness of a suicide attempt is judged in two ways: (1) How harmful was the attempt physically? (2) How strong was the patient's intent to die? An attempt that is serious either physically or psychologically suggests that this patient is more likely to commit suicide than is one whose previous attempt was not so serious. When you are assessing your new patient for suicide potential, you should have these guidelines in mind.

A suicide attempt is physically serious when it results (or could result) in significant bodily harm. By this standard a severed jugular vein, a deep coma, or a gunshot wound to the chest would be a physically serious attempt. But so would be the ingestion of 100 antidepressant tablets, even if the patient's stomach is pumped before coma sets in. Without prompt medical attention, fewer than half that number of antidepressants could be fatal.

At the other extreme are those attempts that are highly unlikely to cause serious harm, let alone death. They include such acts as lightly scratching the wrist and swallowing four or five aspirin tablets. Such behaviors are sometimes called "gestures." They suggest that, in making an attempt, the patient had some purpose other than dying. To make this judgment, you must assess the psychological seriousness of the attempt.

The psychological seriousness of an attempt is assessed apart from its physical implications. Now you want to know what intention lay behind the attempt. Was there a genuine wish to die, or was it a cry for help? Here are some of the possible motives for attempted suicide:

A genuine wish to die
The desire to attract help
Escape from some intolerable situation
Relief from mental distress
An attempt to influence someone

Many patients who have made psychologically serious attempts can clearly state their feelings.

"I'm sorry I didn't succeed."

"I'll try it again."

Others may be less clear, or perhaps ambivalent. For them you must ask:

"What did you think would be the outcome of your overdose?"

For some, your best course could be to infer their intentions from behavior. The patient who attempts suicide under an assumed name, alone in a hotel room, is clearly more serious than one whose attempt occurs at home just before the expected return of a spouse.

Here are some other questions that can help you judge the psychological seriousness of intent:

"Did you impulsively decide to make the attempt or had you been planning it for a while?" *Planning and preparation are usually associated with more serious attempts.*

"Before the attempt, had you written or revised a will, given away property, or taken out life insurance?" *Any of these behaviors suggests planning.*

"Did you write a suicide note?" *More evidence of planning.*

"Was someone with you when you made the attempt?" *A "yes" answer suggests that the patient had arranged a means of rescue.*

"What did you do after you made the attempt?" (Lie down to wait for the end? Call for help? Phone the suicide hotline?) *Inaction of any sort is serious.*

"How did you feel when you were rescued?" *"Anger" sounds more serious than "relief."*

Whatever you learn about these past suicide ideas and attempts, it must be correlated with your patient's current thinking on the subject. It is vital to learn whether your patient has ideas or plans that could prove lethal, especially within the next few hours or days. Ask:

"Have you felt suicidal recently?"

"What have been your thoughts about it?"

"Have you made any plans?"

"What are they?"

"Do you think you are likely to carry them out?"

"When is it likely to happen?"

"Could anything make suicide seem less a possibility?"

As a general rule you should avoid using the term *manipulative* in describing a suicide attempt. For one thing, most patients who attempt (or complete) suicide are somewhat ambivalent about their actions, so nearly every attempt is to some extent manipulative. More important, this term tends to cause clinicians and families alike to relax their vigilance at a time when they may need it most.

Any current ideas or plans that could prove harmful, even lethal, require rapid action. If you are a student, this may mean contacting the treating clinician at once, to be certain that the patient's thoughts and plans are fully known. This action on your part is essential, even if it means violating a confidence or promise of confidentiality you have made previously. *Avoiding suicide and other harm to patients is an absolute duty of every mental health professional. To carry out this duty effectively, all clinicians must feel confident that everyone who has contact with the patient will share vital information. If you must break a confidence to ensure the safety of your patient, be assured that the vast majority of patients will not blame you for your action. In fact, most patients later feel intensely grateful for such a lifesaving "betrayal."*

VIOLENCE AND HOMICIDAL IDEAS

A history of violent behavior is relatively uncommon, but it is at least as important to learn about as suicide. It can have serious implications for patients as well as for intended victims.

If your patient admits to legal difficulties such as arrests or periods in confinement, you will have a natural lead-in to questions about violence. Much violence is domestic, so another good time to inquire is when you learn that the patient has been divorced or has been a partner in a troubled marriage. (Don't forget to ask about beatings or other mistreatment that the patient might have received *from* a domestic partner.)

If no natural lead-in occurs, you will have to ask. As with self-harm, you can work up to the subject gradually:

1. "Have you ever had feelings of uncontrollable rage?"
2. "Have you had any thoughts about harming others?"
3. "Have you ever had trouble controlling your impulses?"
4. "As an adult have you been involved in fights?"
5. "Were you ever arrested for fighting or for other violent behavior?"

Positive answers must be explored.
"What were the circumstances of the violent acts?"
"When did they occur?"
"Who was involved?"
"How did you feel about this?"
"Did the behavior involve substance abuse?"
"What was the effect on the victim?"
"What happened to you as a result?"
"Were you arrested?"
"Were you convicted?"
"How much time did you serve?"

Throughout, try to understand which emotions lie behind your patient's violent ideas or behavior and what might be causing these feelings. These emotions might include, for example:

Anger at the motorist who has damaged the patient's car
Depression that results from genetic inheritance plus heavy drinking
Envy of a co-worker who has won a coveted promotion to vice-president
Frustration that the Internal Revenue Service continues to send dunning notices for an assessment the patient has already paid
Greed when confronted with the possibility of inheriting a large estate
Hatred for an ex-spouse
Revenge for a sister's death at the hands of a mugger

SUBSTANCE ABUSE

At least one of every 13 adult Americans has a problem with substance abuse. The figure is even higher among mental health patients, of whom perhaps 25% abuse substances. Some experience with substances of abuse has become almost a rite of passage for American teenagers. It is so common, and its effects upon patient and environment are so far-reaching, that substance abuse must be covered in the initial interview of every mental health patient, regardless of sex, age, or presenting complaint.

Alcohol

Despite the educational efforts of mental health professionals and 12-step organizations like Alcoholics Anonymous, many people still view substance abuse as a disorder of morals. As a result, patients and interviewers often find this issue difficult to discuss. Perhaps you can find a natural lead-in. The family history might tip you off.

PATIENT: So you can see, my childhood was nearly ruined by Mom's drinking.

INTERVIEWER: Sounds pretty difficult, all right. And what about you—do you do any drinking yourself?

It may be inconvenient just then to change course and pursue a new subject such as the patient's drinking. You might elect to keep on pursuing the childhood history and later refer back to what the patient said about family history:

INTERVIEWER: A few minutes ago you mentioned your mother's drinking. It made me wonder—have you ever been a heavy drinker yourself?

If your patient doesn't raise the subject of drug and alcohol abuse, you will have to create your own opportunity. Alcohol is more socially acceptable, so you can ask about it with less risk of embarrassment. Assume that your patient, like most adults, is no teetotaler. You will be right more often than not, and the assumption of some drinking may ease the stigma if your patient's drinking has been excessive. Find out how often and how much your patient drinks:

"Now, I'd like to know about some of your habits. First, in an average month, on how many days do you have at least one drink of alcohol?"

Note how this interviewer requests a precise answer, framed in terms of days per month. This discourages vague or evasive answers such as "not very much" or "only on social occasions." (You can count the following drinks as having roughly the same alcohol content: a 12-ounce beer, a 6-ounce glass of wine and a 1-ounce shot of 80-proof hard liquor.)

Next you might ask:

"On the average day that you have at least one drink, how many drinks do you usually have?"

These two numbers—drinks per day and days per month—allow you to calculate your patient's average number of drinks per month. As you do more interviews, you will develop a feel for what is usual and what is excessive. More than 60 drinks per month (two per day, on average) is worrisome; more than 100 per month is far above the norm. But even a number below 60 can suggest a drinking problem if many of the drinks are consumed over just a few individual days: Binge drinking is one of the possible patterns of alcohol abuse.

Even if the patient denies current heavy drinking, learn how much drinking there has been in the past. Has the patient been a lifelong teetotaler, or is this a recent change? ("I don't touch alcohol" may mean "I haven't had a drink since Sunday. For breakfast.") Ask:

"Was there ever a time in your life when you used alcohol more heavily than you do now?"

Obtain follow-up information about days per month, drinks per day, and the reasons for stopping.

Alcoholism is a disorder that is defined by its consequences. The amount a person consumes is an important clue, but the diagnosis itself is based on the effects drinking has on the individual and on the environment. Therefore, unless your patient denies ever having a problem with drinking, you will need to ask questions about several categories of consequences.

For medical problems, ask:

"Has drinking caused you to have liver trouble, vomiting spells, or other medical problems?"

"Has a doctor ever told you to quit drinking because of your health?"

"Have you ever suffered from blackouts? That means that the morning after drinking you can't remember what happened the night before." (As demonstrated in this question, be sure to define what you mean by *blackout*—some patients won't know the term.)

For loss of control, ask:

"Have you ever tried to quit drinking?"

"Have you ever set rules about drinking such as 'Never drink before four in the afternoon?'"

"Do you ever gulp drinks?"

"Once you take your first drink, do you have trouble stopping?"

For personal and interpersonal problems, ask:

"Do you sometimes feel guilty about how much you drink?"

"Have you ever gotten into fights when drinking?"

"Has drinking ever caused a divorce or other serious domestic problems?"

"Has it lost you friends?"

For job problems, ask:

"Has drinking ever caused you to be absent from work? Late to work?"

"Have you ever been fired from a job because of drinking?"

For legal problems, ask:

"Have you ever been arrested for alcohol-related behavior?"

"Have you had any arrests for driving while intoxicated?" (Find out what happened in court.)

"Have you ever caused an accident while driving under the influence?"

For financial problems, ask:

"Have you ever spent money on alcohol that should have gone for necessities like food?"

"Have you had any other financial difficulties because of drinking?"

If any of these questions yields a positive response, ask:

"Have you ever been concerned about your drinking?"

"Have you ever thought that you were alcoholic?"

"What has been your longest period of sobriety?"

"How did you achieve that?"

"Were you ever treated for alcohol abuse?"

"What happened as a result of treatment?"

Street Drugs

With street drugs, the procedure is similar. Your questions about alcohol use will lead naturally into this subject. Ask:

"Have you ever used street drugs of any sort?"

As with alcohol, you will want to learn when drug use began and when it ended. Define the type of drug, frequency of use, and its effect on the patient, friends, and relatives.

One problem you may encounter is not knowing the slang terminology for drugs commonly abused. (It is hard to stay completely current: The language of the street keeps changing.)

Hypnotics: downers, ludes, yellow jackets, tranks, reds, rainbows, Christmas trees

Cocaine: snow, coke, rock, crack

Hallucinogens: LSD, acid, PCP, mescaline, peyote, STP

Narcotics: H, horse, smack, junk (heroin); schoolboy (codeine); little D (dilaudid); Miss Emma (morphine)

Marijuana: pot, grass, tea, hash, joint, reefer, Mary Jane

Central nervous system stimulants: uppers, bennies, black beauties, crank, speed

In addition, special names may be used by various ethnic groups or in diverse parts of the country, and the terminology is fluid, changing as new cohorts of users come of age.

Prescribed Medications

Don't forget to inquire into overuse of medicines.

"Have you ever taken more of a prescription medication than your doctor prescribed?"

"Do you ever overuse over-the-counter drugs?"

Again you need to know when, what, how much and what the effects were.

SEXUAL LIFE

Patients expect questions about sex. For most, it's an accepted part of consulting a mental health professional. This line of questioning may make some people feel uncomfortable, so you're usually better off delaying it until later in the interview. Not only will you know the patient better by then but also these sensitive issues will be placed in the context of other necessary psychological, medical, and social information.

Even if your patient's behavior conflicts with your own values, you must be able to discuss it openly, without showing disapproval or censure. Clinicians in training often have difficulty questioning patients about their sex lives. This may relate to their own standards of sexual conduct, which in turn are the result of their upbringing and culture. Here is a point where it is vital to recognize your own standards and acknowledge that your patient has the right to a different set.

During the present illness or the personal and social history, you may have already learned something about the relationship between patient and partner that provides a natural introduction to the subject of sex. If this has not happened or if the patient has no current partner, a straightforward request for information is in order. An open-ended question will provide both comfort for you and scope for the patient to respond: "Now I would like you to tell me about your sexual functioning." The form of this question assumes that most people have sex, and that this is acceptable and normal.

If the first response is a question of the patient's own ("How do you mean?"), you might elaborate as follows:

"I'm trying to learn two things. First, how is your sexual functioning usually? And second, how has it been affected by the problem that brought you into treatment?" (Note that this speech, which deliberately breaks the rule about not asking two questions at once, tells the patient the scope of what you are trying to learn.)

The ensuing discussion should give you the following sorts of information:

At what age did the patient first learn about sex?
What was the nature of early sexual experiences?
At what age did they occur?
How did the patient react to them?

Sexual Preference

Some mental health clinicians prefer to start their inquiries about sex with a straightforward question:

"What is your sexual preference?"

This approach has the virtue of (usually) eliciting a clear answer early, therefore avoiding the possibility of embarrassing misunderstandings later. (Be careful not to assume that a married patient has no history of homosexuality.)

If any patient has such a history, you should try to learn:

Is the patient exclusively gay or bisexual?

If the latter, about what percent of sexual encounters are hetero-sexual?

Does the patient find this sexual orientation comfortable (ego-syntonic) or uncomfortable (ego-dystonic)?

How well has the patient integrated sexual orientation with life-style?

Has the patient wanted or attempted to change?

Although dreams and fantasies are not often productive in an initial interview, the presence of homosexual fantasies may help in the evaluation of patients who remain unclear as to their basic orientation.

Sexual Practices

A great many questions can be asked, and should be asked, when there is a history of sexual difficulty. This extensive list is not one that should be asked routinely. When these questions must be broached, they are often better left until a subsequent interview. Use your common sense. Once you have assured yourself that the patient and partner are happy together and function well sexually, you can probably employ a general question:

"Have there been any problems of a sexual nature that we haven't yet talked about?"

In the event of sexual problems, however, some of the following issues will be appropriate for discussion:

- What are the current sleeping arrangements?
- Have there been problems with intercourse? (Do they necessitate abstinence?)
- Is sex pleasurable for the patient?
- What about for the partner? (Until sex preference and practices are known, it is safer to use *partner* than a gender-specific noun.) *Lack of pleasure is relatively common in women, much less so for men.*

- If married or in a long-term relationship, have there been outside affairs? How many? How often? How recent?
- Does the couple communicate clearly about sex?
- What is the frequency of sexual relations? Has this changed recently, or with age?
- Who usually initiates sex?
- Does the couple use foreplay? How long does it last? What constitutes foreplay? (Talking? Kissing? Genital touching?) *Because many men do not realize that arousal takes longer for a woman than for a man, their female partners may report that foreplay is too brief and that intercourse itself is unsatisfying.*
- If oral sex is practiced, are both partners enthusiastic about it?
- How often does the patient achieve climax? *Anorgasmia (lack of climax) is fairly common among women, who may nonetheless experience strong sex desire. Some can achieve climax only under certain circumstances, such as with masturbation. Ability to achieve climax, like sexual interest, may be decreased by illness (physical or mental) and anxiety.*
- How often does the patient masturbate? Does this represent a problem for either the patient or the partner?
- What method of birth control (if any) does the couple use? Do the partners agree about the timing or prevention of conception?
- Have there been sex partners outside the current relationship?
- Has either partner had any history of sexually transmitted disease?

Common Sexual Problems

Interviewers should be alert for several relatively common sexual problems:

Impotence (inability to achieve or maintain erection). How long ago did it start? Is it total or partial? Does it occur only with specific partners? Has it been medically investigated? Treated? Note that impotence is quite different from lack of sexual desire.

Dyspareunia (pain with intercourse). Common in women, this condition has rarely been reported in men, too. Its cause can be organic or emotional. Is it severe enough to interfere with sexual functioning or pleasure?

Premature ejaculation. When a man too quickly reaches the stage of ejaculatory inevitability (to use the Masters and Johnson term), both partners can experience frustration and lack of pleasure.

Retarded ejaculation. This can be the result of emotional factors, such as guilt, or certain medications (thioridazine).

When learning about sexual problems, ask for specific instances in which the problem arose. If there are problems of technique, get the patient to describe them in behavioral terms: "First I. . .then she does. . .but that usually doesn't work, so we. . . ." As for any nonsexual problem, find out when it began, how often and under what circumstances it occurs, how severe it is (is it worsening?), what has been done about it, and what seems to help.

Paraphilias

Relatively uncommon are the paraphilias, which comprise a number of disorders in which the patient is aroused by a stimulus other than a consenting adult human, or by the humiliation or suffering of the patient or sexual partner. The diagnosis is made only when the desire has occurred repeatedly for least 6 months and when the patient has acted on the urge or has been markedly distressed by it. Almost all such patients are men. They often experience as many as three or more of these urges, which can interfere with the ability to enjoy normal sexual and love relationships. The specific paraphilias are:

Exhibitionism. These patients have fantasies and urges that involve the sudden exposure of their genitals to a stranger, usually a female. Patients who act upon these fantasies don't attempt physical contact with the victim and pose no physical danger.

Fetishism. Fetishists are sexually aroused by inanimate objects, often shoes or women's underwear, which are used by the patients themselves or are worn by a partner for sexual activity.

Frotteurism. Frotteurs are aroused by touching or rubbing against a nonconsenting person. Frottage usually takes place in a crowd and may involve contact with hands or genitals.

Pedophilia. These patients have sexual fantasies and urges about young (usually 13 or under) children. Most pedophiles prefer girls, but some are aroused by boys or by children of either gender. The disorder is usually chronic and may involve various sexual activities including looking, undressing, and physical contact.

Sexual masochism. The sexual fantasies and behaviors of these patients involve being beaten, bound, or otherwise humiliated or made to suffer. When extreme, death from suffocation can result.

Sexual sadism. These patients are sexually aroused by inflicting physical or psychological pain on partners, who may be either consenting or nonconsenting. Such behavior usually increases over time, sometimes to the point that these patients cause severe injury and even death.

Transvestic fetishism. Occurring only in heterosexual males, this disorder involves sexual arousal from dressing in women's clothing.

Voyeurism. Voyeurs ("peeping Toms") are aroused by watching an unsuspecting person who is nude, in the act of disrobing, or having sex.

Other forms of paraphilia. Other paraphilias include sexual arousal from animals, body excretions, cadavers, and "talking dirty" on the telephone.

Sexually Transmitted Diseases

For all patients, be alert for a history of sexually transmitted diseases. Especially ask about risk factors for AIDS: multiple sex partners, sex with drug abusers, or homosexual relationships. If any answer is "Yes," you'll need to ask whether condoms are used. If so, what percent of the time? Has the patient ever been tested for HIV? How recently? What were the results?

SEXUAL ABUSE

Childhood Molestation

A history of childhood sexual experience is distressingly common, especially among mental health patients. Yet this area is often left unexplored, even by experienced clinicians. *Childhood sexual experiences are being linked to an increasing number of adult disorders, including borderline personality disorder, eating disorders, multiple personality disorder, and somatization disorder. (Descriptions of some of these conditions are in Appendix B.)*

Even if none of these conditions is present, memories of early sexual behavior may present concerns that require discussion and reassurance. Therefore, you must ask. But ask in a way that avoids the loaded term *molestation:*

"When you were a child, were you ever approached for sex by another child or by an adult?"

Any positive answer should be explored thoroughly. In particular, obtain the following details:

What actually happened?
Was there physical contact?
How old was the patient then?
How many times did the incidents occur?

Who was the perpetrator?
Was there a blood relationship between perpetrator and patient?
How did the patient react to the incident(s)?
Were the parents told?
What were their reactions?
How have these incidents affected the patient, either during child-
    hood or as an adult?

An occasional patient will give equivocal answers such as "I'm not
sure" or "I really can't remember much about my childhood." Such a
response should alert you that somewhere in your patient's background
may lie experiences too distressing to be tolerated as conscious memory.
Further probing at this time probably won't uncover much additional
information, but do try to identify as exactly as possible the interval
that has been forgotten ("ages 6 through 12" or "throughout junior high").
It may help later with the memory recovery process.

This is one time when you should probably not alert your patient
that you will return to the subject later. A promise to pursue long-buried
traumatic memories may seem threatening and could interfere with the
rapport you are trying to build. Instead, say:

"It sounds as if you have some doubt about this area. That's all
right—nobody remembers everything from childhood. But if anything
about early sexual experiences comes back to you, I'd like to hear about
it later. It could be important."

Do make a careful note to return to the subject in a later interview,
when your relationship is on solid ground.

Rape and Spouse Abuse

For decades (at least) the crime of rape has been seriously underreport-
ed. This fact is probably explained by victims' feelings of shame and
embarrassment and their fear of notoriety. With the publicity of "celebri-
ty rape" trials and our enhanced understanding of victim psychology,
these attitudes may have lessened somewhat in recent years. Nonetheless, it is still all too common that patients (nearly all of them female)
have as adults suffered rape or other forms of sexual abuse. Mental
health interviewers must be able to draw forth the information needed
to determine the best course of action for these patients, many of whom
have been severely traumatized by their experiences.

Usually the preferred first approach is a sympathetic, unstructured
invitation to describe the events and their consequences: "Please tell
me about these experiences." With gentle, probing questions you should
try to obtain the following information:

What were the circumstances? (Surroundings? Patient's age?)
Who was the perpetrator? (Date? Acquaintance? Gang?)
How many times did it occur?
Did the patient know the perpetrator?
Were they related?
Was the use of alcohol or drugs involved? By whom?
What feelings did the patient have at the time?
Who has been told?
Has the story been heard sympathetically?
Has legal action been taken? If not, why not?
What have been the lingering effects of the experiences? (Look for
    fear, anger, shame, anxiety, depression, and symptoms of post-
    traumatic stress.)

Similar multiple emotions can be evoked by sexual and physical
abuse from spouses. Victims may also be reluctant to report this crime
for fear of reprisals, such as further abuse or abandonment.

SUMMING UP

Getting up the courage to cover sensitive subjects is one of the novice
interviewer's more difficult challenges. The material itself is pretty
straightforward: In a short time a student can learn the basic questions
to ask about suicide behavior, substance abuse, and sexuality. To ask questions that our society largely regards as deeply private and in many cases
embarrassing, however, may require the interviewer to cast aside a lifetime of training, personal doubts, and, perhaps, prejudice. Yet the mental
health professional must competently deal with these issues every working day.

10 Control of the Later Interview

During most of the early interview you have encouraged your patient to discuss problems freely. By the time you move on to the personal and social history, you will need to exercise more control over the form of your interview. This will enable you to use your time efficiently to cover all the material and probe the important remaining areas.

TAKE CHARGE

Some patients take direction so well that you can exercise control by gently interjecting an occasional question to serve as a guide. Patients who are only circumstantial or perhaps just plain talkative will need more active measures of control. Others with manic pressure of speech or psychotic suspiciousness may require almost constant redirection.

Of course, you will have to temper your own verbal output. Novice interviewers must be especially wary: Anxiety sometimes causes them to speak too often or at excessive length. Remember that the main purpose of your questions and interventions is to facilitate the flow of information from the patient to you. Formulate your questions clearly and succinctly so that you occupy as little time as possible with explanations.

With the need to cover so much ground, you may not be able to respond as completely as you would like to issues your patient raises. For example, on hearing that your patient was teased as a child, your natural impulse may be to sympathize and ask for examples, effects, and parents' reactions. But perhaps it is late in the session and you still must uncover any history of sexual abuse: You may have to defer some of these natural responses to another session. For now you could briefly sympathize and then indicate your interest by asking about other childhood traumas you want to know about anyway.

PATIENT: . . . so I felt that I was the butt of every schoolyard joke and prank.

INTERVIEWER: That sort of experience can really make a kid miserable. Did you have other sorts of distressing problems as a child—for example, did any one ever approach you about sex?

You should try to avoid abrupt transitions, which can impair rapport. Instead, try one of these techniques:

- You can change the subject with more grace if you first make an empathic comment, as did the interviewer in the previous example.
- Stop taking notes, and put down your pen. If you continue to write, your patient may feel encouraged to continue talking about the same subject.
- If you must interrupt, try raising your forefinger (raising an entire hand seems peremptory) and taking a breath to signal that you need a turn to speak.
- Try moving quickly to get in a word between two of your patient's sentences. Although this requires vigilance and can sometimes be a real struggle, it usually works well, especially if you manage to intervene at the end of a thought.
- If your patient brings up something that you already have covered sufficiently, indicate the need for a change of direction:
    "I'd like to hear more about that later, if we have time. For now, let's talk instead about. . . ."
    "I think I understand about your insomnia. But has your appetite changed any?" (Notice that asking a yes or no question suggests that now you'd like a short answer.)
- Nod or smile when you do get the sort of brief answer you want. This reinforcement will encourage further brevity.

But some patients simply don't respond well to hints. For someone who continues to ramble, you may have to be more direct. A good approach is to state clearly your needs and your proposed solution.
    "For me to help you best, it's important that we cover a lot of ground. That means we'll have to move on now to another area."
    "Our time is a little short. . . ."
    "Let's stick with the main topic. . . ."
    You may have to indicated the new direction more than once before an especially talkative patient gets the message. But keep at it— you must obtain all of your diagnostic material.

CLOSED-ENDED QUESTIONS

In the earlier portions of the interview, open-ended questions are recommended because they help patients communicate with greater clarity and scope. Later in the interview, when you know what sort of specific information may be relevant to diagnosis and therapy, closed-ended questions work especially well.

Closed-ended questions are those that can be answered "Yes" or "No" or that request a specific answer like the age of children or the place of birth. They allow you to pin down diagnostic criteria and clarify previous responses, so you obtain a more complete picture of your patient's problems. They will also help you ascertain significant negatives (such as the *absence* of sexual problems or psychosis); from open-ended questions alone you might not learn that your patient doesn't have these symptoms.

Another closed-ended technique is to substitute a multiple-choice request when your patient can't answer a question that is less well defined:

INTERVIEWER: For about how long have you been using cocaine?

PATIENT: Well, I . . . that is, . . . uh, I don't know exactly.

INTERVIEWER: Well, has it been a week or 2, or more like 6 months, or perhaps a year or more?

PATIENT: Oh, it's been over a year. Maybe 3 years, anyway.

You should also be aware of the potential drawbacks of closed-ended questions. More verbal patients might resent closed-ended questions if they think that you are more interested in the process of getting the information than you are in the person who is supplying it. Also, the yes-or-no format denies patients the chance to give a gradient of response. The answer you get could mislead, rather than educate you. Here is an unfortunate example:

INTERVIEWER: Did you have problems relating to your father when you were a child?

PATIENT: *(Thinking,* "Let's see, I couldn't stand the Old Man, so I never paid any attention to what he said. I guess the answer I can give is. . .") No.

Closed-ended questions can be valuable, but you should avoid suggesting how you would like your patient to answer. These leading questions broadly hint that there are certain standards or behaviors you approve of. A leading question severely limits the scope and validity of the information you will obtain. For example, don't indicate your idea of "average":

INTERVIEWER: How much alcohol do you drink?

PATIENT: Oh, I'd say it's about average.

INTERVIEWER: Two or three times a week?

PATIENT: Well, sure.

A better response for this interviewer would be, "What is 'average' for you?" In fact, beware of any leading formulation that suggests your judgment of what is normal. Instead of "Is your relationship with your father a good one?" try the open-ended "How do you get along with your father?"

Closed-ended questions may actually inhibit some patients from responding fully. This is why they should only be used later in the interview, after you have built rapport and your patient has developed the habit of giving full responses. Closed-ended questions also give you more work to do. While you are doing much of the talking, your patient has the chance to screen out possible replies that are embarrassing or that seem "irrelevant." In consequence, you could be given false or incomplete information.

Nevertheless, this highly structured style of requesting information may be appropriate for patients who are not used to the interview process or for those whose verbal skills have never been well developed. This will apply especially to patients with severe mental illness such as untreated schizophrenia, to some with mental retardation, and to those who, for a variety of reasons, are reluctant to be interviewed in the first place. Such patients may require extensive use of yes-or-no questions.

Regardless of how far you have progressed in the interview, you will probably succeed best if you continue to use both open-ended and close-ended questions. For example, after you have obtained a string of rapid-fire answers that confirm a diagnosis of alcoholism, you might relieve the monotony (and tension) by asking something open-ended:

"That was a lot of questions. Now perhaps you could tell me how you plan to deal with your drinking in the future."

By combining styles you can obtain detailed, structured information as well as encourage your patient to generate important new material, and the combination of styles should help you obtain material that has maximum validity.

SENSITIVITY TRAINING

It is important to remember that highly structured questioning needn't (and shouldn't) be abrasive or otherwise unpleasant. Of course, you can soften any question with a sympathetic facial expression or tone of voice. But you should also phrase your requests to help your patient talk about a variety of sensitive issues:

- "I know that your wife's death makes it hard for you to talk about her." This comment acknowledges that the topic is important enough to pursue despite the patient's obvious distress.
- "How do you think other people would deal with a daughter who's gotten into trouble with the law?" By asking how others might react or feel, you may be able to reduce your patient's sense of personal involvement and responsibility. This particular expression also suggests that the patient is not alone in suffering from this sort of experience. The result could be information that you would otherwise miss.
- "What if you were picked up by the police for drinking—how would you feel?" Using supposition, you help your patient achieve some distance from the emotionally charged situation.
- "Have you ever had the opportunity to tell your wife you were sorry for hitting her?" Here, you soften the question by suggesting that chance might have prevented some praiseworthy action that your patient should have taken, but didn't.

TRANSITIONS

Effective interviewing isn't just asking one question after another. You must also pay attention to the overall coherence of what you and the patient are saying. The sentence or phrase you use to get from one topic to the next is called a *transition*. A careful transition shows that you are paying attention. It also helps your patient understand where you are going. This keeps the patient from feeling blindly herded. Transitions also help you tie the entire story together.

The best transitions are couched in language that flows naturally, as in a conversation. Try to let each question take off from a portion of the previous answer. Whenever possible, use the patient's own words as a vehicle for exploration:

PATIENT: . . . so our finances really changed for the better when my wife got a full-time job.

INTERVIEWER: And what about your relationship—did it change after your wife got a full-time job?

Interviews can't always proceed in a linear fashion. If you are discussing important topic A when B is mentioned, your interview could become scattered unless you get closure on A before moving on. Later, if you reintroduce B by referring to your patient's earlier statement, you will have made a smooth transition. For example:

"A few minutes ago you mentioned that the depression seems to get better when you drink alcohol. Could you tell me some more about the drinking?"

You can use any common factor—time, place, family relationships, a job—to smooth the flow of the conversation:

PATIENT: . . . so it was just after my brother left for Vietnam that my mother died.

INTERVIEWER: And what were you doing at that time?

No one likes to be given the third-degree; patients are no exception. You should therefore try to make your interview feel like a conversation, not an interrogation. Smooth transitions help to create that feeling. But when you have to make an abrupt transition, flag it so the patient realizes that you are changing gears intentionally:

"I think I've got a good picture of your drinking. Now I'd like to move on to something different. Could you tell me whether you've ever had problems with other substances, such as marijuana or cocaine?"

The one time you may feel tempted to make a fairly abrupt transition is if your patient becomes hostile or anxious. Even then, you should attempt to smooth the transition by acknowledging the shift—and the patient's right to whatever upset feelings you may have inadvertently elicited. For example, "I can see that it's pretty upsetting to talk about how your wife ran off with her lover. I don't blame you. It's an area we can easily skip for now. Instead, let me ask you some more about your new girlfriend."

Of course, if it is your patient who abruptly changes the subject, you should try to learn why.

SUMMING UP

When obtaining details of the present illness and personal and social history, clinicians need closed-ended questions to obtain information that is specific and complete. A number of verbal and nonverbal techniques can help direct the patient's responses and maximize the amount of material obtained. Sensitive use of transitions helps convey interest in the patient as a person, despite the clinician's increasing control over the interview process.

Mental Status Exam I: Observational Aspects

WHAT IS THE MENTAL STATUS EXAM?

The mental status exam is simply your evaluation of the patient's current mental functioning. It was traditionally a part of the neurological exam but is now a staple of the initial mental health examination. This and the following chapter discuss the complete mental status exam. The amount of material presented here may seem daunting at first, but once learned it becomes automatic and easy to cover in a few minutes.

The mental status exam is usually divided into several parts. They can be arranged many different ways. Arrange your mental status exam any way you wish, as long as you cover all the parts. Your best bet is to choose a format, memorize it, and perform your mental status exam the same way every time until it has become second nature.

The following format has worked well for many professionals. It divides the mental status exam into two large areas.

Behavioral Aspects

To obtain this material you don't have to ask special questions or perform tests. Mostly you just observe speech and behavior while you are talking to your patient (although in the area of mood there are some questions to ask). The behavioral aspects include

1. General appearance and behavior
2. Mood
3. Flow of thought

Cognitive Aspects

These portions of the mental status exam are concerned with what your patient is thinking (talking) about. Their evaluation demands more activity on your part. They include

1. Content of thought
2. .Perception
3. Cognition
4. Insight and judgment

The cognitive aspects will be described in Chapter 12.

I will define and explain the standard terms you need to know. *Italics* will indicate some of the possible interpretations you might put on this information. Remember that throughout your interview you should be constantly evaluating what you observe of your patient's present behavior against what the history would lead you to expect.

GENERAL APPEARANCE AND BEHAVIOR

You can learn a great deal about a patient just by looking. Most of the following are characteristics that you should begin to notice even before anyone says a word. Start observing as you call your patient into your office or as you greet one another at the bedside.

Physical Characteristics

What is your patient's ethnicity? *Various studies suggest that Hispanic patients report symptoms differently from Anglos. Some diagnoses are more common among, for example, Native Americans. Any patient may have difficulty relating to a clinician of a different ethnicity.*

How old would you say this person is? Do apparent age and stated age jibe? *Age can suggest certain diagnoses. A young patient — late teens to mid-thirties — may demonstrate symptoms of personality disorder or schizophrenia. Older patients are more likely to have symptoms of melancholia or Alzheimer's dementia.*

Notice your patient's body build. Is it slender? Stocky? Muscular? What about posture? (Erect? Slumped?) Are walking and other movements graceful or jerky? Is there a limp? Are there unusual physical characteristics such as scars, tattoos, or missing limbs? How would you assess the patient's general nutrition? (Obese? Slender? Wasted?) *Abnormal thinness suggests anorexia nervosa. Poor nutrition is most often unrelated to mental disorder, but it can indicate a chronic debilitating physical disease, depression, substance abuse or homelessness.*

When you shake hands during your introductions, notice whether the patient's palms are dry or damp. Is the grip firm and hearty, or limp and halfhearted?

Alertness

Your patient's alertness can be graded along a continuum.

- Full or normal alertness implies awareness of the environment and the ability to respond quickly to a variety of sensory stimuli.
- "Drowsiness" and "clouding of consciousness" refer somewhat imprecisely to someone who is awake but less than fully alert. Drowsiness suggests that the patient can be stimulated to full wakefulness. Clouding might be less transient, as in a person who has taken a drug overdose; it carries the implication of greater pathology.
- Stupor is a state of unconsciousness. The stuporous patient will respond with partial arousal to vigorous, repeated physical stimuli such as shaking or pinching.
- Coma is a state from which the patient cannot be aroused at all, even by stimuli such as deep pain or noxious odors.

It is not uncommon to encounter fluctuating consciousness during a single interview session. *Carefully note any fluctuations in level of consciousness; they can affect your interpretation of the formal tests as well as your informal observations of the patient's behavior.*

Some patients will appear to be more alert than is usually considered normal. These people may rapidly and repeatedly glance about the room, as if suspiciously scanning the environment for danger. *Such hypervigilance or hyperalertness is characteristic of paranoid disorder and paranoid schizophrenia.*

Clothing and Hygiene

Is your patient's clothing clean and well cared for or dirty and tattered? Is it casual or formal, contemporary or out-of-date? Is it appropriate to the climate and to the circumstances of your meeting? Notice any jewelry. *Bright colors may suggest mania; something as ordinary as a misbuttoned shirt or coat could indicate dementia. Bizarre dress, such as an adult wearing a Boy Scout uniform, suggests psychosis.*

What is your patient's hairstyle and hair color? Is there any facial hair? What about personal hygiene? *If the patient is disheveled or malodorous, suspect serious illness such as schizophrenia or substance abuse.*

Motor Activity

Try to assess the dominant body attitude: Does the patient appear relaxed or sit tensely on the edge of the chair?

Notice the amount of motor activity. As you talk, does your patient sit quietly? Does this seem to approach immobility at times? *True immobility is rare and can be due to catatonia. Classically a feature of schizophrenia, it is also encountered in a variety of other psychiatric conditions and in patients with frontal lobe brain dysfunction.*

Much more common in mental health patients is excessive motion. Does your patient jiggle a leg up and down or frequently arise from the chair to pace? *Either behavior may be due to* akathisia, *a side effect of neuroleptic drugs, which are often given to control psychosis. Sometimes akathisia can become so severe that a patient literally cannot sit still and spends much time pacing restlessly around the room. Occasional uneasy shifting of position is more likely the consequence of simple anxiety.*

Observe your patient's hands. Are they folded at rest, or are fists kept tightly clenched? Are fingernails dirty, bitten, stained, or carefully manicured? Is there a tremor? *This could be due to anxiety, but tremor of a pill-rolling type is often seen in Parkinson's disease and in pseudoparkinsonism (a frequent side effect of neuroleptic drugs).*

Notice any behavior such as inappropriate scratching, touching, or rubbing in public. Does this person pick at skin or clothing? *One possible explanation is an organic delirium, such as delirium tremens (DTs).*

It is extremely important, especially in chronically ill mental patients, to look for the involuntary movements of face and limbs associated with *tardive dyskinesia.* Are there any twisting or writhing movements of the extremities? What about lip puckering, chewing, facial grimacing, or protrusions of the tongue? These movements may be gross and unmistakable, but more often they will be mild and may be hard to identify. If in doubt, ask to see your patient's tongue: wormlike fasciculations may be the only early sign of tardive dyskinesia.

You may notice other unusual behaviors. Look for any *mannerisms*—unnecessary behaviors that are part of a goal-directed activity. (An example would be the flourish that some people make with a pen before writing something.) *Mannerisms are common and normal; to some degree, we all have them.* Stereotypies are behaviors that are not goal directed. An example would be a patient who repeatedly pauses to make the peace sign to no apparent purpose. *Posturing* is when a patient strikes and holds a pose (such as hand tucked inside a shirt front, like Napoleon) that appears to have no purpose. Purposeless *negativism* may be shown by persistent silence or by turning away from the examiner. In *waxy flexibility* the patient's limbs remain rigid and can be bent only slowly, with pressure from you, as if you were bending a rod of wax or lead. Patients with *catalepsy* will maintain any odd or unusual posture you place them in, despite the fact that you urge them to relax. *Stereotypies, posturing, waxy flexibility, negativism, and catalepsy are rarely encountered today. They usually signify psychosis — most often, schizophrenia.*

Facial Expression

Does the patient smile and generally show normal mobility of facial expression? *A fixed, motionless expression could indicate senility, the rigidity common in Parkinson's disease, or pseudoparkinsonism from taking neuroleptics.* How well does this patient make eye contact with you? *A psychotic patient may stare at you fixedly; in depression, the gaze may seem riveted to the floor.* As you speak, does your patient repeatedly glance around the room, as if noticing something you cannot see or attending to voices no one else can hear? *These behaviors of responding to an internal stimulus may be encountered in patients who have psychoses of various types.* Are there any tics of eyes, mouth, or other body parts?

You should watch for any other behaviors that contradict the information your patient is giving you verbally.

> You notice the motor restlessness of akathisia, when your patient denies taking neuroleptics.
>
> Your patient has a sad face and appears to be about to cry, but claims to feel cheerful.

Voice

As you talk, notice the volume, pitch, and clarity of your patient's voice. Does it have a normal lilt (called *prosody*), or is it monotonous and dull? From the use of grammar can you tell anything about education or background? Does an accent identify the country or region in which the patient was born or reared? Does the patient stutter, lisp, mumble, or demonstrate some other speech impediment? Are there mannerisms of speech, such as words or phrases used habitually? How would you characterize the tone of voice: friendly, angry, or sad?

Attitude toward Examiner

There are several continuums along which you could describe your patient's apparent relationship to you:

Cooperative → obstructionistic
Friendly → hostile

Open → secretive
Involved → apathetic

How far to the left your patient scores on each of these factors will help determine the amount of information you can expect to obtain, as well as the strength of your rapport. In addition, note any evidence of seductiveness or evasiveness.

MOOD

The terms *mood* and *affect* have been variously defined. Nowadays they are sometimes used interchangeably. We will use *mood* to mean the way a person claims to be feeling and *affect* to mean how the person appears to be feeling. Therefore, the term *affect* signifies not only stated mood, but facial expression, posture, eye contact (or its lack), and tearfulness as well.

Mood (or affect) is described in several dimensions: type, lability, appropriateness, and (by some observers) intensity.

Type

What is the patient's type of mood? By that we mean simply the basic quality of mood. In Chapter 7 I presented some 60 expressions of feeling, but they can be boiled down to just a few basic moods:

Anger	Irritation
Anxiety	Joy
Contentment	Sadness
Disgust	Shame
Fear	Surprise
Guilt	

One mood will usually predominate. When it does not, "normal" or "about medium" serves as an adequate description.

Your patient's mood will probably be obvious from what you have already observed. If not, ask:
"How are you feeling now?"
"What is your mood at this time?"
If you detect sadness, you might inquire:
"Do you feel like crying?"
An occasional patient will burst into tears, a response that can be distressing for a beginning interviewer but therapeutic for the patient. Have

some facial tissues available for this situation, and try to learn what feelings lie behind the outburst.

You can also infer a good deal from your patient's body language. Here are a few nonverbal cues to feelings:

Anger: clenched jaw, knotted fists, flushing of face or neck, drumming fingers, extended neck veins, fixed stare

Anxiety: jiggling foot, twisting fingers, affected casualness (such as toothpicking)

Sadness: moistening of eyes, drooping shoulders, slowed movements

Shame: poor eye contact, blushing, shrugging

Some patients have difficulty describing, or even recognizing, how they feel. A few cannot seem to do it at all. The term *alexithymia* is sometimes used to describe this inability of some people to describe their emotions or express their feelings.

Lability

Even normal people will sometimes show two or more moods within a brief time span. For example, at a funny, yet tender moment in a movie or play anyone might laugh and weep, almost at the same time. But wide swings of mood are often abnormal and should be watched for in a mental health interview. Such mood swings are termed *increased lability of mood. Patients with somatization disorder may show dramatic swings of mood from ecstasy to tears, all in a matter of minutes. A patient with manic euphoria may suddenly burst into bitter tears, then rapidly return to bubbling good nature. In the dementias rapid mood swings can be so severe as to deserve the term* affective incontinence.

The opposite picture occurs when the patient shows reduced variation of mood. This lack of response to environmental stimuli is called *flattening* of mood. The term *blunting* has been used as a synonym, although some writers use *flattening* to mean a compressed range of mood and reserve *blunting* to mean a lack of emotional sensitivity. *However the terms are defined, these patients, classically identified as having schizophrenia, seem unable to relate affectively to other people. This relative immobility of mood is also found in severe depression, Parkinson's disease, and other neurological conditions. Blandness of affect, in which nothing much ever seems to ruffle the patient, is classically found in the organic dementias.*

Appropriateness

Appropriateness of mood is your estimate of how well the patient's mood matches the situation and the content of thought. Your judgment will be affected by two cultures: yours and the patient's. Although most people show inappropriate emotional reactions from time to time, a pronounced inappropriateness is common in certain diagnostic groups. *Someone who laughs while describing the death of a close relative may be suffering from schizophrenia, disorganized type. Pathological affect (either inappropriate laughing or weeping) may be encountered in pseudobulbar palsy, which can have a variety of causes, including multiple sclerosis and strokes. Patients with somatization disorder will sometimes talk about their physical incapacities (paralysis, blindness) with the nonchalance that usually accompanies a discussion of the weather. This special type of inappropriate mood is called* la belle indifférence *(French for "lofty indifference").*

Although you should be continually alert for these and other signs of otherwise unexpressed feeling, it is important not to overinterpret. Try instead to relate what you observe to what you hear and to what you yourself might feel under similar circumstances. Are tears warranted by the topic being discussed, or does your patient appear to be unnaturally sad? Does the smile seem genuine, or is it forced, perhaps hiding true feelings?

Intensity

Although the designation is subjective and therefore somewhat arbitrary, you can grade intensity of mood as mild, moderate, or severe. You might also want to note the *reactivity* of a mood: Is it fleeting, prolonged, or somewhere in between?

FLOW OF THOUGHT

The term *flow of thought* is a slight misnomer. What we are interested in is the thought, but what we actually observe is the flow of speech. We assume that the speech we hear reflects the patient's thoughts.

Most of the defects we describe are usually apparent only during the acute phase of illness. They can be grouped into two overall categories, defects of (1) association — the way words are joined together to make phrases and sentences — and (2) rate and rhythm.

Unhappily, not all of these definitions are universally agreed upon by mental health clinicians, so I have tried to adopt a consensus view. However, you will be safest if you record in quotes actual examples of your patient's speech. This will remind you later exactly what the patient said, help anyone who reads your write-up to understand what you mean by the terms you use, and provide a recorded basis for judging future change in thought patterns that may occur with treatment.

Be careful not to attribute undue pathological significance to your patient's manner of speaking. Remember that not everyone who speaks differently from the way you do has psychopathology. Speech patterns can also be affected by neurological or other medical disorders, by cultural influences, and by growing up speaking a language other than English.

Association

First, notice whether speech is *spontaneous* or occurs only in response to questions. In the latter case, you should take some pains to persuade the patient to talk spontaneously.

"I appreciate the fact that you have answered my questions. But it will help us both more if you'll just talk for a while about your problems. That way, I'll get a better feeling for what is bothering you."

If you don't succeed with this, you will obviously be somewhat limited as to the amount of information you can obtain about speech patterns. Record examples of what speech there is, and note the attempts you made to obtain more.

Derailment. Sometimes called *loose associations,* derailment is a breakdown of thought association in which one idea seems to run into another. The two ideas may be related or unrelated. You can understand the sequence of words, but the direction they take seems to be governed not by logic but by rhymes, puns, or other rules that might not be apparent to an observer. What comes out is speech that seems to mean something to the patient but means nothing to you.

"She tells me something in one morning and out the other."

"Half a loaf is better than the whole enchilada."

"I'll never go back to that store again. I don't have enough sand for my shoes."

A special type of derailment is *flight of ideas,* in which a word or phrase from one thought stimulates the patient to take off on another. The thoughts do not appear to be related by logic. The patient will usually completely lose the thread of the original question.

INTERVIEWER: When did you enter the hospital?

PATIENT: I came in on a Monday. Monday is wash day. That's what I'm gonna do—wash that man right outta my hair. He's the tortoise and I'm the hare.

Patients with mania often have flight of ideas associated with push of speech (described later in this chapter).

Tangentiality (tangential speech). These terms describe an answer that seems irrelevant to the question asked. If there is some relationship between question and answer, it is hard to discern.

INTERVIEWER: How long did you live in Wichita?

PATIENT: Even anteaters like to French kiss.

Derailments and tangentiality are both found in psychosis, often schizophrenia, but patients with mania can also exhibit these symptoms.

Poverty of speech. This is a marked reduction from normal in the amount of spontaneous speech. The patient answers briefly when you expect elaboration and, unless prompted, may say nothing for long periods. When this behavior is carried to the extreme of *muteness,* there is no speech at all. *Patients with depression may show poverty of speech. Muteness is more characteristic of schizophrenia, but it is sometimes found in somatization disorder. It must be distinguished from* aphonia *of neurological origin.*

The following terms designate speech pathology that is seldom encountered in clinical interviews. I will define them briefly, but unless you work in a large, back-ward psychiatric hospital you are unlikely to encounter any of these behaviors more than once every few years. Most occur classically in schizophrenia, but any may be found in psychoses of organic origin. When you do encounter an example, be sure to record it and try to learn why the patient has responded that way.

Thought blocking. The train of thought stops suddenly, before it has been completed. The patient can usually give no explanation more adequate than that the thought has been "forgotten."

Alliteration. A phrase or sentence intentionally contains multiple repetitions of the same or similar sounds: "I ran the risk, Doctor Dear, of recognizing revolting rabbits racing in the roadster."

Clang associations. The choice of individual words is governed by rhyming or other similarity of sound, not by the requirements of communication.

INTERVIEWER: Who brought you to the hospital?

PATIENT: My wife, she's the wife of my life, no strife.

Echolalia. In answering a question, the patient unnecessarily repeats words or phrases of the interviewer. This can be fairly subtle, to the point that you may recognize it only after several repetitions.

INTERVIEWER: How long were you in the hospital that time?

PATIENT: How long were you in the hospital? I was in the hospital a long, long time, that's how long I was in the hospital.

Verbigeration. The patient continues to repeat a word or phrase without obvious purpose. "It was deathly still. Deathly. Deathly still. Deathly. Still deathly."

Incoherence. The patient is so disorganized that even individual words or phrases appear to have no logical connection: "Shovel . . . it wasn't the . . . best hatred . . . lifetime." Sometimes this is more colorfully termed *word salad.*

Neologisms. In the absence of artistic intent (such as Lewis Carroll's *Jabberwocky*), the patient makes up words, often from parts of dictionary words. The resulting structure may sound "real," but isn't. "I didn't want him spinning cobwebs all over, so I hit him with my arachnosquisher [a shoe]."

Perseveration. The patient repeats words or phrases, or repeatedly returns to a point that has already been covered or mentioned.

INTERVIEWER: And what was your girlfriend like?

PATIENT: Oh, she had long, blonde hair and she wore it in a pony tail. . . .

INTERVIEWER: Did you feel she supported you when you had that trouble with your ex-wife?

PATIENT: But she wasn't very tall. Just a bit over 5 feet.

INTERVIEWER: What I'd really like is to hear about your relationship with her.

PATIENT: She was pretty, really pretty.

Stilted speech. Accent, phraseology, or choice of words gives speech an unnatural or quaint flavor, as if the patient were someone else entirely. An American who affects a British accent or who frequently uses British idioms might be said to have stilted speech.

Rate and Rhythm of Speech

Patients who speak rapidly, and often at considerable length, show *push of speech* (or pressured speech). Because these patients are often loud and hard to interrupt, they can pose a real challenge for interviewers. Push of speech is usually associated with *decreased latency of response.* In this pattern the period of time between your question and the patient's response is markedly reduced. Sometimes the response seems to come almost before you have asked your question. *Push of speech and decreased latency of response are classically found in patients with mania, who may tell you that their words cannot keep up with their rapid thoughts.*

A patient with *increased latency of response* takes far longer than normal to answer or interjects long pauses between sentences. This speech pattern is called *psychomotor retardation.* When finally offered, the statement itself may be brief and delivered with excruciating slowness. *Increased latency of response is characteristic of severe depression.*

When the timing of syllables deviates from normal, disorders of rhythm of speech occur. *Stuttering* is one such disorder. In *cluttering,* the patient speaks so rapidly as to become tangle-tongued and disorganized. Patients with cerebellar lesions may speak with a rate that is too precisely even, uttering each syllable at the same pace as the last. Those with some forms of muscular dystrophy may speak in clusters or have difficulty uttering syllables.

Other speech patterns occur that usually have no pathological significance at all. Whereas they may be quite noticeable to the listener, the individual who uses them can remain totally unaware of how often they occur.

The term *circumstantial speech* means that much extraneous material is included with the principal message. In this common speech pattern the speaker eventually comes to the point, although often at considerable cost to the listener's time and patience.

In *distractible speech* the speaker's attention may be diverted by stimuli that are extraneous to the conversation. Noise in the corridor or a moth fluttering against a window may send the conversation off in a new, although usually temporary, direction. Distractible speech is usually normal, but it can also be encountered in mania.

Verbal tics are conventional expressions that many people overuse from time to time, usually without realizing it. Such time-fillers are almost always normal, if boring.

"You know"

"I go" (for "I said")

"Basically"

"Really"

SUMMING UP

Mental health clinicians make observations about behavior and general appearance, mood, and flow of thought every time they encounter a patient. For the beginner the real work comes in learning to discriminate the many types of abnormality and to recognize their significance for diagnosis.

12 Mental Status Exam II: Cognitive Aspects

Nearly all of the findings mentioned in the previous chapter are typically made by observation alone. In contrast, the interviewer must use active questioning to elicit most of the material presented in this chapter.

Should You Do a Formal Mental Status Exam?

Some clinicians still fail to assess—or to report—the cognitive aspects of the mental status exam, despite the critical importance of this information to the overall evaluation of any patient. Others feel that it is insulting to ask obvious, routine questions such as "What is the date?" and "Who is the president?" of an adult who seems clearly unimpaired. They choose not to do formal testing without a positive indication, such as a complaint by relatives that the patient has had a memory problem.

Unless you ask, however, you can never be sure that *any* patient is unimpaired. This is why I strongly recommend that you do a formal mental status exam on all patients. You can take some steps to reduce the likelihood of resentment for the patient and embarrassment for you.

• Start by explaining what you are about to do. Stress the fact that these questions are the norm and are not occasioned by something the patient has said or done:

"Now I'd like to ask some routine questions that will help me assess how you think about things. It will only take a few minutes."

Words such as *routine* and *normal* help pull the sting from procedures that might otherwise be taken amiss.

• Use whatever degree of positive feedback seems warranted, as long as you speak no more than the truth:

"That's excellent! This is the best I've seen anyone do calculations all week."

• Respond attentively to any distress these questions seem to cause. If necessary, take a break and return later to any aspect that is troublesome:

"Subtracting sevens in your head is tough. Let's give it a rest and try presidents instead."

• In any case, everyone will feel far more comfortable if you get this portion of your evaluation out of the way at the outset of your relationship. If you delay asking until treatment is well underway, you increase the possibility of embarrassment for you and your patient.

Anyone who observes seasoned professionals doing the formal portions of the mental status exam will find that they don't ask every question of every patient. With time and experience, clinicians learn which tests can be omitted in certain patients and which must be performed every time. While you are still learning, I recommend that you do the entire procedure each time. That way you will learn it all; you will also develop your own sense of what responses are normal for each test. Once you become expert (after your first several hundred exams), you can decide which tests to omit and when.

The mental status exam properly concerns only current behaviors, experiences, and emotions. However, it is often convenient to cover related historical data at the same time. This is the reason that so many of the screening questions begin with "Have you *ever* . . . "

CONTENT OF THOUGHT

Whatever the speaker is interested in at the moment constitutes the content of thought. During the history of the present illness, this will usually be concerned with the problems that caused the patient to seek treatment. But it is vital that you cover several topics of thought with every exam you do. The patient is likely to mention some of these spontaneously, but others you will have to discover by asking screening questions. In order to do a systematic, thorough initial interview, you must keep all of these topics in mind and ask screening questions for each of these major thought abnormalities.

Whenever you are investigating abnormalities of thought, probe gently enough that the patient continues to view you as someone who is sympathetic and friendly. Don't make snap judgments or act surprised at the responses you hear. Remember that bizarre ideas like flying saucers or talking fish may seem as normal to the patient as your own closest-held convictions (even including religion and politics) do to you.

Delusions

A *delusion* is a fixed, false belief that cannot be explained by the patient's culture and education. All portions of this definition must be fulfilled. The patient must have a belief or idea that is obviously false to others of the same culture; it must be unshakable, despite evidence that it is wrong.

"I've been sent to guard the president." (At age 73 this patient was a chronic alcoholic who hadn't worked in years.)

"My husband goes secretly to have sex with the woman across the street. He signals her with the venetian blinds." (Her husband sighed and admitted to the interviewer that he had been impotent for 15 years.)

"My initials are J.C. That means I'm Jesus Christ." (Six brothers and sisters testified that he had been ill for years.)

You can test the strength of your patient's beliefs by asking:

"Is it possible that this feeling is due to some sort of nervous or emotional problem?"

If the patient replies, "No" and perhaps claims instead that the hospital staff has just joined the conspiracy, score the idea as a delusion.

Some patients, when similarly challenged, will agree that another explanation is possible; for them, you would not diagnose a delusion.

"It only seemed as if there was some sort of plot."

"Perhaps it was imaginary, after all."

"My nerves have been bad lately."

Call it a delusion only when the patient maintains an obviously false explanation despite clear evidence to the contrary.

Because the cultural/educational criterion must also be satisfied, a traditional Navajo should not be called delusional for believing in witches, nor should children who write letters to Santa Claus.

With pauses for responses, screen for delusions by asking:

"Have you ever had any thoughts or feelings that people were spying on you, talking about you, or trying to harm you in some way? Have you ever gotten unusual messages? Or had any other thoughts or ideas that others might consider unusual?"

Patients are often aware that other people think their delusional ideas are unusual or strange; they may go to some lengths to hide these delusions. Usually a sympathetic, interested, nonjudgmental manner will relax tensions enough for your patient to discuss these problems about as freely as any others. You may be able to get your patient to elaborate on a delusion and perhaps to volunteer others by asking the noncommittal question:

"How do you know this [the delusion] is the case?"

If you challenge delusions, you risk upsetting the patient. If you accept them, you risk confirming these false ideas in the patient's mind.

You may have to walk a fine line. Of course, you should not show disbelief. If you can avoid it, you shouldn't state any opinion at all. If you are pressed for an opinion you could truthfully state:

"Many people would consider it [the delusion] unusual."

Because this is something the patient already realizes, it comes as no shock; the answer often seems to satisfy. If further pressed, you would have to respond with the truth:

"I think that other explanations may be able to account for your discomfort. You could be mistaken, or it could be some form of nervousness."

Because they are offered tentatively, these explanations often don't provoke much argument. If they do, perhaps you and the patient can amiably agree to disagree.

Once you have detected a delusion, learn all you can about it. The following questions should help:

"How long have you felt this way?"

"What actions have you taken as a result?"

"What other actions do you plan to take?"

"How do you feel about these goings-on?"

"Why do you think is this happening?" ("Why" questions—"Why do you think you were fired?"—are another way that you may be able to elicit delusions.

Finally, is the delusion mood-congruent? By this we mean, Is the content of the delusion in keeping with the patient's mood? This is an example of a mood-congruent delusion:

A middle-aged man hospitalized for a depression who believed he had literally gone to hell. The medical personnel clustered around his bedside were devils who had gathered to administer well-deserved punishment for his sins.

And an example of a mood-incongruent delusion:

An elderly woman, chronically ill with psychosis for many years, who also had ankle swelling due to heart failure. She rather blandly stated this reason for the swelling: In her basement the Nazis had installed gravity machines that pulled her body fluids into her legs.

The presence of mood-congruent delusions should make you suspect a mood disorder; mood-incongruent delusions are more typical of schizophrenia.

Specific Delusions

In the course of interviewing many patients, you will probably encounter a wide variety of delusions. Here are the most prevalent:

- Death. Also called *nihilistic,* this rare symptom is an extreme case of delusions of ill health.
- Grandeur. The false belief is that the patient is someone of exalted station (God, Michael Jackson) or has powers or gifts not possessed by other people (immense wealth, virtuoso musical ability, eternal life). Be sure to distinguish these ideas from joking references: Presidents, kings, and industrial chief executive officers sometimes assume the mantle of prescience or invincibility. To them, "I am God" may be a partly realized figure of speech. *Delusions of grandeur are typically found in mania but may also occur in schizophrenia.*
- Guilt. These patients believe they have committed some grave error or sin, for which they may claim to deserve punishment. *Delusions of guilt are found especially in severe depression and in delusional disorder.*
- Ill health or bodily change. These patients believe they are afflicted by some terrible disease: Their insides have rotted; their bowels have turned to cement. *Delusions of ill health and somatic delusions are occasionally found in severe depression or schizophrenia.*
- Jealousy. The patient's spouse "has been unfaithful." *Delusions of jealousy are classically seen in alcoholic paranoia but are also encountered in paranoid schizophrenia and paranoid disorder.*
- Passivity or influence. Such patients believe that they are being controlled in unusual ways by outside influences such as television, radio, or microwaves. As a result, they can deny responsibility for their behavior. By contrast, some may feel that they can control the environment: What they have for breakfast has influenced the secretary of state to mention Poland in a speech, or their thought waves cause rivers to rise. *Such delusions are typically found in patients with paranoid schizophrenia.*
- Persecution. Patients believe that they are being threatened, ridiculed, discriminated against, or otherwise interfered with. *Such delusions are typical of paranoid schizophrenia.*
- Poverty. Despite evidence to the contrary (money in the bank, a regular disability check), these patients believe that destitution will force them to sell the house and auction their property. *These delusions are found in severe depression.*
- Reference. People are spying upon them, slandering them, or working against them in some other way. These patients "observe" that people whisper about them as they walk past; print or broadcast media contain messages that are intended specifically for them; for example, "On the news hour last night, Jim Lehrer said that a settlement was imminent. This means that I should agree

to the property settlement with my former wife." *Delusions of refer-*
ence are especially common in paranoid schizophrenia, but may be found
in other psychoses, as well.

- Thought broadcasting. The patient's thoughts seem to be transmitted locally or across the nation. *Thought broadcasting is found*
in schizophrenia.
- Thought control. Thoughts, feelings, or ideas are put into the
patient's mind or are withdrawn from it. Closely related to passivity feelings, these delusions have similar import.

PERCEPTION

Hallucinations

Hallucinations are false sensory perceptions that occur in the absence
of a related sensory stimulus. (For example, the patient hears voices
speaking from the fireplace or sees a quartet of purple snakes floating
in the bathwater.) Hallucinations can involve any of the five senses.
Among mental health patients, auditory hallucinations are by far the
most common; visual hallucinations are next.

Screen for hallucinations by asking:

"Do you ever hear voices or other sounds when there is no one
around to produce them? Do you ever see things other people cannot
see?"

Some patients mistakenly respond "Yes" to questioning designed
to elicit auditory hallucinations. This misunderstanding can arise when
they mean only that they hear a voice right now (the interviewer's) or
that they "hear" their own thoughts (although not spoken aloud as in
audible thoughts, which are described later in this chapter). With careful questioning, these false positives are readily distinguished from
genuine hallucinations.

Hallucinations should be characterized as to severity. *Auditory hal-*
lucinations, for example, can be graded on a continuum: Vague noises
→ mumbling → understandable words → phrases → complete sentences.

Here are some additional questions that can help you learn more
about auditory hallucinations:

"How often do you hear any of these voices?"

"Is it as clear as my voice is now?"

"Where is it coming from?" (The patient's head or body? The micro-
wave oven? The hallway?)

"Whose voice is it?"

"Is there more than one?"

"Do they talk about you?"

"What do they say?"

"Do they hold conversations with one another?"

"What do you think the cause is?"

"How do you react?" (Many patients are frightened by their hallucinations; some are only bemused.)

"Do the voices give commands?" (If so, does the patient obey them?)

Audible thoughts is a special form of auditory hallucination in which patients hear their own thoughts spoken loudly enough to be heard by others.

Visual hallucinations can also be graded: Points of light → blurred images → formed people (what size?) → scenes or tableaus. Some of the questions recommended for auditory hallucinations, suitably changed, should be asked of patients who admit to visual hallucinations. You especially want to know when they occur (only when taking drugs or alcohol?) and what the content is. How does the patient respond to these hallucinations? (It can be extremely frightening to perceive faces changing color or form; one woman looked into the mirror and saw that she had become a mushroom!)

Visual hallucinations are especially characteristic of organic psychoses. For example, small animals or lilliputian people are commonly reported by patients who experience delirium tremens when withdrawing from chronic alcohol abuse. Trailing phenomena, in which objects appear to leave a lingering image on the patient's retina, sometimes accompany psychedelic drug abuse. But visual hallucinations can also occur in schizophrenia, early symptoms of which may include intensification of color or changes in the size of objects.

Tactile (touch), *olfactory* (smell), and *gustatory* (taste) hallucinations are uncommon in mental health patients. *These symptoms usually suggest organic psychosis due to such disorders as brain tumor, toxic psychosis, or a seizure disorder. Visual, auditory, and tactile hallucinations may also occur in normal people when they are falling asleep or awakening. They are easily discerned from pathological hallucinations by their exclusive time of occurrence.*

Anxiety Symptoms

Anxiety is fear that is neither directed at nor caused by anything specific the patient can identify. It is usually accompanied by various unpleasant bodily sensations. Other mental symptoms may include irritability, poor concentration, mental tension, worrying, and an exaggerated startle response.

Screen for anxiety symptoms by asking:

"Do you think you worry about things excessively or out of proportion to their real danger to you?"

"Does your family tell you that you're a worrywart?"

"Do you feel anxious or tense much of the time?"

If any answer is "Yes," follow up with some of the questions covered in the section on anxiety disorders in Chapter 13.

When intense anxiety occurs suddenly in a discrete episode, with a rapid increase in these bodily sensations, the patient is said to be experiencing a *panic attack*. Patients often report feelings of disaster, madness, or impending death.

Screen for panic attacks by asking:

"Have you ever had a panic attack—a time when you suddenly felt overwhelmingly frightened or anxious?"

Follow up with the same sorts of questions you would ask for other anxiety disorders (Chapter 13).

Phobias

A phobia is an unreasonable and intense fear associated with some object or situation. Common specific phobias are fears of various animals, air travel, heights *(acrophobia)*, and being closed in *(claustrophobia)*. Common social phobias include fears of being away from home or in open places *(agoraphobia)*, public speaking, eating in public, using a public urinal, or writing when others might see the patient's hand tremble.

To the outsider, a phobia may seem every bit as unreasonable as a delusion. The difference is that, whereas the phobic patient recognizes how unreasonable these feelings are, the delusional patient does not.

Screen for phobias by asking:

"Have you ever been afraid of leaving home alone, or being in crowds, or in public places such as stores or on bridges?"

"Have you ever had fears that seemed unreasonable or out of proportion to you, but that you just couldn't shake?"

In the case of social phobias (such as public speaking), be sure to ask about the development of *anticipatory anxiety*. In this condition, anxiety that is often intense and incapacitating is experienced prior to performing the act that the patient dreads.

Dysmorphophobia is a term sometimes used to describe excessive concern about slight (or imagined) defects in body appearance. Usually these flaws are facial (wrinkles, shape of nose), but they have been reported for nearly every imaginable body part. Because the patient does not avoid the body part in question (of course), the condition is not really a phobia at all. In DSM-III-R the condition itself is called *body dysmorphic disorder*.

Obsessions and Compulsions

An *obsession* is a belief, idea, or thought that dominates the patient's thought content and persists, despite the fact that the patient realizes it is unrealistic and may try to resist it. For example, a middle-aged man had the persistent thought of doing something embarrassing such as standing up and screaming during a church service.

Compulsions are acts performed repeatedly in a way that the patient realizes is neither useful nor appropriate. Often, they are performed in response (or as an antidote) to an obsession.

Counting things repeatedly

Heeding groundless superstitions

Following rituals (such as a set bedtime routine that must be followed to the letter or else it must be started all over again)

A key aspect of obsessions and compulsions is the fact that the patient realizes these ideas or behaviors are senseless and often tries to resist them.

Screen for obsessions and compulsions by asking:

"Have you ever had obsessional thoughts or ideas? I mean thoughts that may seem senseless to you, but keep coming back anyway."

"Have you ever had compulsions—such as rituals or routines that you feel you must perform over and over, even though you try to resist?" (Be ready to cite examples, should the patient ask.)

Some people do not realize that their behaviors—excessive neatness, for example—are at all unusual. Careful questioning may be required to draw them out.

"How neat is your home, your personal belongings?"

"Have you ever gone to bed and left dirty dishes in the sink?"

"If someone sits on your bed after you've made it, do you feel the need to straighten it again?"

A minor degree of obsessional thinking is quite common, so it is important to judge severity. As with phobias, this is best measured in terms of the effect on activities such as school, work, and family life. In severe cases patients may spend many hours a day occupied in pointless handwashing, dressing, or bathroom rituals. As with phobias, ask about onset, duration, treatment, and effect on the patient's life.

Thoughts of Violence

Whether or not there have been previous suicide attempts or violence directed at others, you must learn what the patient is thinking now. Screen for *suicidal ideas:*

"Have you any ideas or thoughts of harming yourself in any way or of killing yourself?"

Most people have had such ideas at one time or another, and a positive answer could indicate only a fleeting thought in reaction to stress or an overwhelming life situation. But it would be an unwarranted, potentially tragic leap of faith to ignore any answer that is even equivocal. You must thoroughly investigate any such ideas you uncover.

Review all the material you have already obtained about past attempts (see Chapter 9). Learn whether or not the patient has current plans and the means to carry them out. You should ask:

"What would it take to make suicide seems less attractive?"
Regard as serious and ominous any equivalent to the answer, "Nothing could." If you encounter this sort of thinking, and add to it evidence of current drinking or depression (feelings of worthlessness, hopelessness, trouble with thinking, loss of energy, guilt feelings), you may have a situation that demands hospitalization, possibly even before the hour is up.

Ideas of homicide or violence present a similar, urgent call to action. The terror of violent ideas is mitigated only by the fact that they are encountered much less often than are suicidal ideas. Screen for thoughts of homicide or violence toward others by asking:

"Have you been feeling so angry or upset that you think about harming someone else?"

Any positive answer *must* be followed up immediately and compared with the historical information you have already obtained. Are there plans or only ideas? Does your patient have the means (firearms, lethal drugs) to carry out this plan? What is the timetable? (This material was covered in greater detail in Chapter 9.)

Worrisome, but Usually Normal

There are a number of symptoms you don't ordinarily have to ask about: Either they are normal or they have no diagnostic import. However, patients sometimes worry about them and bring them up during interview sessions. You should have explanations ready.

Illusions are misinterpretations of actual sensory stimuli. Usually visual, they most often occur when there is decreased sensory input (such as in dim light). Their true nature is readily acknowledged as soon as the patient becomes aware of the mistake. For example, a crack on the wall looks like a frightening snake; once the light is put on, the patient feels immediate relief. Illusions must be distinguished from hallucinations. You can usually accomplish this by obtaining details about such matters as circumstance (dim light) and timing (only when going to sleep). Although usually normal, illusions can be encountered in patients with dementia or delirium.

Déjà vu, French for "already seen," is the commonplace sensation that a person has previously experienced a situation or locale, when that is probably not the case. Most people have had this feeling more than once in their lives, although it can be symptomatic of temporal lobe epilepsy.

Overvalued ideas are beliefs that continue to be held despite lack of proof as to their worth. Like delusions, they cannot usually be challenged by argument or logic; unlike delusions, they are not obviously false. Examples include the superiority of one's own sex, race, political party, or religion. Sometimes overvalued ideas are pursued to a point where they interfere with the individual's functioning, causing suffering to the person or to those around. A common example is racial hatred. Overvalued religious ideas can shade into religious preoccupation, and from there into religious delusions, so the dividing line can be hard to discern. In such a case, note the patient's exact words as a baseline for later review.

Depersonalization is a term that describes an alteration in the perception of one's own self. People usually experience it as a feeling of being detached from body or mind; they may have the sensation of viewing themselves or of being in a dream. Screen for these experiences by asking:

"Have you ever felt unreal? As if you were a robot?"

"Have you ever felt that things around you are unreal?"

Such feelings are reasonably common and usually normal. When these experiences are protracted or repeated and severe enough to cause distress, the individual may be diagnosed as having depersonalization disorder.

CONSCIOUSNESS AND COGNITION

In this section you test your patient's ability to absorb, process, and communicate information. The tests clinicians use are somewhat approximate, but they can serve as a useful guide. If you want quantification, use the Mini-Mental State Exam (Table 5). For greater precision, you can request formal neuropsychological testing by a qualified psychologist.

To introduce these tasks, you might want to restate the reassuring notion that you ask these routine questions of all new patients. Be careful not to describe them as "silly"—you don't want to diminish motivation. Neither should you describe them as "simple," which will only increase the trauma for a patient who has difficulty answering. Remem-

TABLE 5. Mini-Mental State Exam

Maximum score	Score	
		Orientation
5	( )	What is the (year)(season)(date)(month)?
5	( )	Where are we? (state)(county)(town)(building)(floor)
		Registration
3	( )	Name three objects: Allow 1 second to say each. Then ask the patient all three after you have said them. Give 1 point for each correct answer. Then repeat them until all three are learned. Count trials and record.
		Trials _____
		Attention and Calculations
5	( )	Serial sevens. Give 1 point for each correct answer. Stop after five answers. Alternatively, spell *world* backward.
		Recall
3	( )	Ask for the three objects repeated previously. Give 1 point for each correct.
		Language
9	( )	Name a pencil and watch. (2 points) Repeat the following: "No ifs, ands, or buts." (1 point) Follow a three-stage command: "Take a paper in your right hand, fold it in half, and put it on the floor." (3 points) Read and obey the following: "Close your eyes," (1 point) "Write a sentence." (1 point) "Copy a design." (1 point)
_____ Total score		

Assess level of consciousness:			
Alert	Drowsy	Stupor	Coma

From "Mini-Mental State: A Practical Method for Grading the Cognitive State of Patients for the Clinician" by M. F. Folstein, S. E. Folstein, & P. R. McHugh, 1975, *Journal of Psychiatric Research, 12,* 189–198. Copyright 1975 Pergamon Press Ltd. Reprinted by permission.

ber that any test of mental functioning can be traumatic, especially when there is fear of failure. Doing poorly is always stressful, and the patient who stumbles may need support.

"Most people can't perform at their best when they feel under pressure."

"Most patients have some difficulty with that task."
In any case, try to emphasize what the patient is *able* to do.

"You did well on those serial sevens."

"You're doing better than many others have on this test."
(Don't use these supportive comments unless they are true.)

Attention and Concentration

From the entire interview you will already have a good idea of your patient's *attention,* defined as the ability to focus on a current task or topic, and *concentration,* the ability to sustain that focus over a period of time. You can get at these qualities in a more formal way by assigning calculations, which assess ability to focus on a stimulus. Ask your patient to subtract 7 from 100. Once that has been done, request another subtraction of 7 from the result, and so on toward 0. Most adults will finish in less than a minute with fewer than four errors. Remember to consider the patient's age, education level, culture, and degree of depression and anxiety when you assess the performance.

If this task is too difficult (serial sevens does assume some education and facility with math), ask your patient to count backward by 1 from, say, 87 and to stop at 63. This test of attention is less culture bound than serial subtractions. *Reduced attention is found in patients with organic conditions such as epilepsy, dementia, and head injury, as well as in patients with schizophrenia and depression.*

Orientation

Whether or not your patients know their own names (orientation to person) should be evident from the earlier portions of an interview. Test to be sure that your patient is oriented to time and place by asking:

"Where are we now?" (City, state, name of the facility). If this draws a blank, ask what type of a facility you are in. *An answer such as "a library" or "the Lincoln Memorial" suggests severe organic pathology, although you should beware of overinterpreting what you hear from a facetious or otherwise uncooperative patient.*

"What is the date?" Not infrequently, patients will give the correct date and month, but miss the year. Be sure to ask for all components of orientation to time. It is common, and usually without significance, to miss the date by a day or two. This is especially the case in hospitalized patients, who, divorced from their usual routines, tend to lose track of time.

If you detect confusion about time or place, ask about orientation to person:

"Would you tell me your name again?"

Occasionally you will encounter a patient who is not only disoriented, but also tries to hide mistakes by making up responses that sound logical. This is called *confabulation.* If asked whether you have met previously, such a patient might agree, even though it is the first time you have ever laid eyes on one another. *Confabulation is characteristic of patients whose memories are severely impaired by such disorders as chronic alcoholism with thiamine deficiency.*

Language

Language refers to the means whereby we understand and express meaning verbally. The areas of language that are usually assessed include comprehension, fluency, naming, repetition, reading, and writing. Their routine assessment can be quickly done; it is especially important in older patients or in those who are physically ill. It is not uncommon for hysteria, dementia, and other mental conditions to be misdiagnosed when the patient actually has a disorder of language.

- The degree of *comprehension* should already be evident from the way your patient has responded to conversation during the interview. As a simple test, request this complex behavior: "Take a sheet of paper in your right hand, fold it in half, and place it on the floor."
- *Fluency* of language should also be obvious from the patient's use of normal vocabulary and prosody to produce sentences of normal length. Be alert for hesitation, mumbling, stammering, and unusual emphasis.
- Problems with *naming* may be evident if, instead of their names, your patient uses circumlocutions to describe everyday objects. Examples of such a naming aphasia:

Watch band: "The thing that holds it on your wrist."

Pen: "A whatsis for writing."

Screen for aphasias by asking your patient to name the parts of a ball point pen: point, clip, barrel.

- To test *repetition,* ask your patient to repeat a standard, simple phrase, such as "No ifs, ands, or buts."
- *Reading* is quickly tested by asking the patient to read a sentence or two.
- Test *writing* by asking your patient to write a sentence that you dictate.

If you encounter problems with any of these screening tests, you should ask for a neurological evaluation. Your patient's mental condition may be complicated by a significant neurological dysfunction.

Memory

Memory is usually divided into three or four parts. For convenience we will discuss three: immediate, short-term, and long-term. If you feel uncomfortable with asking any of these questions, you can lead into them:

"Have you had any problems with your memory? I'd like to test it."

Immediate memory (the ability to register and reproduce information after 5 or 10 seconds) is more a test of attention, which you may have already accomplished with serial sevens or counting. But you can assess it again on your way to testing short-term memory. Name several unrelated items, such as a name, a color, and a street address. Then ask the patient to repeat these items. This repetition not only assesses immediate memory but also provides assurance that the patient has understood you. Don't mention that there will be a quiz later: Such a warning would invite rehearsal. Then continue with unrelated questions or tasks.

Five minutes later, test *short-term memory* by asking your patient to recall the three items. At 5 minutes most patients should be able to repeat the name, color, and at least part of the address. When interpreting the results of this test, be sure to consider your patient's apparent degree of motivation. *Failure on all three tasks suggests serious inattention due to a significant organic disorder or to severe stress from depression, psychosis, or anxiety.*

You can best assess *long-term memory* from the ability to organize the information necessary to relate the history of the present illness. You will also have a good idea from your patient's facility with dates of marriages, births of children, and so forth—material that you will have elicited in the course of obtaining the personal and social history. Experts disagree as to where the dividing line lies between short-term and long-term memory. Most agree that between 12 and 18 months some sort of consolidation takes place, so that memories stored long-term are not easily forgotten. *Although patients with severe dementias such as Alzheimer's typically retain long-term memories better than short-term memories, if the disease progresses far enough, even long-retained information will eventually be lost.*

Cultural Information

Some texts no longer even mention these tasks, which mainly assess the patient's remote memory and general intelligence. However, these are a traditional part of the mental status exam, so you should have some familiarity with the classical questions.

Name the five most recent presidents, beginning with the current one. Most patients can name four or five, working backwards. (Ask them one at a time. Understandably, many patients find it daunting to be asked to "name the last five presidents in reverse chronological order.")
Who is the vice-president?

Name five large cities.
Name five rivers.

Cautions about interpretation are the same as for subtractions and counting, mentioned previously. Alternatively, you might get quite an accurate picture of your patient's interest, intelligence, and memory by asking about current events: outcome of major sports events, who is running in the next election, and other items of popular cultural significance.

Abstract Thinking

The ability to abstract a principle from a specific example is another traditional test that depends heavily on culture, intelligence, and education. This ability has nothing to do with sanity, as was once thought. Commonly asked abstractions include the interpretation of proverbs, likenesses, and differences. Here are typical proverbs to interpret:

"What does it mean when someone says that people who live in glass houses shouldn't throw stones?"

"Can you tell me what this means: A rolling stone gathers no moss?" Note that a given proverb may have more than one interpretation (gathering moss could be judged as either good or bad). You should accept as correct any logical interpretation.

Similarities and differences are somewhat less culture-bound than proverbs, so you are probably better off asking some of these:

"How are an apple and an orange alike?" (They are both fruit, both spherical, both have seeds.)

"What is the difference between a child and a dwarf?" (A child will grow.)

INSIGHT AND JUDGMENT

Insight refers to your patient's ideas about what is wrong. In the context of the mental status exam, it has nothing to do with theories of etiology or psychodynamics. You could ask:

"Do you think there is something wrong with you?"

"What kind of illnesses do people come here to get treated for?"

"What strengths do you think you have?"

"Do you think you are impaired?"

Insight may be full, partial, or nil; it also tends not to be static, but to deteriorate with worsening illness, and to improve during remissions. *Poor insight is typical of organic mental disorders, severe depression, and any of the psychoses, especially mania and schizophrenia.*

You should also try to get a feeling for your patient's self-image by asking:

"What do you like about yourself?"

Judgment refers to the ability to decide upon an appropriate course of action to achieve realistic goals. Some writers still advise interviewers to assess judgment by asking hypothetical questions such as "What would you do if you found a letter with a stamp on it?" or "How would you react if a fire broke out in a theater when you were attending a performance?" Such abstract questions probably have little bearing on your patient's ability to get along in the world; you are better off avoiding them. There are several questions you can ask to assess your patient's judgment:

"Do you think you need treatment?"

"What do you expect from treatment?"

"What are your plans for the future?"

In the final analysis, your best appraisal of judgment will probably come from the hour or more of history you have just obtained.

When Can You Omit the Formal Mental Status Exam?

The obvious answer, of course, remains "Never." The reason is that unless all your information comes from printed records, you make a great number of mental status observations every time you have a conversation. The question we are really asking is, When can a clinician safely avoid asking the questions contained in the cognitive portion of the mental status exam (the entire contents of this chapter)?

It is seldom risk-free to leave out any test; any time you do so, it must be with the idea of balancing benefits (more diagnostic information) versus disadvantages (your time and the patient's embarrassment). The disadvantages are usually few: Most tests are quick, and most patients will accept with reasonably good grace whatever questions you pose. Nonetheless, here are a few situations in which you could abbreviate your mental status exam by omitting some formal tests of orientation, knowledge, attention, and memory:

Well-organized history. For example, an outpatient who consults you for a relatively non-threatening problem (life stress, perhaps, or marital difficulties) presents a story that is coherent, well told, and devoid of gaps or inconsistencies.

Test results are available. You have a report of recent psychological testing, which will be far more precise than your approximate tests.

The patient is distressed. If the patient has been quizzed recently by other examiners and is embarrassed or angered by repeated requests, you may want to abbreviate your exam. This may be especially true of those who have trouble with certain of the tests.

You should *not* omit any portion of the formal mental status exam under the following circumstances:

Any forensic exam. Such reports may be scrutinized in a court of law; leave no stone unturned.

Any other legal requirements. Commitment proceedings, competency evaluations, and examinations mandated for certain procedures such as electroconvulsive therapy almost always require a complete report.

A benchmark record may be needed. For example, when you may need to evaluate the results of treatment later, you had better have a record of what the patient was like "before."

Any hint of suicidal ideation or threats of violence. Legal consequences and personal consequences for the patient mandate the complete exam.

Major diagnoses. Any major (Axis I or Axis II) diagnosis must be thoroughly investigated.

Inpatient status. Any patient who is sick enough to be hospitalized is sick enough to have a complete workup.

Possible brain injury. Always do a complete mental status exam when there is a history of head injury or neurological illness.

The examiner is a beginner. Performing the complete evaluation over and over will give familiarity to it and facility to the student.

SUMMING UP

Clinicians may infer much of the mental status exam from a patient's behavior and conversation during the interview. They must assess orientation, memory, language use, and higher intellectual functions such as abstracting ability, fund of information, and insight and judgment. The evaluation of abnormalities of perception (hallucinations) and content of thought should be a routine part of every initial interview.

13 Signs and Symptoms in Areas of Clinical Interest

The areas of clinical interest are simply a way of thinking about historical and mental status information. The eight groups that will be discussed here include most of the signs and symptoms a mental health professional can expect to encounter. The areas of clinical interest should help you focus your inquiry on the information you will need to devise a differential diagnosis.

Your job is to obtain the facts necessary to assess the importance of any of these areas you encounter to the overall evaluation. Remember that each of them comprises a number of clinical diagnoses that have symptoms in common. In order to decide which diagnosis fits best, you must inquire about symptoms of each of the disorders you have in mind.

As an example of how this process works, let us consider mood disturbance. Suppose that your patient has complained of feeling depressed, blue, or down in the dumps. You would expect to find some of these symptoms: low mood, crying spells, hopelessness, disordered appetite, change in sleep patterns, feeling worse at certain times of the day, low energy, poor concentration, pessimistic outlook, and suicidal ideas or behaviors. Few depressed patients will have all of these symptoms, but even one of them suggests that your patient could suffer from some kind of a depressive condition. (In Appendix B are diagnostic criteria for the more common mental disorders.) In that case you should learn whether the symptoms and course of the illness will support one of the mood disorder diagnoses. In other words, first get the data. Later, when all the facts are in, you can decide which of the diagnoses best fits the facts.

In discussing each area of clinical interest I will present these features:

1. Tip-offs, a restatement (from Chapter 5) of the symptoms that should alert you to explore further.
2. The main diagnoses, a section that comprises the most important disorders covered by that area of clinical interest plus the principal differential diagnoses.
3. Historical information, which briefly explains the importance of each bit of historical data you should ask about.
4. Typical features from the mental status examination. The current mental status is usually not as helpful as history in sorting out the differential diagnosis, so I have just listed the typical symptoms.

At times it is hard to know where history ends and the mental status begins. For that reason you might find that some features mentioned under one section seem to belong in another. For example, a patient might report some affects that are not observed during the interview.

For many of these diagnoses (marked with an asterisk), there is a brief description and listing of abbreviated DSM-III-R criteria in Appendix B.

PSYCHOSIS

Psychosis means simply that the patient is out of touch with reality, as judged by the presence of hallucinations, delusions, or markedly loosened thought associations. This condition may be either transient or chronic, although with today's treatment methods it is unusual for a person to remain psychotic for extended periods.

Tip-Offs

Symptoms that would make you consider psychosis as an area of clinical interest include

Affect that is flat or inappropriate
Bizarre behavior
Confusion
Delusions
Fantasies or illogical ideas
Hallucinations (of any of the senses)
Insight or judgment that is disturbed
Muteness

Perceptual distortions (illusions, misinterpretations)
Social withdrawal
Speech that is incoherent or hard to follow

Main Diagnoses

A patient who presents with psychosis is likely to have one of three principal diagnoses: an organic psychosis, schizophrenia, or some sort of
mood disorder (either depression with psychosis or a severe mania).
Of those, mood disorders and schizophrenia will be encountered most
frequently. However, a more complete list includes

Schizophrenia*
Depression*
Mania*
Organic psychoses, such as
    Delirium* due to a variety of causes
    Hallucinosis* (e.g., due to alcohol)
Brief reactive psychosis
Schizophreniform disorder
Schizoaffective disorder
Delusional disorder*

Historical Information

Age at onset. Schizophrenia tends to begin early (late teens or twenties); delusional disorder starts in mid to late life.

Alcohol or drugs. Many patients have both psychosis *and* substance
abuse. Check the chronology. If the psychosis began first, schizophrenia with secondary substance abuse is the likely diagnosis. If substance
abuse began first, the psychosis is probably a secondary diagnosis and
schizophrenia is less likely.

Depression. If there is a past or present severe depression, consider
the diagnosis of psychotic depression.

Environmental stressors. Severe stress that precedes the onset of psychosis suggests a diagnosis of brief reactive psychosis.

Family history. Schizophrenia and mood disorders tend to run in families; having a relative with either condition increases the likelihood
of that diagnosis for the patient.

Length of illness. The longer a psychosis has lasted, the more likely
is schizophrenia to be the final diagnosis.

Loss of drive, volition, interest. These symptoms are typical of the later phases of schizophrenia.

Onset. Sudden onset (a few days to a few weeks) suggests an organic or affective psychosis. The longer and more gradual the onset—up to several years in some cases—the more likely is this psychosis to be schizophrenia.

Physical illness. Organic psychoses are associated with a number of health risk factors: endocrine, metabolic, tumor, toxic substance, trauma, and a variety of neurological and medical diseases.

Previous episode with recovery. Mood disorder tends to be an episodic illness; these patients are more likely to recover completely than are those with schizophrenia.

Schizoid or schizotypal premorbid personality. Long-standing character traits such as aloofness, emotional withdrawal, few friends, or odd beliefs or behavior sometimes precede the onset of schizophrenia.

Unemployment or reduced job level. If present for years, and especially if the reduced job level continues after recovery from an acute episode, schizophrenia is more likely than if the patient worked at a high-grade, demanding job until just recently.

Note on first-rank symptoms: A much-discussed set of hallucinations and delusions are Kurt Schneider's first-rank symptoms, any one of which he believed was diagnostic of schizophrenia. Although subsequent scholarship has determined that these symptoms can also be reported by patients with other disorders, you will encounter the concept of first-rank symptoms often enough to warrant a brief listing.

Audible thoughts
Delusional perception, in which a normal observation has abnormal significance for a patient. For example, when a patient was served a grilled cheese sandwich for lunch he "knew" that his aunt was about to die.
Delusions of influence
Delusions of thought control
More than one voice talking about the patient
Voices commenting on the patient's actions
Somatic hallucinations (body sensations produced by outside influence)
Thought broadcasting

Mental Status Examination

Appearance and behavior
  Abnormalities of motion
    Reduced activity
    Pacing
    Posturing
    Rigidity
    Negativism
    Grimacing
    Stereotypies
  Clothing eccentric or disheveled
  Hyperalertness
  Neglect of hygiene
Mood
  Flat or silly
  Perplexity about identity
Flow of thought
  Speech restricted in amount
  Mute
  Incoherent
  Loosened associations
  Illogical ideas
  Preoccupied with fantasies

Content of thought
  Hallucinations: When?
    Where?
    Auditory
      Voices?
      Whose?
      Audible thoughts?
    Visual
    Tactile
    Taste
    Smell
  Delusions
    Death
    Erotomania
    Grandeur
    Guilt
    Ill health or bodily change
    Jealousy
    Passivity
    Persecution
    Poverty
    Reference
Language usually not impaired
Cognition generally preserved
Insight often absent
Judgment may be impaired in
  the acute phase

MOOD DISTURBANCE: DEPRESSION

Depression means a mood that is variously described as blue, low, down in the dumps, or melancholy—as well as depressed. This low mood must be persistent, usually lasting at least a week or two. It is often described as a marked change from the patient's normal mood. The information needed for the history of the present illness addresses both cause of depression (see later) and severity.

Tip-Offs

You should investigate depression if your patient presents any of these symptoms:

Abuse of drugs or alcohol
Activity level that is either markedly increased or decreased
Anxiety symptoms
Appetite changes
Concentration poor
Death wishes
Depressed mood
Interest decreased for usual activities (including sex)
Sleeplessness or excessive sleepiness
Suicidal ideas
Tearfulness
Weight loss or gain
Worthlessness

Main Diagnoses

Many of the same physical diseases that produce psychosis can also lead
to depression. However, the principal problem with diagnosis is differen-
tiating primary depressions (when depression is chronologically the first
disorder to appear) from those that are secondary. (Secondary diagnoses
begin after and are caused by another mental or personality disorder.)
Principal diagnoses to consider are

Major depression (unipolar or bipolar)*
Melancholia*
Dysthymia*
Seasonal mood disorder
Secondary mood disorder

Historical Information

Alcohol and drugs. Substance abuse is a principal diagnosis preceding the onset of secondary depression.

Atypical features. Stress-related depressions classically have symptoms
of excessive sleep (hypersomnia), increased appetite, weight gain; patients feel better in the mornings and when they are with people they
like. These features are called atypical because patients with classical
depressions typically have insomnia, feel better in the evenings, and
complain of decreased appetite and weight.

Change from usual self. Patients who have severe bipolar or unipolar
depressions typically report that the way they feel is a "complete change
from the way I used to feel."

Environmental stress. Any severe environmental stressor can be associated with depressed mood. A depression that remits as soon as the stressor lifts is sometimes called *reactive.* Reactive depressions are usually less severe than depressions that are not stress related and are less likely to require medication.

Family history of mood disorder. This is a classical finding in severe depression; bipolar depression, for one, is at least in part inherited.

Episodic illness. Has there been a previous episode of depression? Did the patient recover completely? "Yes" answers suggest major forms of depression such as bipolar, unipolar, and seasonal mood disorder. A chronic, low-intensity depression that has been present for years is typical of dysthymia.

Indecisiveness. Inability to make up one's mind, even regarding minor details, is also emblematic of severe depression.

Isolation. Withdrawal from friends or family suggests a severe depression such as melancholia.

Mania ever. The distinction between bipolar and unipolar depression is easily made with the finding of episodes of mania.

Neglect of hobbies, activities. Loss of interest in usual activities accompanies severe depression.

Recent loss (bereavement). This is another common environmental stressor; grief reaction is not considered mental disorder in DSM-III-R, but it is often the cause of depressive symptoms.

Seasonal pattern. Some patients report regular onset of depression at a particular season of the year (such as fall), with full remission at another, later season (such as spring). Such patients may be diagnosed as having seasonal mood disorder.

Sex interest decreased. Loss of libido is a classical symptom of moderate to severe depression.

Suicide ideas, attempts. For any depressed patient, ask about psychological and physical seriousness of previous attempts. Are there current ideas about suicide or means for carrying them out?

Trouble thinking or concentrating. These symptoms are usually found in moderate to severe depression.

Vegetative symptoms. Classical for severe depression with melancholia are terminal insomnia (patient awakens early and cannot return to sleep), decreased appetite, weight loss, and low energy (fatigue). Patients tend to feel better in evenings than mornings and don't improve when with people, even those whose company they normally enjoy.

Mental Status Examination

Appearance and behavior
  Tearful
  Decreased attention
    to appearance
  Decreased interest
    in usual activities
  Slowed actions
  Agitation
Mood
  Sad face
  Anxiety
  Guilt feelings
Flow of thought
  Slowing
Content of thought
  Ruminations
  Hopeless
  Worthless

Content of thought (cont.)
  Loss of pleasure
  "Better off dead"
  Death wishes
  Suicide ideas, plans
  Mood-congruent delusions
    Guilt
    Sin
    Worthlessness
    Ill health
    Poverty
  Language not usually affected
Cognition
  Usually intact
  May have "pseudodementia"
Insight and judgment
  May deny feeling depressed
  May deny possibility of
    improvement

MOOD DISTURBANCE: MANIA

Manic patients describe their moods as high, hyper, exalted, excited, or euphoric; sometimes they are mainly irritable. Although mania is a condition that has been well recognized for more than a hundred years, these patients are often misdiagnosed as having schizophrenia. Organic disorders can sometimes present with symptoms of mania.

Tip-Offs

Consider mania when confronted with any of the following symptoms:

Activity level increased
Distractibility
Grandiose sense of self-worth
Judgment deteriorates
Mood that is euphoric or irritable
Plans many activities
Sleep decreased (reduced need for sleep)
Speech rapid, loud, hard to interrupt
Substance abuse recently begun or increased
Thoughts move rapidly from one idea to another

Main Diagnoses

Most manic patients also have episodes of (often severe) depression. Cyclothymia, a milder condition in which high (although not psychotic) moods alternate with depressed ones, is the principal differential to consider. Differential diagnosis includes

Mania* (bipolar mood disorder)
Cyclothymia
Organic mood disorder

Historical Information

Alcohol abuse. This may be an attempt to treat the uncomfortable feelings of being speeded up.

Concentration decreased. Manic patients often start projects that they do not complete.

Episodic illness. A previous episode of mania or depression with complete recovery usually clinches the diagnosis.

Insomnia. This is often experienced as decreased need for sleep.

Judgment deteriorates. This appears as a history of spending sprees, legal troubles, or sexual indiscretions.

Libido increased. Manic exuberance can lead to promiscuity, pregnancy, and the risk of sexually transmitted disease.

Personality change. At the extreme, a normally quiet, unassuming person abruptly becomes boisterous, argumentative, or ill-tempered.

Physical conditions. Disinhibition similar to mania can be encountered after head trauma and in various organic conditions such as brain tumors and endocrine disorders.

Relationships disrupted. Friends and family have difficulty coping with a markedly changed personality.

Sociability increased. Manic patients enjoy parties and other social gatherings.

Work-related problems. Loss of concentration and preoccupation with grandiose plans contribute to decreased performance on the job or in school.

Mental Status Examination

Appearance and behavior
    Excited, agitated
    Hyperactive
    Increased energy
    Flamboyant or bizarre dress
    May be threatening or assaultive

Mood
    Euphoric
    Irritable
    Rapidly changing moods

Flow of thought
  Racing thoughts
  Flight of ideas
  Pressured speech
  Wordplay, jokes
  Loud
  Distractible
Content of thought
  Self-confident
  Increased religiosity
  Full of schemes and plans
  Grandiosity that may be delusional

Language usually not affected
Cognition usually intact
Insight and judgment
  Lack of insight into the fact
    of being ill
  Poor judgment (refuses
    hospitalization, treatment)

SUBSTANCE USE DISORDERS

Substance misuse is defined by the culture in which it occurs. In most segments of our culture, the majority of adults use substances, if only caffeine. Whether we consider a person to be *misusing* a substance depends not simply on the amount or frequency of use but also on the consequences of this behavior. These consequences may be behavioral, cognitive, legal, financial, and physical. Many of these also affect society as a whole.

Tip-Offs

The following symptoms should lead you to consider a diagnosis of substance use:

    Alcohol use greater than one or two drinks per day
    Arrests or other legal problems
    Financial problems: spends money needed for other items
    Health problems: blackouts, cirrhosis, abdominal pain, vomiting
    Illegal substance use
    Job loss, tardiness, demotions
    Memory impairment
    Social problems: fights, loss of friends

Main Diagnoses

In current American usage, these disorders are categorized as dependence (defined later) and abuse, which is a residual classification for patients who have some problems with substances but don't qualify for the diagnosis of dependence. Substance-induced organic mental disorders, the brain syndromes that most people who abuse substances also have at one time or another, will be considered under the area of clinical interest of difficulty in thinking.

The classes of psychoactive substance that are recognized as subject to abuse are defined next. Many substance abusers will use more than one of these classes.

Alcohol*
Amphetamines*
Cannabis*
Cocaine*
Hallucinogens*
Inhalants*
Nicotine*
Opioids*
Psychotomimetics* such as phencyclidine (PCP)
Sedatives, hypnotics, anxiolytics*

Substance abuse can occur as a solitary diagnosis, but it is often associated with another Axis I or Axis II (personality disorder) diagnosis. Those to look for especially include

Mood disorders (depression* and mania*)
Schizophrenia*
Somatization disorder*
Antisocial personality disorder*

Historical Information

Abuse. Abuse describes the residual group of drug users who are not dependent on their drug but who continue to use despite (1) physical danger (such as driving while under the influence) or (2) knowledge that they have problems resulting from substance use.

Activities used to obtain supply. These include drug sales, theft, robbery, and prostitution.

Age at onset. How old was the patient when drug use began? For alcoholism, women may have a much older age of onset than men.

Chronology. If there is an associated mental disorder, which came first? For example, if alcoholism is followed chronologically by depression, the depression is regarded as secondary.

Dependence. Dependence on any substance that can be abused is defined by three or more of the following symptoms. Numbers 8 and 9 don't usually apply to cannabis, the hallucinogens, or phencyclidine.

1. Greater use (larger amounts or longer time) than the patient intended
2. Repeated attempts or desire to control use
3. Activities center on use of the substance of choice
4. Intoxication or withdrawal symptoms frequently interfere with major responsibilities
5. Important activities are preempted by substance abuse
6. Continued use despite knowledge of social, physical, emotional, or job problems that result from it
7. Tolerance (the patient needs more drug to produce the same effect)
8. Characteristic withdrawal symptoms
9. Additional quantities of the substance are taken to avoid withdrawal

Features of dependence and withdrawal specific to each of these drug groups are given in Appendix B.

Frequency of use. How often has each drug been used? Has the pattern changed with the current episode?

Health problems. Has deteriorating health been suggested by evidence such as cirrhosis, stomach disorders, wasting, tuberculosis, or respiratory problems?

Legal problems. Have there been arrests or incarcerations for possession, sales, or criminal activities to finance supply? A history of criminal activity occasioned by the need to obtain money for drugs must be distinguished from antisocial personality disorder. Antisocial personality disorder may be the correct diagnosis if illegal activities have been undertaken when the patient was clean and sober.

Needle sharing. If IV usage is reported, has the patient *ever* used dirty needles? Had hepatitis? How recently has there been a test for HIV?

Organic mental disorders. Complications that are especially likely include hallucinosis, mood syndrome, anxiety syndrome, delusional disorder, and delirium on withdrawal.

Pattern of use. Has there been continuous, episodic, or binge usage? If more than one drug is involved, what is the pattern for each?

Personality change. How has drug use affected the way the patient relates to others? Has there been a general loss of motivation (especially with long-term use of cannabis or hallucinogens)?

Relationship problems. These include divorces, separations, and fighting. An occasional couple stays together *only* because of a common interest in drug use.

Route of administration. Any of the following means can be used: oral, snorting, smoking, intravenous (IV).

Mental Status Examination

Appearance
  Plethoric
  Tremor
  Disheveled
Mood
  Depressed
  Anxious
  Belligerent
Flow of thought
  Often talkative
Content of thought
  Maudlin
  Demanding
  Hallucinations
    More often visual
    May be auditory

Language
  Fluency is reduced (mumbling, slurred speech)
Cognitive
  May show signs of organicity if there is a concomitant organic mental disorder
Insight and judgment
  May reject the diagnosis
  Patients often refuse treatment or sign out against advice

SOCIAL AND PERSONALITY PROBLEMS

Personality *traits* are patterns of behavior or thought that persist throughout adult life. To be termed personality *disorders,* traits must be severe enough to cause the patient distress or functional impairment (social, emotional, or biological).

Tip-Offs

You should consider social and personality problems whenever your patient has any of the following characteristics:

Anxiety
Behaviors that seem odd or bizarre
Dramatic presentation
Drug or alcohol abuse
Interpersonal conflict
Job problems
Legal difficulties
Marital conflicts

Personality disorders must be distinguished from ordinary problems of living that are not mental disorders. The latter can include borderline intelligence, academic problems, marital and other family problems, job problems, and uncomplicated bereavement.

Main Diagnoses

Although many personality disorders have been proposed over the years, only the 11 given below currently enjoy the DSM-III-R blessing. Because they have features in common, they are usually presented in three clusters.

Cluster A. These people tend to be viewed as odd or eccentric. The cluster includes the following personality disorders:
Paranoid
Schizoid*
Schizotypal*
Important differential diagnosis (aside from other personality disorders in this or other clusters) include
Schizophrenia*
Delusional disorder*

Cluster B. These people are seen as dramatic, overly emotional, and erratic. The cluster includes these personality disorders:
Antisocial*
Borderline*
Histrionic
Narcissistic
Important differential diagnoses (in addition to other personality disorders) are
Substance abuse*
Mania*
Somatization disorder*

Cluster C. These patients seem anxious or afraid. The cluster includes the following personality disorders:
Avoidant
Dependent
Obsessive compulsive*
Passive aggressive
Important differential diagnosis (also, other personality disorders) include
Obsessive compulsive disorder*

Other personality disorders (or clusters) may come to the fore in the future.

Historical Information

A large number of traits have been linked to personality disorder. For purposes of description, I have grouped these under several common headings. This list makes no pretense of completeness; it does present traits that clinicians consider significant in defining currently recognized personality disorders. These are some of the traits that should be pursued in the quest of a personality disorder diagnosis.

Callousness. Forces sexual activity on others; takes advantage of others for own gain; humiliates others publicly; uses harsh discipline; takes pleasure in suffering of others.

Carries grudges.

Childhood delinquency. Truancy; starts fights; fights with weapons; runs away; is cruel to animals or people; destroys property; sets fires.

Compliance is excessive. Volunteers for unpleasant tasks so as to be liked by others; agrees with people to avoid rejection.

Concern for others is lacking. Self-centered; unable to recognize how others feel.

Criticism is rejected. Resents useful suggestions; easily hurt by others.

Dishonesty. History of frequent lying; history of stealing, robbery, or conning others.

Impulsivity. Wanders without a fixed abode; sexual indiscretions; shoplifts; reckless disregard for personal safety.

Indecisiveness. Depends on others to make decisions or avoids making decisions; vague about goals.

Indifferent to praise.

Inflexibility. Reluctant to do things that differ from routine; perfectionism that interferes with task completion; preoccupation with rules, lists, order; misses forest for the trees; won't let others do things their way; inflexible about morality, ethics.

Insecurity. Feels uncomfortable when alone; won't get involved unless sure of being liked; fearful of embarrassing self in social situations; exaggerates risks of doing something outside the routine; afraid of being abandoned; feels helpless or uncomfortable, so avoids being alone.

Irresponsibility. Defaults on financial obligations such as family support or debts; unable to hold a job; fails to do a reasonable share of the work; "forgets" obligations; puts things off.

Mood instability. Mood fluctuates more rapidly or more widely than is usually considered normal for the circumstances. May be quick to show anger; "hair-trigger temper."

Physical aggression. Fighting or assaults.

Saves objects of no value.

Sex drive is low.

Sociability is low. Is a loner (prefers solitary activities); uncomfortable in social situations or with strangers; avoids close relationships.

Stinginess. Shows lack of generosity with money or time.

Suicidal ideas or behavior.

Suspiciousness. Reluctance to confide in others; easily slighted; reads hidden meaning into innocent remarks or situations; expects to be exploited or harmed by others; questions loyalty of friends or fidelity of spouse.

Trusts others excessively. Chronically chooses associates or situations that lead to disappointment.

Unstable interpersonal relationships.

Workaholism.

Mental Status Examination

Appearance and behavior
  Lacks sense of humor
  Hypervigilant
  Argumentative
  Appears tense
  Reluctant to confide
  Cold or aloof
  Sexual seductiveness that is
    inappropriate
  Overly concerned with
    appearance, attractiveness
Mood
  Hostile or defensive
  Temper; inappropriate, intense
    anger
  Exaggeratedly emotional speech,
    behavior
  Denies experiencing strong
    emotions
  Feels empty or bored
  Lacks remorse for hurting others
  Shallow, shifting emotions
  Apathy
  Restricted or inappropriate affect
  Cool, aloof, or silly

Flow of thought
  Vague speech
  Odd speech (vague, digres-
    sive, impoverished)
Content of thought
  Expects to be exploited
  Questions loyalty of friends
  Suspects hidden meanings
  Fantasies of success, power
  Ideas of reference (e.g., "as
    if" strangers talk about
    patient)
  Odd beliefs, superstitions or
    magical thinking, illusions
  Uncertainty about identity
    (self-image, sexual orien-
    tation, long-term goals,
    values)
  Frequently requests re-
    assurance or approval;
    fishes for compliments
  Fears being embarrassed
  Judgmental of self and/or
    others
  Unreasonably devalues
    authority figures

Language: no abnormalities
    are typical
Cognition: no abnormalities
    are typical

Insight and judgment
    Exaggerates accomplishments
    Lacks remorse for behavior
    Feels others make unreasonable
        demands
    Overvalues own work; self-impor-
        tant; feels problems are unique;
        sense of entitlement

DIFFICULTY THINKING (ORGANIC MENTAL PROBLEMS)

A wide variety of physical and chemical insults can interfere with thinking. These causes include

Brain tumors
Head trauma
Hypertension
Infections
Metabolic disorders
Postoperative complications
Seizure disorders
Toxic substances/withdrawal
Vitamin deficiency

Tip-Offs

Any of the following symptoms or signs should stimulate further investigation of organic mental problems:

Bizarre behavior
Confusion
Decreased judgment
Delusions
Hallucinations
Memory defects
Mood fluctuates
Toxin ingestion

Main Diagnoses

Physical or chemical brain dysfunctioning produces abnormalities of
behavior or thinking that can be either temporary or permanent. The
types of organic problems include

Amnestic syndrome*
Anxiety syndrome
Delirium*
Delusional syndrome
Dementia*
Hallucinosis*
Intoxication* and withdrawal*
Mood syndrome
Personality syndrome

The important differential diagnoses include those starred diagnoses in the previous group plus

Depression*
Schizophrenia*
Substance abuse disorders*

Delirium and dementia may coexist.

Historical Information

Age at onset. Dementia is most commonly encountered in the elderly; delirium is common in children *and* in older people.

Course. May be stable, fluctuating, deteriorating, or improving. If the damage is structural (such as following massive brain trauma), there tends to be some permanent dysfunction, even though improvement may occur. Patients with dementia (such as Alzheimer's) tend to deteriorate.

Depressive disorder. It is especially important to know about a history of depression and current depressive features because "pseudodementia," one of the possible presentations of severe depression, is a completely treatable mood disorder that is no dementia at all.

Difficulty caring for self. Often this is what drives the family to bring demented patients for care.

Fluctuating symptoms and mental status. Such fluctuations are especially characteristic of delirium.

Head trauma. Recent trauma can produce a subdural hematoma, which produces symptoms days to weeks later. Bleeding inside the skull can also cause an epidural hematoma, which leads to symptoms within hours or days. Also be alert for loss of memory that can result from concussion.

Impulsivity. Demented patients lose the ability to judge what is acceptable behavior; consequently, they act on impulses they would once have suppressed. Delirious or demented patients may try to run away, as a reaction to either fear or confusion. Spending money thoughtlessly can occur, as it does in mania, although in demented patients it may lack the grandiose quality it has in mania.

Laboratory testing. This should be consistent with the suspected cause of any organic mental syndrome.

Memory loss. Defective memory is characteristic of the dementias. Recent memory is affected most often. Long-term memory can also be affected in severe dementia. Some patients try to compensate for defects in memory by making up stories (confabulation).

Onset. The development of symptoms may be rapid or insidious, depending on the cause and nature of the disorder. Rapid onset is characteristic of disorders caused by infectious processes or brain trauma; vitamin deficiencies and brain tumors may develop gradually.

Personality change. Many of the symptoms of organic mental syndromes involve a change from the patient's previous personality. These include outbursts of rage or combativeness, social withdrawal, coarsening of behavior (crude jokes), and neglect of grooming or hygiene. One Alzheimer's patient who had always welcomed racial diversity shouted racist comments. Excessive orderliness (known as "organic orderliness") sometimes develops.

Psychotic symptoms. Delusions, usually persecutory, occur in dementia (Alzheimer's patients often believe that people steal from them). The delusions of organic delusional syndrome may be indistinguishable from those of schizophrenia. Hallucinations (usually visual) commonly occur in delirium.

Sleep–wake cycle changes. Delirious patients are typically drowsy, although some have trouble falling asleep; vivid dreams or nightmares occur. In depression with melancholia, patients typically awaken early in the morning and are unable to get back to sleep.

Suicide attempts. The presence of suicide behavior should cause you to consider the diagnosis of major depression, although attempts (and completions) can occur in the dementias.

Mental Status Examination

Appearance and behavior	Mood
Disheveled	Anger
Tremor	Anxiety
Restlessness	Apathy
Picking at bedclothes, clothing	Bland (shallow) affect
	Depression
	Euphoria

Mood (cont.)
Fear
Irritability
Flow of thought
Slurred speech
Perseveration
Rambling, incoherent
Loosening of associations
Content of thought
Suspiciousness
Current suicidal ideas
Illusions
Psychotic features
Delusions
Hallucinations
(especially visual)
Language
Comprehension decreases
with advancing dementia
Fluency is often preserved,
even with moderately
severe dementia
Naming: aphasias

Cognition
Drowsy, hard to stay awake
Disorientation
Not knowing the date may
be an early symptom of
delirium
Disorientation to place,
person are later symptoms
(especially dementia)
Impaired abstract thinking
(similarities)
Low attention span (easily-
distractible) is found
especially in delirium
Impaired memory
Insight and judgment
Impaired judgment

ANXIETY, AVOIDANCE BEHAVIOR, AND AROUSAL

Conditions in this area of clinical interest have in common anxiety symptoms that result in attempts to avoid the stimulus.

Tip-Offs

Symptoms that would cause you to explore this area include any expression of anxiety or fear, as well as somatic symptoms that suggest breathing or heartbeat problems when there is no known basis for concern.

Anxiety
Chest complaints (pain, heaviness, trouble breathing, palpitations)
Compulsive behavior
Fear of objects, situations, dying, impending doom, going crazy
Nervousness
Obsessional ideas

Panic
Trauma, history of severe emotional or physical
Worries

Main Diagnoses

The principal types of disorder covered by this area of clinical interest include

Panic*
Generalized anxiety*
Phobic*
Obsessive compulsive*
Posttraumatic stress*

Although anxiety symptoms are found in nearly every mental disorder, the important differential diagnoses include

Depression*
Substance abuse*
Schizophrenia*
Somatization disorder*

Historical Information

Age at onset. Most of these conditions begin in a patient who is relatively young. Animal phobias begin in childhood; situational phobias usually begin in the thirties.

Agoraphobia. May occur with or without panic disorder. Occurs in situations from which escape is difficult or embarrassing, such as being away from home, in a crowd, in a car, or on a bridge.

Alcohol or drug abuse. These may be either the cause or an effect of anxiety symptoms.

Anticipatory anxiety. Common in phobias, this sensation of dread is experienced for minutes to hours before the arrival of a feared stimulus (e.g., speaking in public).

Caffeine intake. Excessive coffee (or tea) drinking can cause anxiety symptoms.

Circumstances of panic attacks. How many attacks have there been, and in what period of time? Was it unexpected? (Panic attacks tend to come out of the blue; they should not be diagnosed if they occur only when the patient has been the focus of the attention of other people.)

Compulsions. The most common of these are handwashing, checking, counting, and rituals such as a routine that *must* be followed at bedtime. They may occur as rituals (rules) or as an "antidote" or response to obsessions.

Depressive symptoms. Determine whether these came before the anxiety syndrome, suggesting primary depression, or after, suggesting that the depression is secondary.

Duration of panic attacks. Individual panic attacks last only a few minutes. The period during which a patient has attacks may last for weeks, months, or years.

Frequency of panic attacks. This is usually several times a week.

Life-style constriction. As a result of anxiety, does the patient avoid specific situations or objects? This may be true for phobic disorder, obsessive compulsive disorder, posttraumatic stress disorder, and panic disorder.

Mental content of panic attack. Patients may fear they are going to die, lose control, or lose their minds.

Obsessions. Most common are ideas of (1) harming or killing and (2) swearing (blaspheming). These ideas persist despite the fact that patients recognize the ideas are senseless and foreign to them.

Physical symptoms of anxiety. Most of the same physical sensations occur in panic attacks and in anxiety disorder. They include

Breathlessness	Heart palpitations
Chest pain	Lump in throat
Chills or flushes	Muscle tension
Dizziness	Nausea
Dry mouth	Restlessness
Fatigability	Sweating
Frequent urination	Tremor

Prescription medication abuse. Anxiety patients may resort to this in an attempt to keep symptoms in check.

Social phobias. These phobias typically involve speaking or eating in public, using a public toilet, trying to write when someone is watching, or saying foolish things in public.

Specific phobias. Also called *simple phobias,* the most common are fear of air travel, animals, blood, closed-in places, heights, and injury.

Stressors. A severely traumatic physical or emotional experience is a required precipitant for posttraumatic stress disorder.

Worry. Unwarranted or excessive concern about real life circumstances is characteristic of generalized anxiety disorder. Examples are losing the house to the bank two months before the mortgage is paid off; being fired when one is the "fair-haired child" of the company president.

Mental Status Examination

Appearance and behavior
  Hypervigilance (scanning the environment)
Mood
  Depression
  Anxiety
Content of thought
  Obsessional ideas
    Killing
    Blasphemy
Insight and judgment
  Insight retained that the fear or behavior is unreasonable
  Tries to resist

PHYSICAL COMPLAINTS

Physical illness (anatomically demonstrable heart attacks, asthma, ulcers, allergies, and the like) must always be a prime concern of any clinician confronted with a patient who has somatic complaints. But many patients come to mental health care complaining of physical symptoms for which no basis in body physiology, chemistry, or anatomy can be found. Such symptoms are commonly called *hypochondriacal* or *psychosomatic*. Often, by the time the patient (and family) are finally driven to seek help from a mental health professional, there has already been a full range of medical tests and evaluations. Because of certain features of demographics and symptoms held in common, I have included anorexia and bulimia nervosa in this group.

Tip-Offs

If patient presents any of the following problems you should consider this area of clinical interest:

Appetite disturbance
Depression that is chronic
History that is complicated
Multiple complaints
Physical symptoms unexplained by known illness (especially neuro-
    logical symptoms such as pain, convulsions, sensory loss)
Sexual or physical abuse in childhood
Substance abuse in a woman
Treatment failures that are repeated

Vague history
Weakness that is chronic
Weight changes (up or down)

Main Diagnoses

The principal diagnoses in this area include

Anorexia nervosa*
Body dysmorphic disorder (dysmorphophobia)
Bulimia nervosa
Hypochondriasis
Somatization disorder*
Somatoform pain disorder (chronic pain syndrome)

Other disorders that should be considered in patients who complain of physical symptoms are

Depression*
Panic disorder*
Physical illness
Substance abuse*

Historical Information

Age at onset. Most of the mental disorders in this group begin early (childhood or adolescence). Hypochondriasis usually begins in the twenties, somatoform pain disorder in the thirties or forties.

Childhood physical or sexual abuse. This is so common in patients with somatization disorder that it should always be inquired about.

Chronic pain. In somatoform pain disorder there is no known basis for pain, or the pain is out of keeping with known physical cause.

Doctor shopping. A relentless search for a cure frequently accompanies somatization disorder. It may lead to repeated, fruitless medical evaluations.

Environmental stress. Social problems (marital, job) may impel somatization disorder patients to seek mental health treatment for what they perceive as physical problems.

Fear of organic illness that is not present. The nondelusional idea that the person is ill persists despite (often repeated) reassurances to the contrary. This is the cardinal symptom of hypochondriasis.

Operations. Somatization disorder patients often have a history of multiple surgical procedures; many times, healthy organs are removed.

Organic illness in childhood. Did the patient receive attention for being ill as a child? In some cases this factor may underlie the somatization.

Physical defect (imagined or exaggerated). The essential symptom in body
dysmorphic disorder, these ideas are *not* of delusional intensity. Anorexia
nervosa patients typically regard themselves as appearing overweight,
even when they are demonstrably emaciated.

Review of systems. This is a specialized review of 35 symptoms, any
13 of which are diagnostic of somatization disorder. The complete review
of systems is given in Appendix B. Seven symptoms constitute a useful
screening test. If the answer to all of these seven items is "No," you can
assume that the patient does not have somatization disorder and omit
the full list. Any positive answer necessitates asking the entire list from
Appendix B.

Amnesia
Burning sensation in sexual organs or rectum
Difficulty swallowing
Painful menstruation
Pain in extremities
Shortness of breath (not while exerting self)
Vomiting (not during pregnancy)

Secondary gain. This occurs when a person gains attention or support from being ill; it is classical for somatization disorder and other
somatoform disorders.

Suicide ideas, behavior. These patients often threaten or attempt suicide; occasionally they do kill themselves.

Substance abuse. Misuse of alcohol or drugs frequently complicates
somatization disorder and other disorders in this group.

Mental Status Examination

Appearance and behavior
   Flashy dress
   Ingratiating manner
   Exaggerated mannerisms
   Marked wasting
Mood
   Indifference toward symptom (*"la belle indifférence"*)
   Dramatic presentation
   Anxiety
   Depression
Flow of thought: no abnormalities are typical

Content of thought
    Centers on physical (sometimes imagined) illness
Language: no abnormalities are typical
Cognition: no abnormalities are typical
Insight and judgment
    Overinterprets physical symptoms

SUMMING UP

Areas of clinical interest are a way of identifying signs and symptoms that may be of clinical importance. Especially during the history of the present illness, clinicians should be alert for symptoms in any of these areas: difficulty thinking; substance use; psychosis; mood disorder; anxiety, avoidance behavior, and arousal; physical complaints; and social and personality problems.

14 Closure

An hour usually provides enough time to explore the reasons for seeking treatment and to obtain a great deal of personal background information about your patient. Within this time you should also have conducted a mental status examination. Even though there is still much you would like to know, you probably shouldn't push the interview too much further. You're learning to interview, not testing your endurance, and you need to be fresh enough to keep evaluating what you hear and see. Perhaps your class schedule dictates that you will have to finish next week, or the hour of the day could suggest that you return tomorrow. Or, if both you and your patient still have time and the inclination, just take a coffee break before continuing.

THE ART OF CLOSING

Once you have decided to bring the interview to a close, you need to plan its termination carefully. Closing an initial interview is a minor art form that requires some care. Your patient has just invested considerable hope and confidence in the time you have spent together, and quite reasonably expects some information to carry away from the encounter. The content of that message will depend in part upon your relationship with the patient.

If you are a practicing clinician responsible for this patient's care, you will probably follow these steps: (1) summarize your findings, (2) develop with the patient a plan for future management, and (3) set a time for your next meeting. Whenever it is justified, you should also (4) include a message of hope for the future. Here is an example:

"From what you've told me, it seems that both you and your husband have had a lot of trouble adjusting to the death of your daughter.

161

It's something you haven't talked much about, and you're suffering from the lack of communication. I think I can help, but before we decide on a plan of action I'd like to talk with your husband. You said you thought he'd be willing to come in. Could you ask him to make an appointment for next week?"

The closing phase of your initial interview as a trainee might sound something like this:

"Thank you for spending so much time with me. You really helped me understand about your type of depression. I agree that your therapist is doing everything possible to help. Tomorrow I'd like to ask you more about your family background, if that's all right with you."

You shouldn't expect that you will anticipate everything the patient needs to hear. In any session as intense as a typical initial interview, you are likely to leave unspoken something that is important to the patient. Therefore, it is usually a good idea to learn whether you have omitted anything that should be covered right away. Before you quit, say something that invites comments or questions about your interview.

"Do you have any questions about anything we've said so far?"

"Are there any important issues we haven't covered?"

You may find that something you've left out needs action now—such as additional information about proposed treatment, uncertainty as to the time of the next appointment, or reassurance about prognosis. Try to respond factually to such substantive issues.

Of course, you won't be able to cover everything in a single interview session. Most patients will accept this and will be content to delay other concerns, questions, and items of historical information until a subsequent appointment.

Occasionally, something comes up right at the end of an interview that would require considerable time to cover adequately. Examples:

"What does the future hold for someone like me?"

"What do you think I should do about my son's alcoholism?"

If neither you nor the patient has any time constraints, you can deal with these questions when they arise. But if either of you has another appointment, you will have to delay further inquiry until your next interview.

In either case, consider the possible reasons for this new question so late in the interview. Some patients habitually save important information for closing time. Perhaps they need nearly an entire session to get up the courage to discuss important problems—are they afraid of the solution? Others may come to see their sessions as so valuable that they unconsciously try to prolong them.

You can deal with most of these last-minute items by expressing interest and promising to discuss them during your next session:

"I'm glad you mentioned that. It's something I want to learn more about. Let's make it our first order of business next time."

If the last-minute information is of life-threatening proportions (suicidal or homicidal ideas), you have no choice but to run overtime. If this happens habitually to you, you may need to consider why you neglect to raise these sensitive topics earlier in your interviews.

QUITTING EARLY

A rare patient may try to break off the interview before you've finished. Usually this will be someone who has a character disorder or is psychotic, intoxicated, or under extreme stress, perhaps from sleep deprivation or physical illness. (Sometimes all of the above apply!) Whatever the cause, you suddenly find yourself trying to get information from someone who is putting on a coat to leave. How should you react?

If it is close to the end of the session, point out that you will need only a few more minutes to finish. Then try to accommodate your patient's agitation by selecting only the most important remaining questions to ask.

With a new patient, you don't have much leverage, so try to avoid direct confrontation. If it is early in the interview, especially right at the beginning, the patient might not fully understand the reasons for the interview. Try explaining again. At the same time you can offer some empathy:

"I can see that you have been pretty upset. I'm sorry to be adding to your discomfort, but we do need to talk. It's the only way I can get the information I need to help you."

Your appeal to reason may succeed about half the time. If it doesn't, try switching gears to a discussion of the feelings that have blocked cooperation. As before, lead with an empathic statement.

"You seem pretty uncomfortable. Could you tell me what you are feeling?"

You may learn quite a lot about your patient's fear, anger or discomfort. By pursuing what you have just heard, you may be able to ease right back into the interview.

INTERVIEWER: I can see this has upset you. Could you tell me what you're feeling right now?

PATIENT: *(Rising to leave)* I can't stand it. It's just like the last time!

INTERVIEWER: Were you pretty upset then, too?

PATIENT: Of course I was! You'd be, too, if your therapist treated you the way mine treated me.

INTERVIEWER: It must have made you terribly uncomfortable.

PATIENT: *(Sitting down again)* I was humiliated. And scared.

As in this example, you may hear a good deal about previous attempts at therapy that have gone awry. Be prepared to spend considerable time, in the initial interview and later, digging out the facts about the previous treatment, even though it may have little or nothing to do with the actual reasons the patient has come in at this time.

If all your best efforts fail, respect the comfort and privacy of your patient. Specifically, don't plead, threaten, or imply shame or guilt. If your patient gets up to leave the room, don't use physical restraint. Instead, acknowledge the right to make this decision and your intention to respect it. But promise to have another try soon at this important task of gathering information:

"I can see that we'll have to break it off for now. That's okay—you have a right not to be bothered when you're feeling this bad. But it's really important that we figure out what difficulties brought you here. I can come back this afternoon, after you've had a chance to rest up."

Occasionally, *you* may decide to quit early, well short of an hour. This alternative will seem especially attractive when

- It is late at night, your patient has just been admitted to the hospital, and both of you are exhausted.
- Because of severe psychosis or depression, your patient cannot focus on the interview situation for longer than a few minutes at a time.
- Anger renders your patient unwilling to cooperate.
- You have squeezed a brief interview into an already hectic day. By agreement, you will talk just long enough to discover the major issues and to decide how soon you should meet again.

SUMMING UP

A good closing does not just summarize the interview; it also prepares the patient (and clinician) for the sessions that lie ahead.

15 Interviewing Informants

Most patients can tell you nearly everything you need to know. Whenever possible, you should also obtain information about your patient's present illness from other sources such as relatives, friends, previous clinical records, and other mental health professionals. But some situations virtually demand that you seek additional information or verification of data from informants. Here are a few of them:

- Children and adolescents often lack adequate perspective on their own behavior.
- Even some adults don't know certain important items of family history.
- Patients of any age who feel ashamed of things they have done may conceal historical information that you can learn from family or friends. Examples include episodes of substance abuse, suicide attempts, violence, and criminal behavior of any type.
- Psychotic patients may present delusional interpretations of fact, rather than the facts themselves.
- Childhood health history, often unknown to the patient, can be relevant to mental retardation or specific learning disorders. There may be a history of obstetrical complications during the birth of patients who have a sporadic form of schizophrenia.
- Patients with organic illnesses such as Alzheimer's disease may be unable to give a good history.
- Informants can tell you about cultural norms. This may be the only way to learn that it is normal in your patient's family to believe in astrology or to speak in tongues in church.
- Some patients with character disorder (especially antisocial personality disorder) do not reliably tell the truth.
- Personality disorder doesn't bother some patients much; it is their families and friends who suffer.

- For some, safeguarding a family secret may be more pressing than telling you things that could help with diagnosis or treatment.

Your family conference could reveal characteristics that will help you better understand or manage your patient. For example, high levels of emotional expression in relatives may predict relapse in a patient with schizophrenia.

You will almost always interview the patient first. The only significant exceptions, besides children and adolescents who are brought in by their parents, are adults who lack the capacity to speak for themselves. These include regressed schizophrenics, Alzheimer's disease patients, the developmentally disabled, and those with whom you do not share a common language. But even when you and your patient communicate well with one another, a little time spent with relatives will usually gain you additional perspective on the patient's disorder. This is especially true when a relative comes along for the first visit. This often means that the relative fears that, without help, the entire story may not be told.

OBTAIN PERMISSION FIRST

Before you talk to friends or relatives, you must usually obtain permission from the patient. Most patients consent willingly. The few who demur are usually afraid you will let slip something they have been trying to keep secret. You can often quiet these fears by pointing out that your main job is to seek information, not to dispense it, but that to be of the greatest help you need another person's perspective. Here's how you might phrase your reassurance:

"What you've told me is confidential, and I'll respect that confidence. You have that right. But you also have a right to the best help I can give. For that I need to know more about you. That's why I'd like to talk with your wife. Of course, she'll want to know what's wrong and what we plan to do about it. I think I should tell her, but I'll only tell what you and I have already agreed upon. I won't tell her anything else we've discussed, unless you give me permission in advance."

Once you have reached such an agreement, be scrupulously careful not to divulge additional information. Revealed secrets have an uncanny way of identifying their source. On the rare occasion when you are denied permission, you might suggest that the patient sit in when you talk to the friend or relative. This should calm any fears that you might use the meeting to hatch some sort of plot behind the patient's back.

As a rule, though, you should try to interview the informant when the patient is not present. The privacy will improve your chances for obtaining complete, accurate information, and both you and the informant will feel more comfortable.

There are only a few significant exceptions to the requirement to obtain the patient's consent first. These include patients who are

Minors
On conservatorship or unable to sign consent
Violent
Mute
Acutely suicidal
Experiencing a medical or mental health emergency

Then, when it is clear that the patient does not have the judgment to exercise autonomy, it is your duty to step in and make a decision as to the best course of action. To accomplish this, you will usually obtain information in any way you can.

CHOOSING AN INFORMANT

Because your goal is to obtain as much pertinent information as you can, you will naturally choose an informant who knows your patient well. Spouses usually have the most current information, so if the patient is married or has an intimate relationship of long standing, that is the person you will probably speak with first. But the sort of information you need may dictate a different choice. For example, if you want to know about childhood hyperactivity, you should interview a parent. Another consideration: studies show that relatives who have had an illness similar to the patient's are better able to recognize its symptoms. (Perhaps this is because they have been sensitized to the symptoms and course of illness.) Finally, as we shall discuss later, yours could end up being a group interview with several relatives at one time.

WHAT DO YOU ASK?

You should start by briefly explaining the purpose of this interview. Relatives will readily accept that you need to verify history or to give them information. But they may worry that clinicians have another agenda, such as blaming them or asking them to assume increased responsibility for the patient.

Your earlier discussion with the patient should have given you a considerable knowledge base, so your interview with informants can usually be comparatively brief—anywhere from a few minutes to half an hour. Even if you think you know exactly what questions you want answered, you could be surprised with new information about a problem you hadn't recognized before. That's why you should begin with a brief fishing expedition to learn what the informant knows. Use an open-ended question as bait.

In the example that follows, the patient had spent much of the initial interview talking about her previous episodes of depression. So, when her husband came in, the interviewer had prepared questions about depressive symptoms, treatment, and response. Fortunately, the leading question was open-ended.

INTERVIEWER: What can you tell me about your wife's difficulty?

PATIENT'S HUSBAND: Well, I just hope you can do something about her drinking. She's drunk nearly every afternoon when I get home from work, but she refuses to admit she's got a problem.

Once you've determined that patient and informants identify the same set of problems, you can get down to the business of obtaining the additional specific information you need. It will be of two sorts: (1) questions the patient was unable to answer and (2) items about which there is some confusion in your mind, often due to inconsistency in the patient's story. Here are a few examples of each:

History of mental illness in a parent
The patient's own developmental history
A reappraisal of your patient's drug or drinking history
The patient's symptoms during a psychotic illness
The ability of a patient to provide self-care
Relatives' willingness to provide care after discharge from hospital
A spouse's view of the reasons behind marital discord
Behavior that suggests a possible criminal career
An appraisal of the patient's personality characteristics
Effects on the family of any change in behavior

Even if you don't learn much that is new about the patient, an open-ended session with an informant may help you learn

How well does the family understand the illness?
What has the patient told the informant about the symptoms?

How has your patient interpreted the facts?
Has the patient distorted what you have said?

Of course, if the information from informants conflicts with what you have obtained from your patient, you must decide which (if either) story to believe. You are by no means safe if you automatically accept the informant's version — being a mental health patient should not automatically discredit anyone's testimony. Rather, when you evaluate conflicting stories, weigh the following factors for each informant, including the patient:

How much contact has the informant had with the patient?
How much does the informant appear to remember?
Does the informant seem to be protecting someone (self, patient, or others)?
Does family taboo appear to prevent the informant from discussing sensitive material?
How much is the story being distorted by wishful thinking (for example, about the happiness of a faltering marriage)?
Is there evidence of a halo effect that puts a positive spin on all the patient's behavior?
Does your informant seem well motivated to give you a complete and accurate story?

Afterwards, it is a good idea to discuss the session with your patient. You should provide some idea of what was said, so as to reassure your patient that you have broken no confidences, but how specific or general you are will depend on your taste and your patient's needs. You should also take care not to break any confidences from the relatives.

Here is an example of the sort of feedback you might give your patient:

"I had a very good talk with your wife, Mr. Crenshaw. Her information confirmed what you told me last week about your depression, and I think we all see eye to eye on the need for treatment. As you requested, I didn't say anything to her about the cocaine abuse, but I do think you'll feel better once you've gotten up the nerve to discuss it with her yourself."

GROUP INTERVIEWS

If the family is large and close-knit, you may find yourself interviewing whole groups of relatives. Some clinicians find this difficult, especially when the family is unhappy and expresses itself forcefully. Although it can be difficult to manage a large group of relatives, there are advantages to this approach.

- It is far more efficient than trying to talk with them individually. Although you might sometimes get the family to agree on one spokesperson with whom you will meet, information can be lost or distorted that way.
- The family is part of the environment. A group interview gives you the chance to observe how the relatives interact with one another and, by logical inference, with the patient. Do they treat one another considerately? Do you detect accusations, scapegoating, or guilt in one or more of your informants? Is their concern generally for the patient or for their own comfort?
- In some cases you may elect to interview family and patient together. This obviates all problems with confidentiality, because everyone hears what everyone else says. It also gives you the chance to observe directly how the patient and family interact. Do relatives ignore or answer for the patient? Do they disagree a lot? Fight?
- If you determine that family dynamics are in part responsible for your patient's difficulties, meeting with everyone can help lay the groundwork for eventual change in the home milieu, as an adjunct to therapy.

When meeting with more than one informant at a time, be sure to encourage all relatives to have their say. Often someone will be passive and silent; this is the individual you should try to draw out. It is better to have everyone's input at the beginning, rather than leaving them all to sort out their problems later, when you're not around to help. Of course, you shouldn't make decisions for them and you shouldn't take sides. Your goal should be to facilitate the discussion so all can understand the patient and their common problems.

OTHER INTERVIEW SETTINGS

Telephone Calls

Several studies have shown that you can obtain good-quality information from telephone interviews. If there is no other way to speak with a relative, it is certainly better than nothing. But it is hard to "meet" someone for the first time without face-to-face contact. If you must rely on words and tone of voice alone, you can never extract the nuances of meaning that body language so readily conveys. Furthermore, on the telephone relatives cannot size *you* up. Only a personal interview can convey the warm feelings that allow relatives to know that you are someone they can trust with secret or sensitive information. Finally, consider confidentiality laws. Without visual contact it is more difficult to be sure whom you are speaking with. If you give out information to someone you think is a spouse, but is actually an employer, you could hurt your patient's career and your own reputation.

House Calls

Although the house call has generally gone the way of insulin shock therapy, it can still be a useful tool for the clinician who wants maximum information about all aspects of a patient's milieu. There you can get a feeling for the environment (type of dwelling, neighborhood) *and* the family, which, when relaxed at home, may behave more "normally."

SUMMING UP

The most valuable informants are usually family and friends who know the patient well. By verifying existing information and providing new facts, they can help the clinician obtain a clear, comprehensive, balanced view of both patient and milieu.

16 Meeting Resistance

In most mental health interviews, two individuals work together to achieve a common understanding. But all patients have their own agendas, and sometimes these conflict with the usual goals of the initial interview. The result can be behavior that frustrates your attempts to obtain a complete data base while building rapport.

Resistance is any conscious or unconscious attempt to avoid a topic of discussion. Because nearly everyone feels uncomfortable with some topic or other, resistance is perhaps the most frequent of problem behaviors.

RECOGNIZING RESISTANCE

To counter resistance you must first recognize it. Sometimes this is easy, especially if it comes in the form of an obvious statement such as "I'd rather not talk about that." But many patients feel uncomfortable with open defiance; they may resist you in ways that are sometimes so subtle you will be hard-pressed to detect them. Watch for any of these behaviors that could indicate that your interview may be in trouble:

Tardiness. Being late for the interview is a classic sign of resistance. It is perhaps less common during an initial interview than during subsequent ones.

Voluntary behaviors. Poor eye contact, glancing at the clock, or shifting uneasily while seated suggests that your patient may feel uncomfortable with the topic currently under discussion.

Involuntary behaviors. Flushing, yawning, or swallowing also implies discomfort.

Forgetfulness. Some patients develop a "convenient" poor memory and respond to certain questions with "I don't know" or "I can't remember."

Omissions. The patient leaves out certain information. Unless reliable informants are consulted, even experienced clinicians find this sort of resistance difficult to detect.

Contradictions. Information that contradicts what you thought you learned earlier is relatively easy to spot but may be difficult to reconcile.

Changing the subject. Shifting to another topic of conversation may be an attempt to draw you away from a subject the patient would like to avoid. For example, You ask Mr. Blocker how he feels about his impending divorce; he responds by telling you that his wife's attorney has been bleeding him dry.

Exaggerations. Puffing up their own accomplishments is one way some patients resist facing the truth about themselves. You may not be able to detect individual exaggerations, but with time you begin to discern a pattern of improbable claims.

Diversionary tactics. These include telling jokes and asking to smoke or to use the bathroom. Some patients may try to control the interview by asking about the interviewer's personal life.

Silence. This can be a major indicator of resistance. It should not be confused with the time some patients need to think before responding to a complicated question.

A slight hesitation. Most subtle of all may be a slight hesitation before answering certain questions.

WHY DO PATIENTS RESIST?

Patients may resist telling the whole story to a mental health professional for a variety of reasons. Understanding these reasons often provides the key to breaking up the resistance.

- Preventing embarrassment is probably one of the most common reasons; it may operate especially during an initial interview. This is certainly understandable: Baring your soul to a total stranger is the unnatural antithesis of self-protection. It is especially hard for some people to reveal sensitive material about sex, illegal activities, and any behavior that demonstrates a lapse of judgment.
- Some patients (or their families) are afraid of criticism or worry that you may be shocked by their stories. They have learned to avoid disapproval simply by not risking it: They keep material they consider blameworthy to themselves.
- Some patients may withhold information because they are too afraid of its implications for diagnosis, prognosis, or treatment. The "stigma" of mental illness is one example.

- In a new relationship your patient may not yet feel enough trust to communicate fully with you, especially about thoughts or behavior that might damage a relationship or jeopardize a job or legal status. Unhappily, previous experience may have instigated these fears that a mental health professional might violate confidentiality.
- A patient might altruistically seek to protect a friend or loved one from any of the consequences mentioned previously.
- Some incidents or thoughts may seem too trivial to relate.
- Unconsciously the patient may be testing you to see whether you are smart enough or persistent enough (do you care enough?) to dig out the information that is being withheld.
- Patients may withhold information because of anger, conscious or unconscious, that has any of a number of causes. You may have unintentionally said something upsetting, or the patient may be reenacting with you feelings held for someone else in the past, a behavior called *transference.* Transference is by no means limited to feelings of anger.

Whatever the cause, resistance must not be allowed to persist unexplored and unchallenged. It is the responsibility of the interviewer to try to determine the cause and to remedy it. It can be a serious error to skip important topics or passively to follow the patient's lead.

HOW TO COPE WITH RESISTANCE

Above all else, it is most important that you try to understand (and correct, if you can) the reasons behind the behavior. The first step should be to consider whether you have done anything to provoke the resistance. There may be something obvious that you can deal with directly.

INTERVIEWER: I notice that you seem to have grown quiet, all of a sudden. What seems to be the problem?

PATIENT: Oh, I don't know.

INTERVIEWER: I'm wondering if you're upset that I said I wanted to talk to your husband.

PATIENT: *(Long pause)* Well, I don't understand why you want to.

INTERVIEWER: Could you tell me what you're afraid of?

PATIENT: He wouldn't understand about that affair I told you about. He isn't a bit broad-minded.

INTERVIEWER: Ah, I can see why you're unhappy. I think anyone would be, who worried that her therapist might break a confidence like that one. But that wasn't what I had in mind. The reason I want to talk to him is to learn how *he* views the marital problems you two are having. I think it would help me to understand the whole picture better. Do you think that you could ask him to come in with you for your next appointment?

This clinician's explanation told the patient three things: (1) that the clinician understood her, (2) that she had a right to her feelings, and (3) that her fears were groundless. Finally, it suggested that they continue with their plans.

All too often, however, you will be unable to identify anything specific that can be quickly corrected. Then the approach you take will depend on several features of the resistance itself.

   Its cause
   Its severity
   The form it takes
   The importance of the information you are seeking

Managing Silence

A relatively common example of a mild resistance is the embarrassed silence. You may encounter this reaction to questions about sex (see Chapter 9), but it could occur in nearly any interview situation. Your best first response may be a little silence of your own. You might try glancing away for a few seconds to emphasize your willingness to wait. By saying nothing for a few moments, you give your patient some extra thinking time. (Maybe that's all the silence signified in the first place. But if it is instead an early resistance, you allow the patient time to try to resolve the conflict.)

   However, a prolonged lack of response may establish a precedent for withholding further information later in the interview, and that is not in the patient's best interests. If a decent interval (no more than 15 seconds or so) fails to produce any response, you should probably intervene.

   During the brief silence, your patient's thoughts may have wandered, so your next step should be to refocus the question by asking it again in a slightly different form.

INTERVIEWER: How has your sexual adjustment been?

PATIENT: *(Silently looks at the floor for 15 or 20 seconds)*

INTERVIEWER: I was wondering whether there had been any problems with your sex life.

If the question seems important (the patient's inability to answer suggests that it might be), you should probably persevere. Start by giving the patient control over what will be said and by offering reassurance.

INTERVIEWER: Tell me what you feel comfortable saying about your sex life.

PATIENT: This is really hard for me.

INTERVIEWER: That's all right. It's safe to talk about it here.

Another tactic combines multiple approaches. You might word it something like this:

"A lot of people have difficulty with sensitive issues like this one. I'm really sorry that I have to put you through this, but to help you most, I need all the information I can possibly get. Please try to help me."

In this single speech you have (1) expressed sympathy, (2) underscored the normality of your patient's feelings, (3) re-emphasized the importance of obtaining a complete data base, and (4) issued a personal appeal.

Yet another approach is to try to name the emotions your patient might be having. If you do so correctly, you will help your patient perceive you as an empathetic, perceptive interviewer who can be trusted with secrets. You will maximize your chances of success if you name several possible emotions, as in this example:

"I can see you are having a real problem with that question. Sometimes people have trouble with questions when they feel ashamed. Or sometimes it's anxiety or fear. Are you having any of those feelings now?"

Although you have now asked something that is different from your original question, the two are related. Your patient may be able to respond more readily to the second one.

You want to reinforce in your patient the habit of responding to you, and even a nod is better than nothing at all. Once you have obtained any response, even a silent shrug or frown, you can often parlay it into a renewal of speech.

INTERVIEWER: You must be feeling pretty upset about this. Am I right?

PATIENT: (Nods)

INTERVIEWER: I think maybe we should move on and talk about your education, instead. Does that seem like a good idea to you?

PATIENT: *(Nods)*

INTERVIEWER: Is that something you think you can talk about?

PATIENT: Yes. . .I think so.

INTERVIEWER: That other subject is pretty important, but this clearly isn't the time to talk about it. We can come back to it another time.

Delaying the discussion of difficult material, as in the example just given, is probably one of the most often-used methods of dealing with moderate to severe resistance. The technique sacrifices information for the sake of rapport and the integrity of the interview, so you should use it sparingly. It is important for the patient to understand that the matter isn't closed, only postponed.

An answer of "I don't know" gives you no more information than does dead silence; if repeated often, it can cause an interview to grind to a halt. Occasionally, you might succeed in getting the patient off dead center by responding:

"Well, what do you *think* about it?"

Unfortunately, this often only invites the obvious (and maddening) rejoinder, "I don't know."

If you're not getting much information anyway, you're not taking a big risk by forcing a rare confrontation. You may get some clues as to the reason for the resistance. In this example the patient confronted is a 16-year-old girl:

INTERVIEWER: *(Leans forward and smiles)* Several times when you've said, "I don't know" it's been about questions that I think you know the answer to. What do you think might happen if you didn't hold back?

PATIENT: I don't know.

INTERVIEWER: A lot of kids don't like to talk because they're upset about something. Have you been feeling upset?

PATIENT: Maybe.

INTERVIEWER: *(Smiles)* Maybe we should try to understand that. What were you feeling just a moment ago?

PATIENT: My dumb mother made me come. *(Pauses)*

INTERVIEWER: So it was your mom's idea to come?

This example demonstrates confrontation and naming of feelings, which we have already mentioned. It also suggests several other techniques that can help break through resistance.

- Switch from facts to feelings. Resistance usually has an emotional basis. This interviewer recognized that feelings had to be explored before getting on with the history-taking.
- Emphasize the normal. Patients sometimes conclude that they must be pretty bizarre, just to be under the care of a mental health professional. The patient in this example was made to feel that her interviewer had encountered this behavior before and didn't find it strange.
- Reject the behavior, accept the person. By leaning forward and using warm words and tone of voice, the interviewer clearly indicated both (1) that a different response would be welcome and (2) unconditional acceptance of the patient as a person.
- Use verbal and nonverbal encouragements. Once the patient began to speak, the interviewer encouraged further efforts by a smile and making a suggestion that took off from her "Maybe." Other such encouragements (nods, paraphrasing) were discussed in Chapter 4.
- Focus on the patient's interests. As soon as it became clear that this patient was angry about being forced to come, the interviewer shifted the focus to her relationship with her mother. Subsequently, the session became much more productive.
- Still another technique is to look for a less affect-laden model of the behavior or feelings in question, and discuss the model first. Often this is a similar episode that happened to the patient long ago, but it could be one that affected a friend or relative. Here's how the process works:

INTERVIEWER: Have you been feeling so bad you've thought about harming yourself?

PATIENT: I—I can't say.

INTERVIEWER: It's a pretty upsetting subject, isn't it?

PATIENT: (Nods)

INTERVIEWER: Didn't you say you made a suicide attempt several years ago?

PATIENT: Yes. (Long pause)

INTERVIEWER: What happened then?

PATIENT: I overdosed on my wife's heart tablets. But I threw them all up.

INTERVIEWER: You must have been feeling pretty desperate.

PATIENT: (Nods)

INTERVIEWER: Are you feeling that way now?

PATIENT: I guess so. But I don't like to talk about it. It scares my wife.

With variations, this technique can sometimes ease you into a fruitful discussion after a more direct approach has failed. But if the only result is more resistance, you should probably change the topic completely.

Sometimes patients will fall into this technique spontaneously. When that happens, hear out the past example, then ask:

"Can you see any connection between what happened then and the way you have been behaving just recently?"

Most patients will see the point. For those who do not, you can gently draw the comparison yourself.

Special Techniques

Several other interview techniques are sometimes useful in countering resistance. For the most part these strategies apply in specific situations or to particular types of patients. Novice interviewers will rarely use these specialized techniques.

• Offer an excuse for unfavorable information. By helping out with plausible reasons, you may encourage your patient to be frank about embarrassing or distressing problems.

INTERVIEWER: How much have you been drinking just recently?

PATIENT: Not much. I really don't keep track.

INTERVIEWER: What with all the stress surrounding your husband's death, I thought you might have started drinking heavily again, like what happened several years ago when your mother died.

PATIENT: You're right. I've been so overwhelmed. If I didn't have three or four doubles every evening, I wouldn't be able to get to sleep at all.

• Exaggerate negative consequences that *didn't* happen. By emphasizing the worst possible outcome of a behavior, you diminish the patient's anxiety about what actually did happen.

INTERVIEWER: During that fight did you really hurt your wife?

PATIENT: Well... *(Silence)*

INTERVIEWER: Well, did you kill her?

PATIENT: Nah, I just knocked her around a little bit.

• Induce your patient to brag. Rarely, a patient withholds information about an exploit but seems secretly proud of it. Some interviewers try to encourage frankness by subtly implying admiration for some aspect of the behavior in question.

INTERVIEWER: How much were you drinking then?

PATIENT: Gee, that's hard to say.

INTERVIEWER: You're a pretty good-sized man. You look like you could really put it away.

PATIENT: I've hoisted a few in my day.

INTERVIEWER: I'll bet you could drink them all under the table!

PATIENT: Yeah, I suppose I've won my share of chug-a-lug contests.

This technique can build rapport while it obtains information. Although it is probably innocuous enough when applied to substance abuse, I worry that it might send a message of approval to a patient with personality disorder whose activities include sexual misconduct, fighting, or criminal behavior. If you ever use this technique, be careful not to condone or encourage the behavior itself.

PREVENTION

As with any other problem, no remedy for resistance is as satisfactory as preventing it in the first place. The following strategies should help you avoid having to use the more devious techniques we have just discussed.

- If you can obtain information about your patient's character or style of interacting before the interview begins, you may be better able to modify your approach to difficult topics. Resources include word-of-mouth information from referring clinicians and records from previous hospitalizations.
- Sometimes you can tell right away that your patient is reluctant to talk. A scowl, a sigh, or an upturned gaze may tip you off, even before you begin to speak. If so, perhaps this is the time to break the rule and start with small talk. A few moments of conversation about something you share (the weather or sporting interests) might help identify you as "friendly" and reduce your patient's antagonism. The purpose of small talk—to grease the skids for productive conversation with a potentially difficult patient—suggests two warnings: (1) Politics and religion are never "small" topics. Avoid them like a dirty needle. (2) For any subject, avoid taking a position that might be considered strong or controversial. It could throw you into confrontation that your already challenging interview hardly needs.
- Carefully monitor your reactions to the information you obtain.

If by your speech or facial expression you register surprise or disapproval, you may seriously damage rapport and limit both the quantity and quality of your information.

• Individualize your history-taking technique. Some patients simply won't be hurried. They aren't psychotic or demented; they simply have to tell their stories in their own way. When you encounter such a patient, you might as well forget about your time schedule and relax. You'll get your history—a little at a time—and you'll preserve rapport.

• Preface your mental status exam questions about delusions, hallucinations, and orientation with the remark that these "routine questions" are part of your usual, thorough evaluation. This will help to reduce your patients' concerns that you suspect them of being mentally slow or psychotic.

• If you encounter psychotic material such as delusions or hallucinations, don't argue. You won't win points by refuting what your patient "knows" to be true. But neither should you agree with something you know is false: You don't want to reinforce the psychosis. Instead, ask how long the patient has felt that way, or emphasize your concern for the accompanying discomfort. For example, the patient might be frightened by the content of the hallucination.

YOUR ATTITUDE

As we have noted before, with all patients it is important to understand your own feelings. If you find yourself feeling bored, angry, or disgusted, ask yourself, "Why?" Is there someone this patient reminds you of, such as a supervisor, parent, or spouse? (When therapists' feelings toward patients are carried over from previous relationships of their own it is called *countertransference*.) Perhaps there are features of this patient's personality that remind you of some of your own less admirable traits. Do you have anxiety about your own health, marriage, or family relationships? These feelings are ubiquitous, so even experienced therapists must take care that they do not intrude into their relationships with patients.

A patient who is uncooperative or difficult in other ways creates a special challenge. Clinicians must not let passive-aggressive behavior, sarcasm, or anger precipitate an outburst from them. Negative affect from the examiner, especially when it comes early in the relationship, can imperil an interview and even seriously damage future rapport. If you find yourself feeling uncomfortable during an interview, ask yourself:

"Why should I be feeling so upset?"

"What message am I missing?"

"Whom does this patient remind me of?"

The answers to these questions should help determine what corrective action to take.

SUMMING UP

At one time or another, most patients will resist giving complete information. Clinicians must keep alert for signs of resistance and try to identify its causes. Then they can usually find an interview technique to deal effectively with even very difficult patients. It is important to address resistance when it appears and not simply to move on without trying to determine (and remedy) its causes.

17 Special and Difficult Patients

A variety of attitudes and behaviors can affect the success of your initial interview. Although you won't often encounter these characteristics of patients, your response to them can modify their effect on your interview.

THE VAGUE PATIENT

Instead of information, the vague patient gives you only empty words. Here are a few examples:

The unfocused chief complaint. A variety of concerns may be stated, but none of them seems an adequate reason for seeking treatment.

Overgeneralizations. A single episode of illness may be treated as typical when it is not; one example of a friend's behavior is labeled as "usual." The words *always* and *never* may tip you off to overgeneralization.

Approximate answers. Often, this means that the patient gives you adjectives when you want numbers.

INTERVIEWER: How long have you been drinking?

PATIENT: A long time.

INTERVIEWER: Can you give me an idea of how long?

PATIENT: Well, quite a while.

Sometimes a patient simply seems unable to give precise descriptors.

INTERVIEWER: How did you feel when your stepdaughter arrived for that long visit?

PATIENT: Lousy.

INTERVIEWER: Well, can you describe your feelings then?

PATIENT: I felt terrible.

Dealing with Vagueness

Try first to determine why the patient is vague. Sometimes it may be a function of the particular mental illness. Vagueness of expression is especially characteristic of patients who have mental retardation, psychosis, or personality disorders. But it can also be encountered in almost anyone who is unaccustomed to thinking in precise terms. This may be the first time your patient has tried to express troubling feelings. It may also indicate resistance to the interview; perhaps this patient has something to hide.

Next, you should deal with vagueness by providing structure. Indicate clearly what type of answer or degree of precision you expect.

INTERVIEWER: How much time did you serve in the penitentiary?

PATIENT: Oh, quite a while.

INTERVIEWER: How long was that in months or years?

To the patient who persists in using general descriptions such as *terrible* you might respond:

"What is your interpretation of *terrible?*"

"Could you give me an example of what you mean by *terrible?*"

You may have to pin down some patients with specific questions, perhaps based on the areas of clinical interest (from Chapter 13) or on what you know about specific mental disorders.

INTERVIEWER: What do you mean by *terrible?*

PATIENT: I don't know, I just felt bad.

INTERVIEWER: Can you give me an example?

PATIENT: *(Pauses)* Just really awful.

INTERVIEWER: Well, were you depressed?

PATIENT: Sometimes.

INTERVIEWER: Did you feel anxiety?

PATIENT: Yeah, that's it! I was wound up like a clock!

Whatever technique you use, once you have clarified your patient's meaning, summarize to be sure you have understood:

"So when you said you felt terrible when your stepdaughter arrived for a visit, you were a little depressed, but mainly you felt this sense of overwhelming anxiety."

It may require a lot of prompting to teach the habit of precision to a patient who prefers approximate answers. You could find yourself resorting to multiple-choice questions. Early in the interview the un-focused, rambling patient may require you to use focused, short-answer questions. If the vagueness persists despite your best efforts, suspect some source of underlying resistance. To explore the reasons for this resistance, you might have to risk a confrontation. Try:

"In order to help you I really need a more definitive answer. Is there some reason you are having trouble answering my questions?"

Inability to Generalize

A problem related to vagueness is that some patients cannot general-ize experiences. When you ask them to give you a broad picture, they respond with tiny vignettes.

You can try to deal with this by redefining what it is you are after. Words like *common, often,* and *usual* may help you teach your patient what you want.

INTERVIEWER: Do you have a lot of trouble dealing with anger?

PATIENT: Last week I got really burned at my mother-in-law, threw a fit.

INTERVIEWER: What I'd like to know is, is this pretty common for you?

If your patient cannot generalize, you may have to make do with several examples from which you distill the generalization yourself. Then summarize aloud to make sure that you are correct.

LYING

As a part of the therapeutic contract, the patient agrees to tell the truth. At the beginning of your relationship with any patient, you should as-sume that this will be the case. Unfortunately, for a variety of reasons it doesn't always turn out this way.

Patients may lie when they are frightened, ashamed, worried, or angry. To a degree these emotions probably apply to most people who seek the help of mental health professionals. Other patients may lie for social gain: to get or keep a job, to avoid punishment, or to feel more respected. Those who habitually lie without discernible cause, although popularized as "pathological liars," are probably a small minority.

Any of several clues should warn you that your patient might not be telling the truth.

- The history is inconsistent with the known course of the disorder you suspect. For example, your patient denies ever being hospitalized despite a long history of severe manic symptoms.
- You ask about any behavior that would make most people feel ashamed or guilty. Common examples include drug use, sexual problems, suicidal behavior, and violence, any of which could provide incentive for shading the truth.
- The patient tells a story that is internally inconsistent; for example, a patient who never passed eighth grade claims to have held high-level executive positions.
- You suspect a severe personality disorder. A childhood history of delinquency progressing to adult criminality would make you suspect antisocial personality disorder. These patients often display little regard for the truth.
- Despite ample opportunity and objective justification, your patient denies all negative personal attributes; for example:

An embittered, 40-year-old woman is a college graduate stuck in a dull secretarial position. Her life has apparently been loveless and friendless. But when you ask her what she would change about herself, if she had it to do over again, she replies, "Nothing."

- Your patient seems to exaggerate lifetime accomplishments.

Dealing with Lying

As with other forms of problematic behavior, dealing with suspected lying requires a delicate touch. You need accurate information to make a diagnosis, but open confrontation risks early rupture of the relationship. (In ongoing therapy you would eventually have to deal with the need for trust in your relationship. Although treatment is not the principal goal of the initial interview, you don't want to do or say anything that will impede your later ability to work constructively with your patient.)

Before settling on any course of action, it is often worthwhile to ask for a restatement of what your patient just said. Perhaps you misunderstood; perhaps the patient misspoke. Another obvious approach is to ignore the lie and seek the truth elsewhere—from records or informants, for example. You may be able to arrive at the truth by piecing together a careful, year-by-year history of work, education, and social activities. Although it takes time, life-history detective work can be interesting and rewarding for the mental health interviewer.

Should you feel that a confrontation over the issue of misinformation is warranted, formulate your questions in a way that avoids making accusations. Couch them in terms of resolving a misunderstanding
or clearing up your own confusion: "Something puzzles me. You just
said that you hadn't had any problems with drinking, but your previous record here mentions two emergency room visits in the past year
for intoxication. Can you help me out with that?"

You can use something of the same approach—a gentle request
to help you understand—toward the related behaviors of exaggerating
and minimizing symptoms.

HOSTILITY

Of all the problem behaviors, hostility—anger directed toward
someone—is usually the easiest to spot. The patient's feelings are clearly
shown in a scowl, clenched fist, tone of voice, or content of speech. Even
those patients who resolutely smile regardless of their emotions will
usually betray their underlying feelings by a set jaw or by tension in
the voice. Whatever its manifestations, hostility must be dealt with immediately and effectively. To do less jeopardizes your entire interview.

The possible causes of hostility are numerous. Here are a few, some
of which have already been mentioned as causing other problem behaviors:

Fear of illness. These patients reject the notion that they are ill by
rejecting their need for a caregiver.

Displaced emotion. Perhaps it isn't you or the present situation at fault,
but a boss, spouse, or previous mental health professional that lies behind the hostility. You become the innocent target of negative transference.

Fear of intimacy. This reason may be especially relevant in a mental
health interview, where hostility could serve to "protect" the patient from
making unwanted revelations.

Fear of dependence. Some patients resent having to seek help for any
problem. For them, hostility may be a mechanism for keeping a safe
distance from people they view as wielding power. Perhaps this stems
from previous experiences of being socially "one-down."

Habit. Whatever the initial cause, some people have become habitually aggressive and hostile in their social interactions. They may have
learned this as a way of maintaining control over others.

Unempathic interviewer. In addition to the foregoing "patient-
centered" causes, consider the effect of an interviewer who appears un-

involved or disinterested. Most mental health patients already bear a considerable burden of negative emotions. If they must also cope with someone who is supposed to behave therapeutically, yet doesn't come across as empathic, the natural reaction might well be added hostility.

Negative emotions usually make their owners feel uncomfortable; hostility makes friends and acquaintances feel that way, as well. Because this reactive discomfort also applies to mental health interviewers, your first impulse may be to change the subject quickly. That strategy could succeed if the problem is anger or resentment stirred up by your line of questioning. But true hostility tends to be generalized more than anger; you're unlikely to deal with it successfully by ignoring it.

Handling Hostility

Hostility warns you that before continuing, you must confront your patient's feelings. To advance your interview effectively, you must make your confrontation nonthreatening and nonjudgmental. Here's how you might accomplish it:

INTERVIEWER: Why did you come here?

PATIENT [A tall, heavyset, 28-year-old man]: Why was I brought here, you mean. And why should I tell you? You're the third one I've talked with this afternoon!

INTERVIEWER: I'll bet you're getting sick of talking about it. I don't blame you.

PATIENT: You don't blame me, you just bug me.

INTERVIEWER: I don't mean to bother you. I can see that anyone as upset as you are must have a lot on his mind.

PATIENT: You've got that right.

INTERVIEWER: What is it? It must be pretty awful to get you this stirred up.

PATIENT: It's that, all right. *(Pauses)* My wife left me.

Although this patient's angry words were directed toward the interviewer, the underlying reason for the hostility was much more personal. By excusing the behavior and sympathizing with the feelings, the interviewer could side with the patient and break through to the core of his hostility.

Note how different reactions from the interviewer would only produce additional negative feelings:

"Look, I'm only trying to help you." (Yields guilt)

"If you don't talk about it, you'll never get over it." (Anxiety)

"Don't bark at me! I haven't done anything to you." (More hostility)

This last response brings up a point that is sometimes forgotten. Hostility is contagious; if you aren't wary, it can infect you. A sharp retort might be the natural response under the circumstances, but it could ruin your interview. (This might be the outcome your patient was trying to provoke all along.) It may help you maintain your composure if you remember that you have known your patient too short a time to have provoked any personal animosity. Any verbal attack must therefore be the product of your patient's own problems.

If you are talking to a voluntary patient who demands to leave, it is possible that you will never complete the interview. But if your patient is being held involuntarily on a closed hospital ward, time will be on your side.

A 20-year-old man was admitted against his will. In the following dialogue, notice how the interviewer doesn't argue, but instead agrees with the patient's every statement, giving each request a twist that requires the patient's cooperation:

PATIENT: Look, I don't want to talk to you or any other shrink. Just get me the hell out of here!

INTERVIEWER: That's what I'm trying to do. My job is to help you get out of here. But the law says that I can't let you go until I've decided it's safe. And I . . . .

PATIENT: Don't give me any of that crap. I want out of here now!

INTERVIEWER: *(Getting up to leave)* I'll be glad to start working on it as soon as I get the information I need from you.

PATIENT: You mean, I've got to stay here all night?

INTERVIEWER: *(Moves toward the door)* Well, it could be several days.

PATIENT: Wait a minute! You can't just leave me here!

INTERVIEWER: I'll be glad to come back when you're ready to talk.

PATIENT: I'm going to sue you for every nickel you've got!

INTERVIEWER: We'll help you get legal representation tomorrow. But it would be quicker if you'd just decide to cooperate.

This interviewer left the room but returned 20 minutes later at the request of the patient, who subsequently did cooperate fully—and was released a few hours later.

Defusing hostility can be a supreme test of any interviewer's professionalism. To pass it, you must continually monitor your own feelings and respond in ways that address your patient's emotional needs, not your own.

POTENTIAL VIOLENCE

Patients are only infrequently hostile to the point of violence. Although mental health workers are hardly ever severely injured by a patient, most of us have been shaken up or struck at least once during our careers. At best, this is an unsettling experience that should be avoided whenever possible.

Unfortunately, it is hard to predict who will become violent. Such patients may include those with schizophrenia (especially paranoid type), mania, organic mental disorders, personality disorders, and, when acutely intoxicated, substance abuse disorders. You should be especially vigilant when you are interviewing someone who may have any of these diagnoses.

Regardless of diagnosis, keep in mind several safety principles. (These comments apply strongly to female interviewers, whom some patients will treat as especially vulnerable targets.) Remembering that no one cares as much about your safety as you do, here are some of the preventive steps you should consider:

• Try to review any documentation before you interview your new patient. Be especially wary of those with a history of past violence or who seem to have a condition that suggests poor impulse control: Psychosis, current intoxication, and antisocial behavior are obvious candidates.

• Ideally, an interview room in a mental health emergency facility will have two doors, both of which open outward. Even if this is not the case, arrange the seating in any office you use so that the patient is never between you and your escape route.

• When meeting a new patient for the first time, try to have a security guard available, especially if it is late at night and there are few other people around.

• Many clinics have panic buttons installed under the desk top in their offices. If your setting is one of those, be sure to familiarize yourself with its workings and the expected response.

• In doubtful circumstances, leaving the door to the interview room open will also provide you a sense of security and give the patient an added reason for restraint.

• Watch carefully for these signs of heightened tension: clenched fists, loud or quavering voice, angry words, narrowed gaze, or sudden bursts of activity.

Suppose that, despite your best efforts at forming rapport, your patient displays evidence of unremitting hostility. Of course, you will have to break off the interview, but try to do it in such a way that you preserve some basis for a future relationship. You might say something along these lines:

"I'm sorry. I'd really like to work with you, but right now you seem to be pretty upset. Perhaps we can get together again later."

Then leave the room quickly and notify the security staff. Remember that it is nobody's job to face single-handedly a hostile, possibly violent patient. It is trite but true that there is safety in numbers, and it is always your responsibility as a mental health professional to promote safety—your patients', your co-workers', and your own.

THE CONFUSED PATIENT

Patients who are confused from dementia or delirium present an unusually vexing challenge to the interviewer. They may think and speak slowly, mix up the chronology of events, forget important facts, or have difficulty following your instructions. Their own frustration with poor performance sometimes precipitates hostility. Because the data you obtain from them are too few and too unreliable, it is hard to make a valid diagnosis. Sometimes you will conclude your interview with little to show for your efforts.

The best solution to this frustrating experience is a preventive one. Before the interview, obtain all the information you can from collateral sources such as relatives, physicians, other mental health workers, and previous hospital records. Then you can concentrate on doing a thorough evaluation of the patient's mental status.

Even without collateral information you can take several steps to facilitate your interview with a patient who is confused:

Introduce yourself slowly and distinctly. Before you begin your questions, make sure the patient understands who you are and why you are there. These steps will help prevent any *additional* elements of confusion:

Try not to rush. It is better to get a few reliable facts than a lot of inaccurate "information."

Use short sentences. Long speeches only compound the confusion.

Choose your words carefully. Jargon and slang may be especially treacherous for the confused patient.

Avoid shorthand phrases. A confused patient may take your question "Have you been hearing voices?" in its most literal sense.

Ask for repetition. If you wonder whether your question was understood, ask the patient to repeat it.

Ask about the events of a single day. If you aren't having much success with your usual questions, ask your patient to tell you about
the day's activities, or about a typical day's schedule.

Keep smiling. At a time when you lack information, you don't want
the appearance of irritation to rob you of rapport.

OLDER PATIENTS

Being old does not by itself constitute a disability. Too often interviewers forget this and assume that patients who are older are also confused,
deaf, or feeble. Although you should always try to show appropriate concern, older patients justifiably resent being needlessly patronized, moved
around, and shouted at. Don't let their advanced age deter you from
asking questions about activities usually associated with youth. These
people are old, not extinct. Many of them still enjoy sex, abuse drugs
or alcohol, or even worry about caring for their own parents.

However, there are a number of special considerations to keep in
mind when you interview older patients:

• You will probably need more interview time just to get through
the sheer volume of material. During a lifetime that spans many decades, the average older patient has accumulated more experiences, both
good and bad, than has the average younger patient. You'll especially
need to allow more time for your older patient's personal and social
histories. And because the mental health problems of senior citizens
are more likely to be complicated by medical disorders, you'll need to
spend extra time obtaining general health information.

• A stylistic change seems to take place somewhere during the
seventh or eighth decade of life. Personality traits become accentuated.
Older patients tend to reminisce a lot—perhaps it helps them to feel
better to review happier early periods of their lives. Young interviewers should try to accommodate themselves to this slower pace. Speak
distinctly, allow more response time, and suggest additional interview
sessions if you need them to finish gathering data.

• Older patients have some unique problems. Young interviewers
may have difficulty focusing on problems with which they have had no
personal experience. The economics of living on a fixed, reduced income is one example; trying to fill many leisure hours may be another.
Even ordinary activities such as meal preparation and arranging for
transportation can burden someone who has become isolated or
withdrawn.

• Watch out for instances of elder abuse. This problem, which can include neglect, exploitation, and rights violations as well as physical and psychological abuse, probably affects more than one million people over the age of 65 each year. It is especially likely to occur when an older person has recently become more dependent on a caregiver, who is often the one who does the abusing. You can screen for instances of elder abuse by asking the following questions:

"Are you afraid of anyone at home?"

"Has anyone at home ever harmed you?"

"Has anyone made you do things you didn't want to do?"

Abuse should be reported to the adult protective service appropriate for your state. In some states failure of health care practitioners to report the physical abuse of older patients is a misdemeanor punishable by a fine or jail term.

• Older patients have suffered a variety of losses, which multiply with the passing years. They include loss of health, jobs, income, status, friends, and family. Children have moved away; homes of many years have been sold when the patients move to retirement communities. Perhaps there is no telephone, producing loss of contact with others. Each of these losses demands special sensitivity. That means not only being sympathetic but also keeping alert to the possibility of denial. Some patients will have difficulty admitting, even to themselves, the waning of their capabilities and prospects. The result may be overgeneralization or vagueness that you must counter with careful requests for more complete information. Here is an example:

INTERVIEWER: How often do you see members of your family?

PATIENT: Oh, pretty often.

INTERVIEWER: For example, when did you last see your son? I understand he lives just across town.

PATIENT: Well, it's been about 6 months, actually.

OTHER BEHAVIORS AND PATIENTS

Blindness

Blind patients can communicate just as well as people who can see. What they can't do is read the body language clinicians normally use to help convey concern and directions. With blind patients you will have to use your tone of voice to indicate that you care and take extra pains to put into words what you want them to do. If you get up or change positions, describe your movements. This will help answer questions before they are asked and tell your patient that you are a considerate interviewer who is sensitive to special needs.

Deafness

Most deaf patients will communicate quite well if you speak distinctly and slowly, while looking right at them (this facilitates lipreading). Don't hide your lips behind your hand or a piece of paper. Of course, you wouldn't ordinarily smoke, eat, or drink anything during an interview, but here is one more reason not to. Don't shout: Most patients with a significant hearing impairment use hearing aids, and loud noises only distort the sound. As with blind patients, be careful not to talk down to the deaf: They may be handicapped, but they are not children.

Foreign Language

If you must communicate through an interpreter, be sure to look at the patient when speaking. Don't say, "Ask him if he. . . ." Rather, ask the patient directly, and then let the translator speak. (The same rules hold for interviewing deaf patients who communicate through someone who signs.)

Crying

A patient who becomes tearful can slow things down for awhile, but in the long run this may even facilitate the flow of information about emotions. A quick touch on the arm (one of the few times I recommend physical contact other than a handshake between patient and therapist) lets the patient know of your concern. Offering a fresh facial tissue serves the same purpose. A few moments of silence may be enough to allow the patient to regain composure with dignity.

Humor

Jokes can go a long way toward reducing tension, but patients will some-times shroud their concerns in humor. This may be a way of conveying a concern in such a way that the clinician won't give it serious (there-fore potentially threatening) consideration. In any case, listen careful-ly when your patient treats sensitive material with a light touch: There may be more cause for concern than is first apparent.

Rambling

Some patients are remarkably circumstantial. Left to their own devices, they will tell you far more than you want to know. Although circumstantial speech is not usually pathological, it carries with it too much chaff for the amount of wheat. Rapport may also suffer when you endure talking that has no purpose, so you should probably intervene if your patient rambles. To attempt a graceful transition, try to let your intervention take off from something your patient has said. For example, in response to a question about drug usage, this patient spent several minutes discussing the drinking habits of a cousin:

PATIENT: . . . So I don't think I've ever seen her after 6 p.m. when she wasn't in the bag. Another thing, . . .

INTERVIEWER:: *(Interrupting)* But what about *your* drinking?

The clinician had to intervene this way several times before the patient finally started sticking to the point.

Somatic Concerns

Some patients, even those who do *not* have somatization disorder, firmly believe that their symptoms are physical in nature. Despite what their physicians have told them, they cling to the idea that their problems can be solved by drugs or surgery. There is little value in explaining the probable emotional origin of these complaints: Even after repeated failures such a patient will continue to search for medicines and operations that will produce relief. Without arguing, you can point out that physical approaches haven't helped (not enough, at any rate) and that talking about the patient's feelings may relieve some of the anxiety that inevitably accompanies illness.

The Overtalkative Patient

Patients who are overtalkative seem to dominate an interview, even if they don't intend to. (Those with mania are notorious in this respect.) You may be able to handle irrelevant comments by only smiling an acknowledgment as you continue with your line of questioning. A more explicit gesture, such as a finger to your lips, may help even a boisterously manic patient talk less. Sometimes you may have to set firm limits, perhaps in the form of a direct confrontation:

"You have a lot to say that is very interesting. But our time is short, and we still have a lot of work to do. Let's try hard to stick to the subject."

If your patient isn't usually overtalkative, could this be an attempt to avoid a specific topic of conversation? Or consider the patient who harps on one theme, even when you try to change the subject. In these two instances, you need to reevaluate the importance of a theme to the patient. Confrontation is again the most direct method, but it should be phrased diplomatically:

"It seems to me that the subject of sex is difficult for you. Am I right?"

"We seem to be stuck on the issue of your son's accident. What else about it is important to you?"

In cases of extreme overtalkativeness you may be forced to ask only yes-or-no questions and to resist vigorously any attempt at amplification.

Psychosis

In emergency rooms and admitting wards of hospitals you will often encounter patients who are so severely psychotic that they cannot communicate well. They are tangential or have some other thought disorder, and the connections they make between ideas are so illogical that you cannot make much sense of them. You should certainly ask such patients to try to explain their thinking, but the answers may be of interest more for the psychopathology they show than for any historical information they contain. For history that is accurate and relevant, rely on informants or a chart from a previous admission. You can also ask the patient later, after the psychosis has abated.

Some patients may lack insight into being ill because of psychosis or a severe character disorder (such as antisocial personality); others may be drug abusers who are in denial. Patients without insight often feel no compelling reason to be interviewed. Unless you have some leverage (legal, family pressure), you probably won't obtain much in the way of useful information from them.

Muteness

Muteness has several possible causes.

Neurological. A number of neurological problems can cause patients to be mute. Be sure that the patient is fully conscious and alert.

Depression. In the case of severe depression, the patient may not be completely mute, just showing a long latency of response.

Conversion. A patient with mutism as a conversion symptom (hysterical mutism) may be able (willing) to produce a grunt or throat-clearing sound. With patience, coaxing, and praise for progress you may eventually parlay these sounds into syllables, words, phrases, and sentences.

Psychosis. Someone who is severely psychotic may heed voices that threaten reprisals for talking with real people. Head nods and shakes in answer to your yes-or-no questions may help you to make this diagnosis. This same patient, given a pencil and paper, may be willing to write answers to your questions.

Gain. Could this patient have a reason to *appear* mute (or psychotic)? Motives such as avoiding punishment and achieving financial gain (insurance, worker's compensation) are the most obvious. A clue to such behavior (I hesitate to use the word *malingering* because it is pejorative and hard to prove) would be provided if your patient was overheard speaking normally with other patients or staff. If relatives or friends are present, ask them to leave before you continue your interview. Patients sometimes reveal secrets to a stranger that they could never bear to share with their families.

Seductive Behavior

This is less likely to be a problem during the initial interview than during subsequent therapy sessions. However, the potential for seduction is always there, especially when the interviewer is male and the patient is female. (Studies have shown that the vast majority of health care workers who become involved with their patients are male, although female clinicians are by no means immune.)

If you notice seductive behavior that is directed toward you, ask yourself the usual questions: Why is this patient behaving this way? Is it a need to feel attractive? Over the years has aggressive sexual behavior been reinforced with material or emotional rewards? The answer may be buried beneath memories too remote to uncover in a year, let alone in a single interview.

Seductive behavior may be as subtle as a significant glance, as suggestive as provocative clothing, or as direct as a request to be held or kissed. Regardless of its form, the meaning of seductive behavior is always the same: Danger for the interviewer and danger for the patient. This is because the overt message of seductive behavior ("Embrace me") is often quite different from what the patient really feels ("Help me; protect me"). If a health care professional responds literally to the request for physical contact, the patient may feel outraged and retaliate accordingly.

The best preventive approach to seductive behavior is to maintain appropriate distance. Address each patient by title and last name, and expect your patients to do the same for you. You can also discourage excessive familiarity if you stick to business and avoid discussing matters personal to you. If you are a male who does physical exams as a part of your job, be sure that a female attendant is in the room with you at all times when you are examining a female patient of any age. If you are a female examining a male, have a male attendant with you.

The Dying Patient

Patients who expect to die soon, either immediately or in the near future, are often angry or depressed; sometimes they may deny what is happening to them. It is sad if friends and relatives begin to shun them; it is a tragedy if their therapists also refuse to talk frankly about death and the future.

Always ask your patients who are dying about their feelings and reactions to this universal experience. Besides a full range of (often conflicting) emotions, you will find that they still experience everyday fear, envy, love, hope, and joy. They certainly have regrets and memories; many feel lonely. And each has a lifetime of experiences and emotions that must be sorted out as carefully as if this person were going to live forever.

HOW TO RESPOND WHEN THE PATIENT ASKS. . .

"How do you feel about me?" This question is usually a request to be reassured that you like or accept the patient. You can give it, but try to throw in some information or instruction that might provide more substantive help. Here are two examples:

"I think you're a very nice person who is having a terrific problem with her marriage. It's going to be very important to get your husband to come in for some sessions."

"I think it took a lot of courage to sign yourself into the hospital. Now let's work together hard on that drinking problem."

"Do you think I'm crazy?" The answer to this can be hard or easy, depending upon whether the patient is psychotic or not. If the latter, say so. If the former, try to avoid a direct confrontation (your claim that this is psychosis would probably only be rejected, anyway). Instead, you could respond with a question of your own:

"Why do you ask that?"

"Are you afraid of that?"

You could give an answer that sidesteps the question:

"I think you are clearly troubled by what has happened to you."

"You are having some unusual experiences, but we can help this."

"What should I do about [any concern the patient has]?" If this question can be answered simply, then do so. Then again, it may be a request for more help than a student can give or than any clinician can reasonably provide during an initial interview session. In that case, try to define what will be necessary (more information, more time) and when you might be able to provide it.

"What's wrong with me?" (and you don't know). First of all, try not to feel insecure. As we shall see, no firm diagnosis can be made in about 20% of initial interviews, and even experienced clinicians are sometimes baffled initially. If you think there are some good possibilities that won't frighten or threaten the patient, state them. If you need more data, say so. A good, generic response would go something like this:

"It's clear you're having a serious problem with [patient's chief complaint]. We need to get more information, so that together we can work out the best plan for you."

"Have you ever experienced anything like this yourself?" Most patients are interested in their therapists' personal lives, and sometimes you may feel tempted to share something of yourself with your patient. (The temptation may increase after the first few interviews, when you have come to know your patient better.) Although I am not one of those who believes that a therapist should reveal nothing personal under any circumstances, I do agree that self-revelation can be fraught with difficulty, especially for the beginner. Certainly in an initial interview you will progress further and feel more comfortable if your own life and personality are not at issue. You can answer any personal question by gently redefining the purpose of the interview. At the same time, be careful to show that you are not upset that your patient has asked the question:

"A lot of patients wonder about the people who interview them. It's perfectly normal to be curious. But we should concentrate on getting as much information as we can that will help me to help you with your problem."

SUMMING UP

Of course, all patients are special, and every patient is unique. But some can be especially difficult in that they are vague, hostile, untruthful, confused, or even violent. Such patients offer mental health professionals the opportunity to hone the skills of accommodation and persuasion and to practice the virtues of patience and tolerance.

18 Evaluation

With all interviews completed, you begin the task of evaluating your information. It should be organized in a form that is useful for making recommendations and for communicating with other professionals. These tasks will be our concern in the final three chapters of this book.

DIAGNOSIS AND DIFFERENTIAL DIAGNOSIS

Some practitioners view diagnosis as denying the individuality of the patient; sometimes this is called "pigeonholing." Others consider diagnosis to be an important guide for recommending treatment, predicting the course of illness, advising relatives, and communicating with other mental health professionals. Whether or not this opinion is consistent with your usual way of thinking, current mental health practice— hospital record rooms, third-party payers, and sometimes patients themselves—will often require you to make a diagnosis. Regardless of your professional discipline, it will pay you to learn to make the best diagnosis possible.

The importance of *accurate* diagnoses can hardly be overstated. At best, incorrect diagnosis will delay treatment; at worst, ineffective (or even dangerous) treatment may result. Inaccurate diagnosis also risks giving a prognosis that is either too gloomy or too optimistic for the individual patient. Planning then will suffer—planning about marriage, jobs, childbearing, buying insurance, and the myriad other tasks that mental illness can interdict.

Once made, diagnostic errors can be difficult to reverse. Diagnosis is passed along from one clinician to another, from one chart to the next. It may be many years before a clinician with fresh perspective takes the time to review a chronic mental patient's history. All of these difficul-

ties can be avoided if you take the utmost care to make the right diagnosis in the first place.

Accurate diagnosis usually poses few problems. Most patients clearly
meet the criteria for a major diagnosis with which the majority of professionals would agree, and most do not meet criteria for other, confound-
ing diagnoses. But about 20% of the time the situation is less clear-cut.
You may have insufficient information to make any diagnosis, or your
patient may seem to meet the criteria for several diagnoses.

That is why most health care professionals state their impressions
in terms of a *differential diagnosis* — a list of diagnoses that are possible
and should be considered for any given patient. You should include
in your differential diagnosis every disorder you consider even remotely
possible. This is true all the more if you are in some doubt as to the
correct diagnosis. You will have the best chance of selecting the right
diagnosis if your working list is broad and inclusive.

In constructing your differential, you should arrange all the possible diagnoses in decreasing order of likelihood, beginning with the
one you consider to be most important. Sometimes called the *best diagnosis,* this is the one that most satisfactorily explains all of the historical
data, signs, and symptoms of illness. All elements of the history and the
mental status examination should support your differential diagnosis.
Even if you believe there is only a small chance that your first diagnosis is incorrect, you should list other diagnoses to "rule out" or disprove.
That list, with your reasoning behind the order in which you have placed
the various possible diagnoses, is what creates the "differential."

Evaluating Your Information for Diagnosis

For an experienced clinician, the differential diagnosis unfolds like the
plot of a novel, right during the course of the examination. But the
welter of information can seem daunting to the beginning diagnostician, who may need help in sorting it all out.

The First Interview is not intended as a textbook of diagnosis; there
are many good works that will serve that function. However, you will
find a brief summary of the principal diagnostic features (and abbreviated DSM-III-R criteria) in Appendix B. The purpose of this chapter
is to explain the principles that should guide you in choosing the most
appropriate diagnosis for your patient.

PRINCIPLES TO USE IN MAKING A DIAGNOSIS

In sorting through their initial interview information, clinicians use
a number of principles to help them decide which data are the most

important for diagnosis. These principles should allow you to select from the mass of available data those facts that you will emphasize in making a diagnosis.

History Is Better than Cross-Sectional Observation

This powerful principle is a corollary to the venerable truism "The best predictor of future behavior is past behavior." It encourages you not to depend upon impressions made at a single point in time, but to base your judgments on data that describe the longitudinal course of illness.

To illustrate the importance of this principle, consider the example of a woman who complains of severe depression. If all you know is how she looks and feels at the moment she appears in your office — low mood, tearful, slow speech, perhaps suicidal ideas — you will have difficulty making a diagnosis or recommending treatment. You can't even say for sure how seriously ill this patient is. But here's how data from her history could help you:

- The recent death of a spouse or other close relative might suggest that this is a grief reaction.
- Years of heavy drinking would make you suspect that this depression is secondary to alcoholism.
- If you learn that your patient has recovered from several previous episodes of depression, you should suspect recurrent unipolar depression.
- A lifelong history of feeling some depression might lead you to a diagnosis of dysthymia.
- Previous episodes of mania would be diagnostic of bipolar mood disorder.

Recent History Is Better than Ancient History

This principle advises you not to accept passively *any* previous diagnosis; instead, check your impressions against recent information. It reminds you that symptoms early in a patient's course of illness may have prompted a diagnosis that was either not specific enough or downright incorrect. For example:

A teenaged girl is diagnosed as having an anxiety disorder from which she recovers. Three years later she has an episode of illness during which depressive symptoms are prominent, and a diagnosis of unipolar depression is made. Only at age 27, when she has her first episode of mania, is she ultimately diagnosed as having a bipolar mood disorder.

Collateral Information May Be Better than History from the Patient

Of course, this will usually be the case for children and adolescents, but sometimes adults can also be unaware of their family histories or details about their own development. Patients with psychosis or personality disorder may not have enough perspective to judge accurately many of their own symptoms. In any of these situations, the history you obtain from people who know your patient well may strongly influence your diagnosis.

Signs Are Better than Symptoms

Signs (what you observe in your patient's behavior) are subject to your interpretation; inevitably your own past experiences and attitudes will influence how you read these signs. However, symptoms (what the patient tells you) are subject not only to your own interpretation but also to your patient's impressions and distortions. For example:

> A patient denies auditory hallucinations, but during your interview frequently glances around the room and pauses to say, "Huh? What?" This appears to be a response to something or someone you cannot hear. The sign (distractibility) is more trustworthy than the symptom (the patient's denial of auditory hallucinations).

Objective Assessments Are Better than Subjective Judgments

This is similar to the signs/symptoms principle just given. If anything, it is stronger. It reminds us to be wary of making a diagnosis based upon intuition (or hunch) rather than upon scientific criteria. For example, the diagnosis of somatization disorder, as made by DSM-III-R criteria, can help predict how well the patient will be doing in 5 or 10 years, the response to treatment, and other features of the illness. But there may be no predictive value at all to a clinician's intuitive statement: "This person seems hysterical." (Your definition of *hysterical* may be entirely different from mine; neither definition is likely to be based on scientific criteria.)

Crisis-Generated Data Are Suspect

Although the stress of crisis may reveal valuable insights about someone's character and behavior, the one-shot format of the initial interview provides no reference point from which to judge what behavior is normal for a given patient. As a result, the clinician can easily become confused by patients who, intentionally or not, may inaccurately report how they felt or behaved during stress, for example,

The combat veteran who reports great heroism (or lack of it) under fire

The rejected suitor for whom the entire world seems bathed in despair

The lottery winner who has forgotten the twin miseries of her divorce and her diet

DIAGNOSTIC HIERARCHIES

The foregoing principles should help you choose a diagnosis. But for some patients, two or more conflicting diagnoses may seem possible; for others, the data after the first interview may be insufficient to make even one diagnosis. Yet, case histories must be written up and treatment plans formulated, so you must decide on one diagnosis to put at the top of your differential. For these reasons the concept of the diagnostic hierarchy was developed.

Why Use a Diagnostic Hierarchy?

The diagnostic hierarchy is based on the assumption that there is value in assigning some order of priority to the list of any patient's possible diagnoses. The main benefits are utilitarian.

1. A hierarchy tells you where to direct your further diagnostic efforts. For example:

You think your patient with psychosis could have organic mental disorder, schizophrenia, or a mood disorder. With organic mental disorder at the top of the differential, you first request a neurological evaluation to help rule out a mass lesion in the brain.

2. It tells you what to treat first. Many patients present with a number of symptoms; the differential diagnosis can help you decide how to formulate your treatment approach. For example:

A young mother presents with depression and anxiety symptoms. Depression is your "best diagnosis," so you recommend a course of cognitive therapy and antidepressant medication. The symptoms quickly resolve and the patient doesn't require antianxiety medication or behavior modification therapy.

3. It places less treatable conditions last, so it helps avoid labeling a patient, perhaps forever, with a poor prognosis diagnosis unless it is fully warranted. For example:

An elderly woman is admitted at the request of relatives, who say she is demented. Although her poor memory could be due to Alzheimer's dementia, you suspect that she could have a pseudodementia due to depression.

Rational Diagnostic Rules

Overall, the diagnostic hierarchy gives clinicians a tool for thinking rationally about patients, even if their symptoms are confusing or contradictory. The four rational rules you can use to help you arrange diagnostic possibilities into a hierarchy are given here, approximately in descending order of importance:

1. *Organic mental disorder* preempts all other diagnoses that could produce the same symptoms. The importance of this rule is dictated by the potentially life-and-death nature of organic illnesses and their sometimes urgent need for treatment. For example:

A young woman's parents complain that she has recently become promiscuous and talks to herself as if hallucinating. These symptoms could be produced by a psychosis, such as mania or schizophrenia, or by a physical disease, such as a brain tumor. Obviously, the patient must first be evaluated to learn whether she has a life-threatening tumor.

If there is any possibility that your patient has an organic mental disorder, it is vital that you place that diagnosis at the top of your differential. Conditions (with some examples) that can underlie and cause an organic mental disorder include

Birth trauma (cerebral palsy)
Circulatory (strokes, aneurysms)
Dementias (Alzheimer's, Creutzfeldt-Jakob, kuru, HIV)
Diseases of unknown cause (amyotrophic lateral sclerosis, systemic lupus erythematosus, multiple sclerosis)
Endocrine (hypothyroidism or hyperthyroidism)
Epilepsy
Head trauma
Infections (neurosyphilis)
Inherited conditions (Huntington's chorea)
Metabolic
Nutritional (various vitamin deficiencies)
Poisons (toxins, alcohol, street drugs, mercury)
Tumors

2. The fewer the diagnoses, the better. This rule (referred to as *par-simony*) dates back a hundred years to the time of the pioneer German psychiatrist, Emil Kraepelin. It advises you to explain all of your find-ings by a single diagnosis, if this is possible. Failing that, make the smallest number of diagnoses you can. Here is a typical example:

> A man with a 20-year history of heavy drinking complains of audi-tory hallucinations. He says he feels as depressed as he did a de-cade ago when he attempted suicide. Although you could make three independent diagnoses (mood disorder, psychosis, and sub-stance abuse), the most parsimonious formulation is that he is a chronic alcoholic who is having a secondary depression and with-drawal hallucinations. The parsimonious diagnosis has important implications for treatment and prognosis: The hallucinations and depression should diminish, or even clear completely, once he has dried out.

Of course, you should make more than one diagnosis whenever it is warranted. (Two mutually exclusive diagnoses such as bipolar dis-order and schizophrenia would not be diagnosed in the same patient.) But the parsimony rule is powerful for its logic and simplicity and be-cause it has important implications for prognosis and treatment. Ac-cepted for years, it deserves to be strongly considered in devising your differential diagnosis.

3. Give priority to the disorder that has been present longest. Cli-nicians have also used this rule (*chronology*) for years as an aid to diag-nosis. Its most obvious application is to patients who have depression plus some other psychiatric diagnosis. Often at issue is whether the depression is an independent primary mental disorder or is secondary to another illness. One example was the alcoholic man mentioned previ-ously. Here is another:

> A young woman has multiple somatic symptoms and depression. The two prominent diagnostic possibilities are (a) a mood disord-er in which somatization is a prominent symptom (in which ag-gressive treatment with antidepressant medication or cognitive therapy might be in order) and (b) somatization disorder with a secondary depression (in which medication would be contraindi-cated). A clinician might be able to make the distinction from his-tory alone. If the depression started first, diagnose *a;* if the somatic symptoms antedated the depression, then diagnose *b.*

Keep in mind that an Axis I disorder (e.g., schizophrenia or depres-sion) is *never* diagnosed as secondary to an Axis II personality disorder.
The chronology rule is logically compelling and widely applica-ble. Most clinicians probably use it in practice more than they realize.

4. If none of the foregoing rules applies, use the *safety* rule. All diagnoses can be placed somewhere on a safety hierarchy. At the top are diagnoses such as the mood disorders, which are considered safe because they imply an excellent outcome (they remit spontaneously or readily respond to treatment). At the other end of the spectrum are the riskiest diagnoses; they can be difficult to treat or have serious sequels or a deteriorating course. The schizophrenias and Alzheimer's and AIDS dementias are among the most serious diagnoses you can make.

Clinicians can argue about the exact placement of various diagnoses on this list, but most would agree with the approximate rankings given in Table 6. If one of the diagnoses you are considering is higher on this list than the others, the safety principle advises you to choose first the one that is more treatable and has a better prognosis.

OTHER CONSIDERATIONS FOR DIAGNOSIS

Percentages

All of the preceding rules are rational; that is, they use the information inherent in the history and presentation of the individual patient. But if none of them resolves your diagnostic dilemma, you might be able to get some help from percentages. This principle is based on the truism that common things occur commonly. In training programs this

TABLE 6. Hierarchy of Conservative (Safe) Diagnoses

Most favorable (most treatable, best outcome)
    Recurrent unipolar depression
    Bipolar mood disorder
Middle ground
    Alcoholism
    Panic disorder
    Phobic disorder
    Obsessive compulsive disorder
    Anorexia nervosa
    Drug abuse
    Borderline personality disorder
Least favorable
    Schizophrenia
    Antisocial personality disorder
    AIDS dementia
    Alzheimer's dementia

From *Boarding Time: A Psychiatry Candidate's Guide to Part II of the ABPN Examination* (p. 95) by J. Morrison and R. A. Muñoz, 1991, Washington, DC: American Psychiatric Press. Copyright 1991 by the American Psychiatric Press, Inc. Reprinted by permission.

is sometimes facetiously expressed, "When you hear hoofbeats in the street, think of horses, not zebras." The principle of percentages advises you that, all other things being equal, you should place at the top of your differential a disorder that occurs commonly in the population from which your patient is drawn.

> Schizophrenia, bipolar mood disorder, and substance abuse are encountered frequently in public hospitals and clinics, where most mental health professionals in training are likely first to see patients.
>
> Young adults are likely to abuse drugs, whereas older adults are more likely to abuse alcohol.
>
> Older patients are more likely to have Alzheimer's dementia or depression; younger patients more often have schizophrenia.
>
> There is a significant chance that a younger demented patient on a medical ward of a major city suffers from AIDS dementia.

In fact, most of the seriously ill mental patients can be diagnosed with one of only a few disorders: depression, mania, schizophrenia, dementia, and substance abuse. But be careful to base your decisions on percentages *only* if none of the rational rules applies to your patient.

Scientific Validity of Diagnosis

Here is another consideration that might help narrow your search for a diagnosis. The past two decades have witnessed remarkable strides in our ability to identify and diagnose mental disorder. Using scientific criteria, clinicians can now agree about many diagnoses that would once have caused them to argue. These are embodied in the revised third edition of the *Diagnostic and Statistical Manual of Mental Disorders* (DSM-III-R). This volume, published by the American Psychiatric Association, has been used increasingly by mental health caregivers of all professions worldwide.

But not all the disorders described in this manual made it there strictly on their scientific merits. Because DSM-III-R was formulated and written by committee, its apparently objective criteria often represent a compromise, sometimes between widely disparate points of view. Politics has occasionally entered in, resulting in the adoption of some personal views of powerful leaders in American mental health.

None of this should be interpreted as detracting from the merits of this document, taken as a whole. But clinicians should keep in mind that some diagnoses have greater validity than others. Although DSM-III-R lists over 250 disorders, relatively few of them have been studied well enough to give them a strong claim to scientific legitimacy. If you

TABLE 7. Most Valid Diagnoses, in Descending Order of
Frequency Expected in a General Mental Health Population

Common
    Primary mood disorder, depressed
    Alcohol dependence
    Bipolar mood disorder
    Schizophrenia
    Recurrent unipolar mood disorder
    Somatization disorder
    Borderline personality disorder
Less common
    Panic disorder
    Dementia, including Alzheimer's, multi-infarct, AIDS
    Antisocial personality disorder
    Obsessive compulsive disorder
    Mental retardation, if specific etiology; e.g., Down's syndrome,
        phenylketonuria
    Agoraphobia
    Anorexia nervosa
Rare
    Learning disorders
    Transsexualism
    Tourette's syndrome
    Autism
    Delusional disorder

From *Boarding Time: A Psychiatry Candidate's Guide to Part II of the ABPN Examination* (p. 92)
by J. Morrison and R. A. Muñoz, 1991, Washington, DC: American Psychiatric Press.
Copyright 1991 by the American Psychiatric Press, Inc. Reprinted by permission.

formulate your differential diagnosis principally from these most valid diagnoses, you will not only simplify your own job but also choose for your patient diagnoses that have strong predictive power. Table 7 lists these best-studied conditions, arranged according to the frequency with which you can expect to encounter them in an adult clinic or mental hospital population. They are the diagnoses that you can make with the greatest confidence in their predictive ability.

Many other diagnoses are in current use; some of them are intensely popular despite their limited validity. Appendix B offers a compilation of most of the diagnoses that are frequently made, well founded, or both.

RESOLVING DIAGNOSTIC UNCERTAINTY

In 80% of patients your initial interview should lead to a definite diagnosis that you believe is correct. But you must still decide how to categorize the other 20%.The information you have about your patient may be powerful enough to help you select a leading candidate, or "best diagnosis," for the top of your differential diagnosis. Several factors may be especially helpful.

Length of Illness

Here is another restatement of the truism that the best predictor of future behavior is past behavior. It is most likely to help when you choose between schizophrenia and a mood disorder, a situation that arises rather often. For example:

> A woman has symptoms of mood disorder and psychosis, but neither predominates. If she has been continuously ill for several years you might choose schizophrenia, which is almost always a chronic illness. But if she has been ill for only a few weeks, or if she had a previous episode of illness that remitted completely, a mood disorder would seem much more likely.

More Symptoms

Even if strict criteria do not allow you to make a firm diagnosis, the sheer number of symptoms may strongly suggest a certain diagnosis. A typical example:

> A psychotic patient has been ill for less than 6 months. If this patient has multiple symptoms of psychosis—perhaps auditory hallucinations plus several delusions *and* a schizoid premorbid personality—you will be more likely to favor the diagnosis of schizophrenia than if the patient has had only auditory hallucinations.

Presence of Typical Features

This principle is based on another maxim: If it quacks and waddles, it's probably a duck, even if you've never seen it fly. For example:

> An 18-year-old woman has a dramatic and ingratiating manner and complains of a number of physical problems that seem to have no anatomical or physiological basis. You suspect somatization disorder, but she lacks sufficient symptoms to fulfill the criteria. (She may well develop enough additional symptoms in a year or more.) Because two of her complaints are nonepileptic "seizures" and "blindness" when she can really see quite well, you put somatization disorder at the top of your list.

Absence of Atypical Features

Hallucinations and disordered thinking are symptoms typical of schizophrenia and of organic mental syndromes; a patient with these symptoms could have either disorder. But disorientation and other cognitive deficits are atypical of schizophrenia. Finding neither of these symptoms in your patient should increase your suspicion that schizophrenia, not an organic psychosis, is the correct diagnosis.

Response to Treatment

Usually the effect of any treatment, whether it is a prescribed medication, psychotherapy, or some other intervention, doesn't give you much specific information about diagnosis. There are several reasons for this.

A given treatment might affect the course of many illnesses.
Patients may improve whether or not they are treated.
Other factors that you haven't noticed may promote improvement.

But in at least one instance—the use of lithium in bipolar mood disorder—the relationship between treatment and outcome is specific enough that you can draw conclusions about diagnosis from response to therapy. Here's how it works:

A 25-year-old man was admitted to the locked ward of a mental hospital. Restrained by a straitjacket, he rambled on about being "the Avenging Angel of Satan." Schizophrenia and mania both seemed likely until the clinician spoke with the patient's sister, who believed that he was well for many months when taking lithium. Bipolar mood disorder was immediately moved to the top of the differential diagnosis.

More Information

Of course, the best approach to diagnostic uncertainty is to gather more information. Usually this means interviewing other people (friends, relatives, former therapists) who know the patient well and can provide a more complete account of personality and symptoms. Additional history will usually settle the issue, whether the problem is one of too little information (the patient is disorganized, secretive, unaware, forgetful, or psychotic) or too much information (the patient is deceitful or tries too hard to please by answering every question positively). However, more information may not solve your problem under the following circumstances:

Atypical course. The history or course of the patient's illness doesn't clearly suggest any one diagnosis. More information adds richness, but not clarity, to the picture.

Too soon. It is so early in the patient's illness that symptoms adequate for diagnosis have not yet appeared.

The Power of "Undiagnosed"

Sometimes you simply cannot decide between two or more possible diagnoses. Then is the time to invoke the power of "undiagnosed." This means that the label you give your patient is some variant of "mentally ill, but currently undiagnosed." There are several advantages to using this term.

- It allows you to recognize that your patient is ill without forcing you to embrace a definitive diagnosis.
- You decrease the risk of giving your patient an inaccurate diagnosis that may be pejorative (such as schizophrenia or Alzheimer's dementia). This is especially important in an era when mental health records are increasingly likely to be reviewed by insurance companies, other health care professionals, and patients themselves.
- It leaves open the question of diagnosis, so you keep thinking about your patient. The diagnosis should become clear later, when you have obtained more data or when enough time has passed to clarify the picture.

Be careful not to apply diagnostic criteria too strictly. Patients are not "cases"; they are people who have problems that often can be classified as disorders. But a patient may have symptoms and a course of illness that, at least temporarily, defies classification. Then there is the need for the best clinical judgment possible to decide how (or whether) to initiate treatment.

Finally, remember the possibility that a patient may have no mental disorder at all. In my practice, this has been a rare phenomenon; in treating over 15,000 patients, I have encountered it only a few times. Marriage or family counsellors may encounter it more frequently. Because it can happen, be alert: Don't let your patient be subjected to a diagnosis, possibly one with serious consequences, when none is deserved.

ASSESSING PERSONALITY

Personality (or character) traits are patterns of behavior that can be detected as early as the first few months of life. They shape behavior throughout life and may become even more pronounced with advancing age. These traits govern relationships with friends and lovers, bosses, and colleagues, as well as with more casual social contacts. They are responsible for much of what makes each person different from the other 5 billion humans on this planet.

Character traits so prominent that they interfere with a patient's social functioning are termed *disorders of personality.* They are recorded on Axis II of DSM-III-R. Most patients with personality disorders also have at least one Axis I disorder. (Note that behaviors that are present only during an episode of an Axis I disorder by definition cannot be considered part of a personality disorder.) Because most Axis I disorders are better studied and better defined than are Axis II disorders, they usually take precedence when predicting such matters as course of illness and response to treatment.

In assessing personality, it is important not to focus solely on weaknesses, but on strengths as well. For example, how would you describe your patient's intelligence? Previous success? Coping skills? Support system? Don't let your quest for psychopathology blind you to the predictive power of a normal premorbid personality. A preponderance of positive character traits suggests that your patient will be less inconvenienced by the current illness, will enjoy better social support while ill, and, once the current siege has lifted, will have a better chance for eventually returning to complete mental health.

Recognizing Personality Disorder

A personality disorder is more a way of life than an illness. It implies long-standing behavior that causes problems for the patient. It often has its roots in childhood and may stem either from environmental influences or from the patient's inherited genetic material. Sometimes both causes are implicated.

Personality disorders should be diagnosed on the basis of repeated behaviors that suggest interpersonal conflict or maladjustment. Your patient may use certain phrases that will tip you off:

"All my life I have. . . ."

"As long as I can remember I have. . . ."

You might also observe something in your patient's speech or behavior during the interview—arguing or requesting to smoke—that makes you suspect a long-standing problem with character or behavior.

A better indicator of personality traits is the history, as it is related by the patient and, especially, by informants. For example, from the employment history you could learn something about your patient's adherence to the work ethic: Consider the age of first employment, number of jobs, unbroken pattern of employment, and history of moonlighting. From the marital history you can learn about your patient's fidelity and capacity for forming relationships. Throughout the history you will have examples of how your patient has responded to various stressors.

But remember that a person can have distressing social problems that are not caused by personality disorder. A tyrannical boss can create dissention at work; a psychotic spouse can wreak havoc with a marriage. Every day, kids use drugs and the stock market swallows someone's savings. It is lifelong patterns of behavior, attitudes, and human interactions that define a personality disorder.

PERSONALITY DISORDERS

The 11 personality disorders currently defined in DSM-III-R are listed next. The five that are asterisked are generally considered to have better validity than the rest. These five are described in greater detail in Appendix B.

*Antisocial.** The irresponsible, often criminal behavior of these people begins in childhood or early adolescence. Pathological childhood behavior includes truancy, running away, cruelty, fighting, destructiveness, lying, stealing, and robbery. As adults they may in addition default on debts, fail to care for dependents, fail to maintain monogamous relationships, and show no remorse for their behavior.

Avoidant. These timid people are so easily wounded by criticism that they hesitate to become involved with others. They may fear the embarrassment of showing emotion or of saying things that seem foolish. They may have no close friends, and they exaggerate the risks of undertaking pursuits outside their usual routines.

*Borderline.** These impulsive people make recurrent suicide threats or attempts. Affectively unstable, they often show intense, inappropriate anger. They feel empty or bored, and they frantically try to avoid abandonment. They are uncertain about who they are and unable to maintain stable interpersonal relationships.

Dependent. These people have trouble starting projects or making independent decisions, even to the extent of agreeing with others who may be wrong. Often preoccupied with fears of abandonment, they feel helpless when alone and miserable when relationships end. They are easily hurt by criticism and will volunteer for unpleasant tasks to gain people's favor.

Histrionic. Overly emotional, vague, and attention-seeking, these patients need constant reassurance about their attractiveness. They may be self-centered and sexually seductive.

Narcissistic. Narcissistic people are self-important and often preoccupied with envy, fantasies of success, or ruminations about the uniqueness of their own problems. Their sense of entitlement and lack of empathy may cause them to take advantage of others. They vigorously reject criticism, and need constant attention and admiration.

*Obsessive compulsive.** Perfectionism and rigidity characterize these people. Often workaholics, they tend to be indecisive, excessively scrupulous, and preoccupied with detail. They insist that others do things their way. They have trouble expressing affection, tend to lack generosity, and may even resist throwing away worthless objects they no longer need.

Paranoid. These people expect to be threatened or humiliated; other people's behavior seems to confirm these expectations. They may be quick to take offense and slow to forgive; often they have few confidants, question the loyalty of others, and read hidden meaning into innocent remarks.

Passive-aggressive. Such persons resist performing adequately in social or work situations by putting things off, working slowly, sulking, performing poorly, forgetting obligations, and claiming that too much is being demanded of them. They resent useful suggestions and think they are doing an excellent job. They may unreasonably criticize authority figures and hinder the work of others by failing to do their fair share.

*Schizoid.** These patients care little for social relationships, have a restricted emotional range, and seem indifferent to criticism or praise. Tending to be solitary, they avoid close (including sexual) relationships.

*Schizotypal.** Such patients have so much difficulty with interpersonal relationships that they appear peculiar or strange to others. Lacking close friends, they are uncomfortable in social situations. They may show suspiciousness, unusual perceptions or thinking, an eccentric manner of speaking, and inappropriate affect.

SUMMING UP

Accurate mental health diagnosis is facilitated by a number of rules and principles, most of which are logical and empirically derived. But for many patients, clinicians cannot reliably record a final diagnosis until there has been follow-up period sufficient to be sure that the "best diagnosis" is stable. For most patients the ultimate proof of diagnostic accuracy is the test of time.

19 Making Recommendations

Practicing therapists generally communicate their recommendations directly to the patient at the end of the first interview. As a student you will probably write up your findings before presenting your opinions about treatment and prognosis to your supervisor. In either case, what you suggest will depend heavily upon diagnosis and the nature of the treatment you propose.

CHOOSING TREATMENT

Fortunately, mental health patients and their therapists today can draw upon a variety of effective biological, psychological, and social treatments. Most of these are not specific for any one diagnostic category; rather, they can be applied across a spectrum of diagnoses. The available somatic and nonsomatic treatments are listed in Table 8. For most diagnoses there are one or two treatments that are more effective than others. Textbooks will spell out which treatments are most likely to help in specific diagnoses.

Following are a number of questions to assist you in formulating a treatment plan that should help your patient:

- First, is any treatment likely to reverse the course of this disorder? Unhappily, the answer is sometimes "no." That may be the case for disorders such as Alzheimer's dementia. Although many such patients can be made more comfortable, and the social consequences of their symptoms can be lessened, the lack of adequate specific treatment means that you may not be able to prevent the progression of disease. In antisocial personality, a chronic disorder of character that affects perhaps 1% of young men (and far fewer young women), no treatment has yet proved superior to the passing of time.

TABLE 8. Outline of Mental Health Treatment Modalities

Psychological

Individual
  Cognitive
  Insight-oriented
  Analysis
  Short-term
Group
  Disease-oriented (Alcoholics Anonymous, lithium clinics)
  General medication clinics
  Family therapy
  General support groups
Behavioral
  Simple reassurance
  Systematic desensitization with reciprocal inhibition
  Mass practice
  Ward token economies
  Thought stopping

Biological

Drugs
Electroconvulsive therapy
Light therapy
Psychosurgery

Social interventions

Vocational rehabilitation
Social skills training
Education of family
Placement in a facility for acute, intermediate, or chronic care
Involuntary commitment
Conservatorship

• How certain is the diagnosis? Treatment has the greatest chance for success when it is based on clinical studies of reliably diagnosed patients. Your confidence in' any treatment program will rise in proportion to the certainty that you have made the correct diagnosis. In general, treatments that are risky, complicated, expensive, or take a long time to complete should be reserved for well-diagnosed patients who have not responded to simpler measures.

What about the use of experimental treatments? A useful rule is that it is acceptable to use proven treatments in uncertain diagnoses, and experimental treatments when diagnosis is certain; it is generally

not acceptable to use unproven treatments when the diagnosis is uncertain.

Diagnosis is important in deciding treatment, but it is by no means
the only determining factor. Some patients are so ill that treatment must
be started even without a definite diagnosis. Acute psychoses provide
the most frequent examples: Even while clinicians argue about bipolar
disorder versus schizophrenia, for the patient's safety and comfort, neuroleptic drugs must be started. Some problems may merit intervention,
even though no well-defined diagnosis is likely *ever* to be made. Marital
discord is an example.

• How urgent is treatment? For most hospitalized patients the answer is, urgent enough to begin at once. For outpatients, the need may
be less immediate. In general, the urgency for treatment will increase
under any of the following three conditions:

1. The number of symptoms is increasing. For example, the patient,
   who has had anxiety attacks for years, has recently also complained of depression, loss of appetite, and trouble sleeping.
2. The symptoms are getting worse. For example, in the last few
   days this same patient has had recurrent thoughts of suicide.
3. The symptoms lead to consequences that are more alarming. For
   example, for the past week this same patient has felt unable to
   go to work and has now resigned after 13 years with the same
   firm.

The three rules just cited can also help you decide which disorder to
treat first, in the event that your patient has multiple concurrent diagnoses.

• How costly is the treatment? This question implies not only
financial expense but also the cost of unwanted effects of treatment.
Of course, the patient's ability to pay must be considered. You wouldn't
recommend prolonged psychotherapy for a self-supporting student who
has no medical insurance. Someone who is fully covered by a health
care maintenance organization or private or government insurance program may be able to afford the latest in antidepressant medication,
whereas a self-pay patient may request an older, generic drug.

When selecting treatment, you must also consider whether the
wanted effects of the treatment outweigh its unwanted effects. This warning applies especially to prescription medications: Will rapid heartbeat
or wakefulness cause your patient to "forget" the evening dose? Can some
other side effect result in injury, or even death? What about interactions with other medications?

• Does the therapy you are considering have relative contraindi-
cations? These are problems that might make you reluctant to use a

treatment but that do not absolutely prohibit it. Common examples are drug allergy, the possibility of interaction with another medicine, and the use of electroconvulsive therapy for patients with known heart disease. You would also be reluctant to recommend intensive psychotherapy for patients who have a low capacity for insight or who are unreliable about keeping appointments. In fact, a history of noncompliance with treatment reduces still further the desirability of any treatment that is risky or complicated.

• Have you considered all feasible treatment modalities? Therapists of all professions feel most comfortable recommending those approaches they themselves use. Although this is understandable, it breeds the danger that a given patient might not be considered for a treatment that could work well, but with which the therapist has had little experience. The best prophylaxis against the therapeutic rut is an attitude of flexibility.

> Psychiatrists expert in psychopharmacology must be ever-alert to the possibility that, for a given patient, family therapy might prove quicker, safer, and more effective than drugs.
>
> Social workers and psychologists should keep in mind the indications for which drug therapy should be recommended.

The fact that most mental and emotional disorders probably have multiple causes should encourage all clinicians to consider using more than one therapeutic modality for individual patients.

ASSESSING PROGNOSIS

The term *prognosis* has Greek roots meaning "to know in advance," which is, of course, impossible. But scientific progress over the past three or four decades has greatly improved our ability to predict outcome for individual patients. We'll discuss this in a few moments, after first defining what it is we are trying to predict.

Areas Defined by the Term *Prognosis*

The term *prognosis* commonly implies a number of meanings.

> Symptoms. Will they be relieved partly or completely, if at all?
> Course of illness. Will it be chronic or episodic? If the latter, will there be one episode or many?
> Response to treatment. How rapidly will this occur? Will it be slight, moderate or complete?

Degree of recovery. Once the acute episode has been arrested (either by treatment or by the passing of time), will the patient's previous personality be completely restored or will there be residual deficits?

Time course of illness. How long will recovery take? If the illness is episodic, how long is the patient likely to remain well between episodes?

Social consequences of the illness. What will be the effects on the patient's job performance? Family life? Independence? Will financial support be needed? If so, for how long? Does this illness imply the need for conservatorship or other special legal proceedings? How will it affect the patient's ability to vote, to drive a car, or to enter into contracts?

Are other family members at risk for this illness? If it is hereditary, what degree of risk do you predict for first-degree relatives? How should you advise the patient who asks about having children?

A number of factors help us make accurate predictions. Unfortunately, no one knows how strongly any one factor will influence the outcome in any given case. Because each can be important, I have simply tried to list them all, in no particular order.

• DSM-III-R diagnosis. Axis I diagnoses are usually more important than Axis II disorders; they are more traditional and generally better substantiated. Axis II diagnoses (the personality disorders) may be especially important for prognosis if no Axis I diagnosis exists or if none can be made with certainty. If your patient has more than one diagnosis, it is important to keep them all in mind when discussing the various aspects of prognosis.

• Availability of treatment for the primary disorder. If effective treatments exist, are they likely to be used? Geography can be an important factor: Does the patient live close enough to a center where effective treatment is offered? Another factor is the patient's financial condition, as demonstrated by this widely discussed example: Clozapine, a drug effective for schizophrenia, was introduced in the early 1990s at a cost of nearly $10,000 per patient per year. Many patients could not afford it until heavy pressure was brought to bear on the manufacturer to reduce the cost of laboratory monitoring.

• Duration and course of illness. Once again, past behavior predicts future behavior.

If there have been past episodes of illness (such as a mood disorder), you can predict with some confidence that there will be future episodes.

A patient who has already been ill for many years has scant chance for complete recovery.

• Previous response to treatment. As a predictor, previous treatment response is only as good as the previous treatment. If in the past your manic patient has been treated only with neuroleptics, you can upgrade your prognosis by an order of magnitude once lithium therapy is begun.

• Compliance with treatment. Even effective treatment is worthless if the patient refuses to accept it. Be sure to consider both Axis I and Axis II diagnoses as well as past treatment history in estimating treatment compliance.

• Available social supports. Prognosis varies directly with the number of bridges the patient has left unburned. Consider all of these resources for help: family of origin, spouse, children, friends, support groups, physicians, and religious organizations. Besides providing comfort, they can help to ensure that the patient continues in treatment and avoids harmful influences such as drugs or alcohol.

• Premorbid personality. As was noted in the previous chapter, premorbid personality is directly related to prognosis. Once patients recover from an acute episode of mental disorder, they tend to resume premorbid levels of functioning. Those who maintained friendships, worked well at their jobs, and provided adequately for their families will probably do so again. All else being equal, parallel predictions are usually warranted for those who premorbidly functioned at lower levels.

• Highest recent level of functioning. If productively engaged in work or school during the past year, your patient will probably regain that status once the current episode of illness has been resolved. Of course, this assumes that a deteriorating or chronically debilitating illness has not supervened. DSM-III-R has formalized the scoring of recent functioning in the Global Assessment of Functioning, which is reproduced in Table 9.

RECOMMENDING FURTHER INVESTIGATION

Further study may be necessary to confirm or rule out specific diagnoses. Resources for this information include

A review of prior hospital and other records
Laboratory tests, including radiographic studies
Formal neuropsychological testing
Interviews with relatives

TABLE 9. Global Assessment of Functioning

Code	Description
90 : 81	Absence of minimal symptoms (e.g., mild anxiety before an exam), good functioning in all areas, interested and involved in a wide range of activities, socially effective, generally satisfied with life, no more than everyday problems or concerns (e.g., an occasional argument with family members)
80 : 71	If symptoms are present, they are transient and expectable reactions to psychosocial stressors (e.g., difficulty concentrating after family arguments); no more than slight impairment in social, occupational, or school functioning (e.g., temporarily falling behind in school work)
70 : 61	Some mild symptoms (e.g., depressed mood and mild insomnia) OR some difficulty in social, occupational, or school functioning (e.g., occasional truancy or theft within the household), but generally functioning pretty well, has some meaningful interpersonal relationships
60 : 51	Moderate symptoms (e.g., flat affect and circumstantial speech, occasional panic attacks) OR moderate difficulty in social, occupational, or school functioning (such as having few friends, or conflicts with co-workers)
50 : 41	Serious symptoms (e.g., suicidal ideation, severe obsessional rituals, frequent shoplifting) OR any serious impairment in social, occupational, or school functioninng (such as having no friends or being unable to keep a job)
40 : 31	Some impairment in reality testing or communication (e.g., speech is at times illogical, obscure, or irrelevant) OR major impairment in several areas, such as work or school, family relations, judgment, thinking, or mood (e.g., depressed man avoids friends, neglects family, and is unable to work; or a child frequently beats up younger children, is defiant at home, and is failing at school)
30 : 21	Behavior is considerably influenced by delusions or hallucinations OR serious impairment in communications or judgment (e.g., sometimes incoherent, acts grossly inappropriately, suicidal preoccupation) OR inability to function in almost all areas (e.g., stays in bed all day; no job, home, or friends)
20 : 11	Some danger of hurting self or others (e.g., suicide attempts without clear expectation of death, frequently violent, manic excitement) OR occasionally fails to maintain minimal personal hygiene (e.g., smears feces) OR gross impairment in communication (e.g., largely incoherent or mute.)
10 : 1	Persistent danger of severly hurting self or others (e.g., recurrent violence) OR persistent inability to maintain personal hygiene OR serious suicidal act with clear expectation of death
0	Information inadequate to judge

From *Diagnostic and Statistical Manual of Mental Disorders* (3rd ed., rev., p. 12) by the American Psychiatric Association, 1987, Washington, DC: APA. Copyright 1987 by the American Psychiatric Association. Reprinted by permission.

Further interviews and study of existing records usually cost nothing. They often provide new or corroborative information that can rapidly advance your understanding of your patient. Because testing costs both time and money, its use should be justified by the facts of each individual case. Rarely cost-effective are tests that are ordered as a part of an admission routine and not in response to a perceived need.

When laboratory or psychological testing is involved, it should be justified on the basis of these factors:

- Cost of the test. The range can be enormous, from nothing at all to thousands of dollars.
- Risk of the test. Pencil-and-paper psychological tests have essentially no risk; some invasive procedures carry a risk to health and even to life itself.
- Value of the test. How strongly confirmatory will the results be? A costly lab procedure that has a good chance of nailing down the diagnosis is probably worth the expense; a routine urinalysis that has no bearing on the diagnosis is too expensive by far.
- Prevalence of the disorder. Routine testing for rare disorders is not cost-effective. However, this does not mean that you should avoid ordering confirmatory tests for uncommon disorders that seem possible on the basis of history or physical exam.
- Complexity of the question to be answered. If the patient's illness is relatively simple and straightforward, you may well be able to omit laboratory testing completely.
- Will the procedure facilitate treatment? It is well and good to know what's wrong; it is better to learn how to fix it.

MAKING REFERRALS

You are likely to recommend mental health therapy that is directed specifically at your patient's complaints. You should also keep in mind the range of other treatments and referrals that may be needed, either to help manage the presenting complaints or to deal with social, psychological, and biological problems that are incidental to the main problems.

Many organizations and individuals can help you manage nearly any problem you may encounter. This is fortunate, because no therapist has the training and experience to do it all alone. It is vital that you know the limits of your own capabilities and refer for outside help those portions of each patient's difficulties that can be better treated by others.

How much outside help is needed will depend on these factors:

Type of problem. A clinician whose training neglected behavior therapy techniques may need some assistance with a patient who presents with obsessions or phobias.

Acuity of the problem. Mild depression may respond to cognitive therapy; a severe depression may require the services of a clinician skilled in psychopharmacology.

Strength and extent of support network. The most obvious example, a homeless patient, will require far more in the way of social services than one who lives with relatives.

Degree of patient's desire and cooperation. Obviously, a patient's refusal to be hospitalized limits the scope of services that can be brought to bear.

The clinician's training, experience and available time. I strongly recommend that students try to gain familiarity and experience with as many types of treatment as possible.

Although many of the resources mentioned in this chapter have traditionally been provided or arranged by social workers, all mental health professionals should be aware of the type of services that are available in the geographic area where they work. Too, clinicians in private practice will often find that they must arrange for their own referrals. Of course, you can use only the services you know about, hence this listing.

Mental Hospital

Although lay people often consider hospitalization to be a last resort, in several situations the modern mental hospital is the most sensible recourse.

For patients who are dangerous to themselves
For patients who are dangerous to others
For patients who are unable to care for themselves
When the desired treatment is available only there
When the patient must be removed from the environment
When intensive evaluation/observation is required

Clinicians tend to be quite conservative when it comes to protecting their patient's lives. At least regarding suicidal ideas, which are probably the most frequently cited reason for hospitalization, most clinicians would agree that it is better to err on the side of overhospitalization.

Shelters

These are vital resources for patients who do not need to be hospitalized but who for various reasons cannot live at home. Specialized shelters
are operated for battered women, runaways, and the homeless (men,
women, families) and for the protection of children.

Other Therapists

No one can know everything; wise clinicians know their own limitations.
If you practice group therapy and your patient need chlorpromazine,
of course you will refer to a physician for medication. If drug therapy
is your forte, it is important to refer your patient for forms of psychotherapy in which you are not expert.

Legal

Legal assistance may be needed for problems that might either cause
or grow out of the mental disorder; sometimes, the legal problems may
be unrelated. If your patient has inadequate resources and needs services as varied as drawing a will or fighting criminal charges, a referral
to Legal Aid Society may be necessary. If the problem concerns elder
abuse or child abuse, refer to Adult Protective Services or Child Protective Services, respectively. Their numbers can usually be found in
the county government listings in the telephone books of most major
cities.

Support Groups

Their name is legion. Many of these groups are modeled after the famous Alcoholics Anonymous twelve steps. Most cost nothing and many
are nearly ubiquitous, having chapters throughout the country (in some
cases, throughout the world). The name of the group usually describes
its function.

> Adult Children of Alcoholics
> Adults Molested as Children United
> Al-Anon (families)
> Alateen
> Alcoholics Anonymous
> Batterers Anonymous
> Gamblers Anonymous
> Narcotics Anonymous
> Overeaters Anonymous

Parents Anonymous (parents who have abused their children)
Parents Without Partners
Recovery Inc. (emotional problems)

Other Resources

Acute substance abuse treatment. Detoxification services are usually
available through referral from county mental health centers.
Medical evaluation. Available at county, state, city, and private hospitals for evaluation of rape, trauma, HIV testing, and diseases
of any type.
Vocational services. Including evaluation for disability, job training, and unemployment compensation, these services can be ac-
cessed through state and county employment offices.

SUMMING UP

The whole point of the initial interview is to allow a clinician to make
predictions for and about the patient. Clinicians are most interested
in the following predictions: Which of the many available modalities
of treatment is most likely to be effective? Are there problems that will
benefit from referral? What is the likely outcome with treatment and
without it?

20 Communicating Your Findings

Somewhere, sometime, a mental health clinician might conceivably do an evaluation and provide a complete course of treatment without saying a word to anyone but the patient. If ever it happened, this rare event would probably take place in the office of an isolated private practitioner. But the demands of insurance carriers, government agencies, and health care maintenance organizations make it increasingly likely that, regardless of who you or your patient may be, you will have to communicate your findings to someone.

THE WRITTEN REPORT

Even the most expert of clinicians collect their data somewhat haphazardly. It is therefore necessary to organize your findings before reporting them. For written and oral reports, the organization of material will be about the same. Written reports are usually the more complete, so they will be discussed first, and in far greater detail. In Appendix D you'll find a sample written report for the patient whose complete interview is transcribed in Appendix C.

Identifying Data

The identifying data provide the reader with a framework upon which to construct a mental image of the patient whose history you are reporting. In the first line or two of the report, you state the basic demographic data, including name, age, sex, race, marital status, religion, and any other item that seems relevant. In the military, identifying data also include the patient's rank; in a Department of Veterans Affairs hospital you might note whether the patient has a service-connected disability.

In any case, you should note that the patient either is new to your facility or has been seen there before.

The Chief Complaint

As described in Chapter 2, the chief complaint is the patient's stated reason for coming to treatment. It is often written as a direct quote, but sometimes it is paraphrased or summarized—especially if it is vague, long-winded, or multifaceted. Occasionally a clinician cites two chief complaints: one from the patient and another, suitably identified, from a relative, friend, or other informant. This double reporting is especially useful for patients who are too confused or too uncooperative to respond appropriately when you request the information.

Informants

Briefly state the names of those from whom you have obtained your information, and estimate the reliability of each. Besides the patient, mention relatives, friends, other health care workers, and old charts—anything or anyone you have used to help round out your picture of the patient.

History of the Present Illness

This section is the most important of the entire written report. When writing up the history of the present illness, keep in mind several rules.

• This should be a chronological history. Like all good stories, this one should have a beginning and an end. In most cases it will begin with the onset of the first episode of illness. Some clinicians carefully mark that point with an opening phrase something on this order:

"Mr. Turner was well until age 32, when he suffered the first of several episodes of depression."

Note that in this single, economical sentence the reader is alerted to (1) the principal area of clinical interest (mood disorder: depression), (2) the age of onset, (3) the fact that the problem has recurred, and (4) the fact that the patient spent a decade of his adult life in good health prior to the onset of this illness. Once your narrative is under way, it should proceed more or less chronologically, ending with the reasons that prompted your patient to enter treatment at your facility at this time.

Patients who have been repeatedly admitted to one facility for the same condition may prompt an interval note, abbreviated to avoid needless, lengthy repetition from one chart to the next:

"Since age 32 Mr. Turner has had five admissions to this medical center for severe depression, each of which has been successfully treated with electroconvulsive therapy. Since his most recent discharge 2 years ago, he had been living independently and working at his trade of commercial illustrator. Two weeks ago he noted the lethargy and loss of interest in work that usually heralds the onset of an episode of depression. . . ."

- Support your best diagnosis. This means that the material you feature should reflect the criteria (in North America, DSM-III-R) for the diagnosis you think most likely. For example:

Your patient has symptoms of both depression and psychosis. You believe that melancholia with psychosis is the most likely diagnosis, so the history of the present illness emphasizes the findings that your patient is never psychotic except during a profound depression.

This is not to say that you should try to hide ambiguities or evidence of competing diagnoses. But your write-up should, insofar as is consistent with the data, form a picture in which history, mental status, and diagnosis are mutually supportive portions of a consistent whole.

- If the story is complicated, try to disentangle it. One way to accomplish this is to leave until later details that do not support your best diagnosis. Perhaps this less relevant information can be included later in the personal and social history. You could also present distinct (although possibly intersecting) themes as separate paragraphs in your history of the present illness. After describing your patient's depressive illness, which was actually the cause of his hospitalization, you might continue as follows:

"In addition to his depression, Mr. Turner has also had a problem with cross-dressing. This began at about the age of 6. . . ."

- Edit your material. If you have just sat through an hour-long interview and read an old chart that is as thick as the Chicago Yellow Pages, you may have learned far more than most readers will need to know. To boil down your material, you can summarize previous treatment in a line or two, categorize hospitalizations (so many for mania, so many more for depression), and list symptoms of a typical episode. This saves your reader from multiple repetitions of essentially identical information.

"At that time [of his first episode of depression] he first noticed lethargy and lack of interest in his work as a commercial illustrator. Over the next few weeks he became increasingly anorectic, lost 10 pounds, and suffered insomnia that caused him to get up and pace the floor early each morning. This symptom pattern has been repeated during subsequent episodes."

As Platt and McMath (1979) have noted, "The present illness should be an elaboration of these primary data, not a saga of medical care."

• Include significant negatives. When investigating various areas of clinical interest, you asked many questions to rule in or rule out certain disorders. Some of the negative answers were important in helping to decide which diagnosis on a differential list was the most likely. Such answers are called *significant* (or *pertinent*) *negatives;* they should be reported in your history of the present illness, along with the important positive answers:

> "Although Mr. Leeborg said that he felt severely depressed in the week since he lost his job, he denied insomnia, loss of appetite, or lack of interest in sex."

• Report your findings in plain language. Your readers may include people who are unaccustomed to the sometimes perplexing jargon of the mental health field. Short sentences and active verbs will demonstrate the clarity of your thinking. Avoid abbreviations other than those commonly used in professional journals.

• The patient is a person, not a "case." Many clinicians consider it bad form to refer to patients as "this manic" or "this schizophrenic." Always strive to refer to your patient as "this person" or "this patient." Such wording helps to preserve the reader's feeling for the humanity of your patient.

Personal and Social History

To keep things orderly, you should adhere as closely as you can to chronological sequence when you present this information. Begin with birth and early childhood and proceed through education, military experience (if any), sexuality, marriage, work history, legal history, and religion. You can use either a paragraph or outline style; the former will be more convenient if you dictate, the latter if you write your history by hand.

In this section, strive to present a reasonably complete picture of your patient's background. Even so, you should generally omit data already covered in the history of the present illness. Edit out the anecdotes and trivial details with which patients inevitably illustrate their life stories. You should include pertinent negatives such as the absence of childhood sexual abuse in a patient you suspect of somatization disorder or borderline personality disorder. Also include important past positives—such as previous drug or alcohol abuse—that you might have omitted from the history of the present illness because they no longer affect your patient's life.

Family History

Although it is properly a part of the personal and social history, family history is traditionally reported in a separate paragraph. Perhaps we do this to emphasize the biological and environmental effects families have on the development of the adult individual. Include the data you have obtained for physical as well as mental disorders. When reporting the latter, be sure to include not just the diagnosis but also whatever data you have obtained that would substantiate (or refute) that diagnosis. For example:

> "Although Mrs. Garwaith's father had been diagnosed as having schizophrenia, he had twice been treated in hospital and released, apparently recovered and able to resume the demanding occupation of singing waiter. These details suggested a diagnosis of mood disorder."

If the patient was adopted or if the family history is completely negative, say so and move on.

Past Medical History

Mention any operations, major medical illnesses, medications, and hospitalizations for non-mental health reasons. List any allergies, especially to medications. If there are none, say so — this information may assume importance, should drug therapy become an issue for your patient. If you have not already done so, mention any habits such as the use of tobacco or alcohol.

Review of Systems

Mention any positive responses to your questioning about past or present physical problems. If somatization disorder has been a consideration in the differential diagnosis, list the symptoms you scored positive in that disorder's specialized review of systems (see Appendix B for details).

Mental Status Examination

For many patients much of the mental status exam will be normal and can therefore be covered briefly. The order in which you report the various areas is not as important as the fact that you mention each, if only to show that you have considered them all. In describing your patient's mental status, keep in mind which details would be needed to support (or refute) the diagnoses included in your differential diagnosis. You

should report not only positive information but also the important negatives that allow you to place diagnoses higher or lower in your
differential.

Describe the patient's general appearance and clothing; contrast
apparent age with stated age. Be sure to mention all aspects of affect.
If type of affect is unremarkable, "about medium" will do as a descrip-
tor, but also mention lability and appropriateness. When you are trying to describe abnormalities, don't use general terms such as *bizarre*
or *peculiar,* which carry none of the flavor of the patient's behavior or
appearance. Instead, take the trouble to choose words and phrases that
are truly descriptive: Instead of "The patient's clothing was bizarre" say,
"The patient was dressed in a tutu and body stocking hand-stitched from
old flour sacking."

Remember that written mental health records are legal documents.
They can be subpoenaed by attorneys and requested by patients themselves, so be careful that your tone and wording will withstand scrutiny.
Avoid jokes, complaints, or other comments that should be kept private. If you need to express an opinion that could be considered pejorative, qualify the statement by admitting that this is your inference.

"He *appeared* to be intoxicated. . . ."

"Her manner *seemed* seductive. . . ."

Under flow of thought, be sure to mention any abnormalities of
association as well as rate and rhythm of speech. Use direct quotes, both
to show the flavor of the patient's speech and as a baseline for judging
later change.

The findings you report under content of thought will generally
mirror what you have already mentioned in the history of the present
illness. You should also mention all the other possible contents of
thought that were not present. Whereas many patients have no content
of thought that is psychopathological, all (except those who are completely mute) do say something. Whatever it is, you should describe it
briefly:

> "The patient's content of thought largely concerned his past infi-
> delities and the fact that his wife was about to leave him. There
> were no delusions, hallucinations, obsessions, or phobias."

When your patient has language deficits, state what they are but
also give an example of what you mean.

> "Although Mrs. Treat was able to comprehend simple instructions
> and spoke with good fluency, she demonstrated a naming aphasia:
> she could not name the clip and point of a ballpoint pen, and she
> called my wristwatch 'a time thing.'"

In reporting cognitive abilities, it is not sufficient simply to mention that the patient was "normal" or "intact." You should note what tests you made, the responses given, and how you interpret the responses. How far off were any incorrect responses? Do circumstances mitigate the errors? For example, if your patient could not recall a name, a color, and a street address after 5 minutes, can this be explained on the basis of poor concentration due to depression? Was abstracting ability impaired? If so, what was the test you used and what was the response? In reporting serial sevens, note the number of mistakes and the rapidity with which the calculations were done. Did the patient use finger-counting as an aid to this calculation?

In reporting insight and judgment, you will usually have to make an interpretation (such as excellent, good, fair, poor), but be sure to cite your reasoning:

> "Miss Rafael's insight seemed poor in that, despite her clearly manic symptoms, she denied ever being ill a day in her life. However, her judgment was fairly good: She did agree to remain in hospital 'for tests.' She even said that she might resume taking her lithium."

RECORDING YOUR DIAGNOSIS

In the United States the standard for psychiatric diagnosis has been DSM-III and its successor, DSM-III-R. Both are scheduled to be replaced by DSM-IV in 1994. These documents, devised by committees of experts and strongly grounded in empirical research, specify that each patient be assessed in five areas. Each area, called an *axis*, contains information to help describe the patient's current mental health status. The first three of these areas contain the actual diagnostic information:

Axis I are the major clinical syndromes, *not* including personality or developmental disorders. Most of the mental health patients you will see will have at least one Axis I diagnosis. These syndromes include the depressions, psychoses, anxiety disorders, substance abuse disorders, and other clinical entities that mental health clinicians so typically diagnose and treat. If more than one diagnosis is appropriate, include them all, but list first that which was mainly responsible for the current evaluation.

Axis II are the personality disorders and developmental disorders, such as trouble with reading. If the diagnosis that occasioned the current evaluation is on Axis II, it should be followed with the words *principal diagnosis*. Axis II helps us maintain sight of long-standing characteristics that define the person we have interviewed.

Axis III comprises all physical diagnoses that contribute to your understanding of your patient, for example: asthma, diabetes, obesity, and temporal lobe epilepsy.

Axis IV is a scale for rating the severity of psychosocial stresses that may have occurred during the past year and that may have caused or worsened the patient's mental condition. This rating is based on the amount of stress an average person might experience in similar circumstances. The scale varies from 1 (no stress) to 7 (catastrophic); it is given in Table 3.

Axis V, the global assessment of functioning, rates the patient's overall functioning. Two ratings can be made: one that is current and one that describes the highest level of functioning during the past year. The scale runs from 90 (highest) to 1 (lowest) and is given in its entirety in Table 9.

FORMULATION

In the case formulation, the clinician attempts to synthesize all that has been learned about the patient's past so as to point the way toward a better future. There are several reasons for preparing a formulation:

To focus your thinking about the patient
To summarize the logic behind your diagnoses
To identify future needs for information and treatment
To present a brief summary of the patient

A number of formats can be used; some of them are so involved that they risk presenting again all the material you have just covered. The method presented here combines the advantages of brevity, completeness, and simplicity.

Of the various sections of the formulation, the two most important are the differential diagnosis and the contributing factors: They contain the original thinking you will do in putting together all the material you have gathered.

A sample formulation, presented piecemeal, follows.

Brief Recapitulation

Following some minimal identifying data, state the symptoms and course of the patient's present illness as based on the facts in the history of the present illness and the mental status examination. Draw from all parts of your report as needed:

"Mrs. Juneau is a 27-year-old married woman with two previous hospitalizations for a psychosis that has been previously called schizophrenia. For 3 weeks she has stayed in her room, fasting and 'preparing for the end of the world,' which she says she has caused. Her husband brought her to the hospital when he became concerned about weight loss."

Differential Diagnosis

Each of the possible diagnoses in your differential is presented with the principal arguments for and against it. State the authority for your diagnoses (it will probably be DSM-III-R or successor). Include Axis I and Axis II diagnoses.

"*Depression.* Mrs. Juneau feels sad, hopeless, and guilty for some unspecified sin she committed before she was married. She has been anorectic, nearly sleepless, and has had a 10-pound weight loss."

"*Schizophrenia.* She is delusional now; during a previous episode she has believed she was put on earth to save the Jews."

"*Substance abuse.* She drank heavily during her two psychotic episodes, but has never continued drinking once the psychosis has resolved."

"*Organic delusional syndrome.* History of head trauma 8 years ago."

Best Diagnosis

State the diagnosis you favor and why you have chosen it. Note that your best diagnosis may not be the one highest in the hierarchy. The most notable example of this is that an organic disorder, if one is possible, must always be ruled out first, but it frequently is not the most likely diagnosis:

"Mrs. Juneau is probably in the depressed phase of bipolar disorder. Her previous episodes of psychosis resolved completely; her husband reports that even without maintenance medication she was well in the interim. All of her psychotic symptoms appear to be congruent with her mood at the time. Head trauma was 8 years ago and without sequel, and there are no other indications of organicity. Her abuse of alcohol appears to be only in response to her psychotic episodes, which in retrospect were probably mania with psychosis."

Contributing Factors

Here you describe how the various factors you have identified contributed to the development of your patient's main problems. Where applicable, mention biological, dynamic, psychological, and social factors. Depending on the material you have identified, this section could be long or short:

> "A biological basis for Mrs. Juneau's illness may be seen in the family history: Her mother suffered from recurrent depressions. A psychological precipitant may be the death of her father 2 months ago. Medical expenses from previous episodes of depression may be contributing to the depth of her current depression."

Further Information Needed

Briefly cover the interviews, tests, and records you may need to firm up the diagnosis:

> "Records will be requested from Mrs. Juneau's previous admissions to see whether the symptoms she had then could be those of mania. Consider CAT scan to rule out sequel of old head injury."

Treatment Plan

Outline your recommendations for treatment. For Mrs. Juneau they were as follows:

Biological
    Lithium 900 mg/day to prevent recurrence of mania
    Fluoxetine 20 mg/day for depression
    Trifluoperazine 5 mg as needed to control psychosis
Psychological
    Psychotherapy, focused on feelings of guilt and grief
Social
    Assistance with financial planning
    ? Referral to Alcoholics Anonymous
    Education of Juneau family regarding bipolar disorder

Prognosis

What is the likely outcome for this patient?

> "Mrs. Juneau is expected to recover completely. Prophylactic use of lithium may prevent subsequent episodes."

THE ORAL PRESENTATION

A verbal presentation of your interview material generally follows the same pattern as the written report. Usually, it is briefer. In fact, any oral presentation that goes on longer than 5 or 6 minutes risks boredom and inattention from your listeners. However, you should present a complete, rounded portrait that demonstrates how well you understand the patient.

You can also demonstrate how well organized you are. For a formal presentation you should outline your findings on a small note card. This will speed you through your presentation, jog your memory when needed, and save you the discomfort of flipping back and forth through your patient's chart as you search for items of information.

When making an oral presentation, be prepared with your diagnosis and differential diagnosis. You should have clearly in mind the reasons for choosing your best diagnosis; some instructors will ask you to defend it with data and logic. See Chapter 18 for help with this material.

COMMUNICATING YOUR IDEAS TO THE PATIENT

Even though you may see no outward indication, your patient will probably be feeling apprehensive about the results of your findings. This is why you should plan to discuss them with the patient just as soon as you can. Many clinicians do this at the end of each initial interview. Complicated problems may require more interviews or time to review materials. Even then, some sort of interim report will be appreciated, even if it is only a few sentences.

What you tell the patient will be governed to some extent by the patient's capacity to understand; this in turn may be heavily influenced by the disorder itself. But most patients can understand and appreciate the truth, which is what you should always try to communicate. I used to feel reluctant to give a patient or family the diagnosis of schizophrenia because it carries an ominous prognosis. But after a few such encounters I discovered that patients tend to accept this diagnosis about as well as any other, and I stopped worrying.

If you follow a few simple rules when communicating your findings, your message will stand a better chance of being both heard and accepted.

Outline the problems. By doing so, you give assurance that you really do understand why the patient has come for help. In the event that you don't understand as completely as you thought, the patient has the opportunity to educate you further.

Give a diagnosis. State your best diagnosis in terms appropriate for this patient. If you are unsure of the diagnosis, say so. Then state how you plan to resolve your uncertainty (more tests? a therapeutic trial?).

Keep it simple. Bear in mind what the patient really needs to know, and convey that. This isn't the time to teach a graduate course in diagnostics.

Don't use jargon. The information should be transmitted in terms the patient can understand. If you use a lot of four-dollar words, you risk losing part of your message while the patient deciphers the code.

Keep asking for questions. You'll ensure good communication and you'll be able to evaluate how the message was received if you keep asking for feedback.
"How do you feel about this?"
"Do you have any questions so far?"

Emphasize the positive. With the many therapeutic approaches mental health professionals have at their disposal, even gravely serious problems such as schizophrenia and bipolar disorder can be helped in some way. Even when you can't do much for the patient who is rapidly sliding into dementia, you may be able to help the family cope.

Show your compassion. Watch for changes in the patient's affect as you give information. Acknowledge the patient's feelings and offer sympathy and suggestions as to how things might improve. Remember that all people need the feeling of hope.

Discussing Treatment

First and foremost, the treatment plan you arrive at should be structured as a collaborative effort between clinician and patient. Although this approach requires more initial effort, in the long run everyone will benefit.

A patient who buys into the plan is more likely to cooperate with it enthusiastically. Compliance will be enhanced: There will be fewer forgotten appointments, missed doses of medicine, treatment failures, and dropouts from therapy. If something goes awry and treatment doesn't work, the patient is less likely to lay the blame on the clinician.

When you are drawing up the treatment plan together, here are several points to consider:

- Discuss the options. It is human nature to feel more in control when there are choices. Therefore, you should run through a complete list of the possible treatment options. One obvious choice that is seldom mentioned is no treatment at all. I often start with this one because it allows me to discuss in concrete terms what I foresee as the outcome of no treatment (or inadequate treatment). This serves as a useful benchmark against which to measure the potential drawbacks and benefits of the other choices.

- Mention the drawbacks. No treatment is free of them. Medicines have side effects, psychotherapy takes time, group therapy involves other people, and behavior modification requires considerable effort and anxiety. All of them are expensive. Negative aspects of treatment are unpleasant to contemplate, but patients need to know these things so they can make a rational choice. Many states have laws that require patients to be told about alternatives to somatic treatments such as drugs and electroconvulsive therapy.

- You can favor one option. Most of the time you will probably convey your opinions directly. But for patients who need to defy authority or who strongly desire a particular form of therapy, you may want to exert your influence more subtly. For example, you can find good news about drug therapy for the patient who needs it:

"You won't have to wait forever to gain control of your symptoms."
You can also find good news for the personality disorder patient who *doesn't* need drugs:

"You won't have to give up control of your own body."
Neither of these statements is untrue, and they can both promote one of the goals of mental health professionals: to encourage patients to accept what will help them.

- Make sure the patient understands the options. Most patients will, but under stress people can have difficulty focusing their full attention on what they are being told. If you have any doubts that your instructions about treatment were heard, ask the patient to repeat what you have said.

Discussion with the Family

Families that are close will want to know what can be done for the patient. Many relatives have had considerable experience in dealing with mental health professionals, and this experience has not always been a happy one. Their experience this time will usually be in direct proportion to

The amount of contact they have with you
The degree to which they feel they have input

How caring you appear
The patient's opinion of you and the treatment plan

You can avoid problems of confidentiality if you *and* the patient meet together with the family. Of course, if you need more information, then you should probably have a portion of your family session with the patient absent.

If this is your first meeting, you might start out by asking what the family already knows about the disorder. This helps you learn about their prior assumptions and therefore avoid discomfiting them with information that directly contradicts what they may have been told earlier. For example, if a previous clinician diagnosed schizophrenia and you believe that the diagnosis should be bipolar mood disorder, you might want to emphasize the psychotic symptoms that both therapists have regarded as key.

Subsequently, your approach to the relatives should be pretty much the same as you used for the patient. Let them know that you have negotiated an agreement about treatment. Describe the treatment plan, including its strong and weak points. It is especially important for relatives to know what to watch for: Side effects and wanted effects of treatment may be more apparent to them than to the patient. Be sure to tell relatives how to get in touch with you, and emphasize that you want all three groups—you, the patient, relatives—to work together as partners in problem-solving.

What If the Plan Is Rejected?

With the stress of mental illness in the family, it is not uncommon for someone—usually the patient, but sometimes a relative—to reject the treatment plan. If it is a relative or friend, and you and the patient agree about how to proceed, move ahead with the plan. But say something to the relative that shows you have considered the dissenting point of view:

> "I'm glad you told me that you don't want your brother hospitalized. But he and I both feel it is the safest thing to do right now, so I think we should go ahead with it. I hope you'll visit him. You know him better than just about anybody, so I'll need your eyes and ears to help me judge how he is progressing."

If your patient is the one who balks at treatment, proceed with a series of steps that might resolve your impasse:

1. Try to discover what about it is not acceptable, and then offer reassurance. For example, side effects of treatment may be tolerable if the patient can be reassured that they are short term.

2. Identify the areas that you do agree about. If it is the need for *some* treatment, proceed with the next step.

3. Learn what therapeutic measure the patient will accept. If it is something you feel will not be harmful, just not helpful (psychotherapy alone for a moderately severe depression, for example), you may agree to try it for a specified period. At the end of that time the patient may agree to proceed with your original recommendation.

4. You may agree to an experimental trial, with the proviso that you will monitor the results carefully and stop or change treatment if the patient feels dissatisfied.

5. Offer to request a second opinion. This may be especially helpful if a trusted friend or relative is influencing the patient to reject your recommendation. But keep an open mind: Your consultant may recommend something entirely different from what you had in mind.

6. Finally, it is possible that either the patient or the family may reject treatment you consider to be essential. I will proceed with a course of treatment against the wishes of either the family *or* the patient (in the case of one who is involuntarily hospitalized). But if both patient *and* family reject my advice, I will usually feel unable to work effectively with this patient. Then I will decline to proceed; instead, I will try to help the patient find another clinician.

SUMMING UP

Clinical findings and recommendations are useful only insofar as they are shared with others. The written report is standard; the oral report is a fixture of the training of many professionals. Most important is the manner and thoroughness with which this material is communicated to the patient and family.

Appendix A:
Summary of the Initial Interview

Information	*Process*

Openings and Introductions

Introduce yourself	Your initial goals
Explain your role in patient's care	Teach respondent role to patient
Outline time, goals of interview	Help patient feel comfortable

Chief Complaint

Ask why patient came for treatment	Request for chief complaint is directive but open-ended

Free Speech

Allow several minutes for patient to amplify on reasons for coming	Early part of interview is non-directive
Listen for areas of clinical interest	Establish rapport
Difficulty thinking (cognitive disorders)	Adjust your demeanor to patient's needs
Substance use	Monitor your feelings
Psychosis	Show your positive affect clearly
Mood disorders (depression and mania)	Use language patient can comprehend
Anxiety, avoidance behavior, and arousal	Don't criticize patient or others
Physical complaints	Maintain appropriate distance
Social and personality problems	Don't talk about yourself
Summarize presenting problems before moving on	Call patient by title and last name
	Encourage flow with silent encouragements
	Maintain eye contact
	Nod or smile when appropriate

Information	*Process*
	Verbal encouragements
	"Yes" or "Mm-hmm"
	Repeat patient's own word or
	words
	Ask for more information
	Re-request information if patient
	doesn't respond at first
	Briefly summarize
	Reassure patient when indicated
	Must be factual, believable
	Use body language
	Correct any misconceptions about
	physical, mental symptoms

History of the Present Illness

Describe symptoms	Establish the need for truth
Type	It's for patient's benefit and for
Onset and sequence	yours
Severity	Reassure about confidentiality
Frequency	"If you can't discuss something,
Duration	don't lie; just ask to talk about
Context	something else"
Stressors	General principles
Vegetative symptoms	Restate what patient says to be
Sleep	sure you understand
Appetite and weight	Don't phrase questions in the
Diurnal variation	negative
Previous episodes	Avoid asking double questions
When	Encourage precision
What symptoms?	Keep questions brief
Recovery complete?	Watch for new leads
Previous treatment	Use terms patient can understand
Type	Probe for details
Compliance	Use direct questions
Wanted effects	Avoid "why" questions, as a rule
Side effects	Limit to one to two confrontations,
Hospitalizations	late in session:
Consequences of illness	"Help me to understand"
Marital and sexual	Mix open- and closed-ended requests
Social	Open-ended increase validity
Legal	Closed-ended increase
Job (disability payments?)	information
Interests	Elicit feelings best with
Discomfort	Facilitate uninterrupted speech

Information	*Process*
Feelings about symptoms, behavior	Open-ended questions—"Could
Negative and positive	you tell me more about that?"
How does patient cope with	Direct requests for feelings—"Tell
feelings?	me about your depression"
Defense mechanisms	Also obtain feelings with
Acting out	Express concern or sympathy—"I'd
Denial	feel angry, too"
Displacement	Reflection of feelings—"You must
Dissociation	have felt frantic"
Fantasy	Watch for emotional cues in
Intellectualization	voice, body language—"You
Projection	looked sad just now"
Repression	Interpretations—"Sounds like the
Splitting	way you felt as a child"
Reaction formation	Analogy—"Did you feel this way
Somatization	when your mother died?"
Devaluation	Reduce excessive emotionality with
Explore areas of clinical interest	Speak softly yourself
	Closed-ended questions
	Redirect comments that change
	topic
	Re-explain what information you
	need
	Ask whether patient understands
	what you want to know
	Break off interview only as last
	resort

Personal and Social History

CHILDHOOD AND GROWING UP	Take charge of interview
Where was the patient born?	Encourage shorter answers with
Number of siblings and sibship	nods and smiles
position	Directly state when you need to
Reared by both parents?	know about something
How did parents get along?	different, but...
Did patient feel wanted as a child?	Make an empathic comment first
If adopted	Raise a finger to interrupt
What circumstances?	Stop taking notes
Extrafamilial?	If above steps don't work
Health as a child?	Be direct: "We'll have to move on"
Education	Use more closed-ended questions
Last grade completed	Use multiple-choice questions
Scholastic problems?	Transition to new topics
Activity level?	Use patient's own words

Information

School refusal?
Behavior problems in school?
Suspension or expulsions?
Sociable as child?
Age dating began?
Sexual development
Hobbies? Interests?

LIFE AS AN ADULT

Living situation
  Currently with whom?
  Where?
  Finances
  Ever homeless?
  Support network
    Family ties
    Agencies help out?
Marital
  Number of marriages
  Age at each
  Problems with spouse?
  Number of children, age, and sex
  Stepchildren?
Work history
  Current occupation
  Number of jobs lifetime
  Reasons for job changes
  Ever fired? Why?
Military
  Branch, years of service
  Highest rank attained
  Disciplinary problems?
  Combat experience?

Legal problems ever?
  Civil
  History of violent behavior
  Arrests
  Underlying feelings
Religion: Which? Different from
  childhood?
  How religious now?

Process

Acknowledge an abrupt transition:
  "Let me change the subject,
  now"
Watch for distortion
Record significant negatives

DEALING WITH RESISTANCE
Do not allow yourself to become
  angry
Switch from discussing facts to
  feelings
Reject the behavior, accept the
  person
Use verbal and nonverbal
  encouragements
Focus on patient's interests
Express sympathy
Reassure patient: Feelings are
  normal
Emphasize need for complete
  data base
Name the emotion you suspect
  patient is having
If patient is silent, obtain nonverbal
  response first
Focus on less affect-laden model of
  patient's behavior
If confrontation is used: nonjudg-
  mental, nonthreatening
Last resort: Delay the question

RISKIER TECHNIQUES
Offer an excuse for unfavorable
  information: "All that stress
  probably made you want to
  drink"
Exaggerate negative consequences
  that didn't happen: "Nobody
  died, did they?"
Induce patient to brag
"Any activities for which you could
  have been arrested, but
  weren't?"

Information	*Process*

Leisure activities
  Clubs, organizations
  Hobbies, interests	

Sexual preference and adjustment
  Learning about sex: details
  First sexual experiences
    Nature
    Age
    Patient's reaction
  Current sexual preference
  Current practices: details
    Pleasures
    Problems
      Birth control methods
      Extramarital partners
  Paraphilias?
  Sexually transmitted diseases?
  Abuse?
    Childhood molestation
    Rape
    Spouse abuse
	"Please tell me about your sexual
	  functioning"
	
	Lead into questions of abuse
	  carefully:
	  "Were you ever approached for
	  sex?"
	  Avoid terms *abuse* and *molestation*

Substance abuse
  Type of substance
  Years of use
  Quantity
  Consequences
    Medical problems
    Loss of control
    Personal and interpersonal
    Job
    Legal
    Financial
  Abuse of prescription
    medications?
	Assume that all adults will drink
	  some
	Ask about past as well as current
	  use

Suicide attempts
  Methods
  Consequences
  Drug or alcohol associated?
  Psychological seriousness
  Physical seriousness
	You can work up to this gradually:
	  "Have you ever had any
	  desperate thoughts? Any ideas
	  of harming yourself?

Information	*Process*

Personality traits
  Evidence of lifelong behavior
    patterns
	Assess personality by
	  Patient's self-report
	  Informants
	  History of interaction with others
	  Your direct observation

Family History

Mental disorder in close relatives
Describe parents, siblings, and
  patient's relationship with them
Other adults, children in childhood
  home
	"Has any blood relative — parent,
	  brother, sister, grandparent,
	  child, aunt or uncle, cousin,
	  niece or nephew — ever had any
	  mental illness, including
	  depression, mania, psychosis,
	  mental hospitalization, severe
	  nervousness, substance abuse,
	  suicide or suicide attempts,
	  criminality?"

Past Medical History

Major illnesses
Operations
Medications for nonmental problems
  Dose
  Frequency
  Side effects
Allergies
  To environment
  To medications
Nonmental hospitalizations
Childhood physical, sexual abuse?
Risk factors for AIDS?
Physical impairments
	Important for *all* mental health
	  workers to obtain

Review of Systems

Disorders of appetite
Head injury
Convulsions
Unconsciousness
Premenstrual syndrome
Specialized review for somatization
  disorder
	Positive responses in these areas
	  have especial relevance to
	  mental health diagnoses.
	
	See Chapter 13 and Appendix B

Information   *Process*

Mental Status Exam

Appearance
  Apparent age
  Ethnicity
  Body build, posture
  Nutrition
  Clothing: Neat? Clean? Style?
  Hygiene
  Hairstyle
Alertness: Full? Drowsy? Stupor?
    Coma?
General behavior
  Activity level
  Tremors?
  Mannerisms and stereotypies
  Facial expression
  Eye contact
  Voice   Observed during history-taking
Attitude toward examiner
Mood
  Type
  Lability
  Appropriateness
  Intensity
Flow of thought
  Word associations
  Rate and rhythm of speech
Content of thought
  Delusions
  Hallucinations
  Anxiety
  Phobias
  Obsessions and compulsions
  Suicide and violence
Orientation: Person? Place? Time?   "Now I'd like to ask some routine
Language: Comprehension, Fluency,   questions. . . ."
    Naming, Repetition, Reading,
    Writing
Memory: Immediate? Short-term?   "How has your memory been? Do
    Long-term?   you mind if I test it?"
Attention and concentration
  Serial sevens
  Count backwards

Information	*Process*
Cultural information	
Current events	
Five presidents	
Abstract thinking	
Proverbs	
Similarities and differences	
Insight	
Judgment	
	Closure
	Summarize findings
	Set next appointment
	"Do you have any questions for me?"

Appendix B:
Description and Diagnostic
Criteria for Selected Disorders

Brief descriptions of typical symptoms and course of illness are given here for those mental disorders that are not only better studied but also, for the most part, common. With the exception of the personality disorders, all of the conditions discussed here are Axis I disorders. At the end of each section I have paraphrased and simplified the DSM-III-R criteria, which, in the original, are often so complicated as to discourage students from using them. For complete, formal diagnostic criteria, see the relevant sections of DSM-III-R.

DEPRESSIVE DISEASE

Depression is a disorder of mood in which the patient feels abnormally low-spirited, down in the dumps, sometimes melancholic. There are sensations of great distress and of being out of control of mood, often to the point of suicide. Depression can take a number of forms, each of which has been given a name—and sometimes several different names. These forms of depression are often overlapping, so that a given patient may actually be classifiable into more than one category. Prominent features of the more important varieties of depression will be given here.

Major Depression

This designation simply means that the patient has depressive symptoms and that they are more severe than if they are due to dysthymia. These patients usually describe themselves as feeling depressed, but sometimes all they can identify is a feeling of irritability or a loss of enjoyment or interest in usually pleasurable activities. In any case, there is a definite change from the patient's previous level of functioning. Depressed patients typically complain of a number of associated symptoms. These include increased or decreased appetite, often with consequent gain or loss of weight; increased or decreased sleep; agitation; psychomotor retardation; fatigue or decreased energy; feelings of worthlessness or guilt; trouble concentrating; and thoughts of death, death wishes, and sui-

Portions of this appendix are adapted from the *Diagnostic and Statistical Manual of Mental Disorders* (3rd ed., rev.) by the American Psychiatric Association, 1987, Washington, DC: APA. Copyright 1987 by the American Psychiatric Association. Adapted by permission.

cidal ideas. Often there is diurnal variation of mood, with the patient feeling better in the morning or at night.

These symptoms may be mild, perhaps resulting in only minor inconvenience; when it is severe, sometimes to the point of psychosis, melancholia may be diagnosed (see later in this appendix). Perhaps 25% of depressed patients also have episodes of mania.

Abbreviated Criteria for Major Depressive Episode

Depressed mood or loss of interest or pleasure that represents a change from previous functioning for 2 weeks plus five of

Depressed mood
Loss of interest or pleasure
Significant (5% of body weight in a month) weight gain or loss, or change in appetite
Insomnia or excessive sleep
Psychomotor agitation or retardation
Fatigue or loss of energy
Feelings of worthlessness or excessive guilt
Indecisiveness or loss of concentration
Recurring thoughts of death or suicidal ideas or attempt

The mood disorder is not due to bereavement or organic factors.

There are no significant delusions or hallucinations without depression, and the patient doesn't have a schizophrenia-like illness.

Melancholia

This severe form of depression is less likely to be associated (at least, in the mind of the patient) with a precipitating stressor. Therefore, it has sometimes been called endogenous depression. These patients may have multiple episodes of depression from which they recover completely; they are likely to have relatives who have also suffered from depression. When ill, they take little pleasure in their usual activities and may not be much cheered by people whose company they normally enjoy. They may awaken early in the morning, well before it is time to arise, and feel worst at that time of day. They may eat little, and they sometimes experience profound weight loss. They may have little insight into the fact that they are ill: Even if they have recovered completely from previous episodes, they often strenuously deny that recovery is a likely outcome. As a result, they are often at severe risk for suicide attempt; perhaps 15% ultimately kill themselves.

Abbreviated Criteria for Melancholia

The patient meets the criteria for major depressive episode.
There are at least five of

Loss of interest or pleasure
Doesn't feel better when something good happens

Depression is worse in the morning
There is early-morning awakening
Psychomotor retardation or agitation
Loss of appetite or weight loss
No personality disorder before onset of depression
A previous depressive episode with complete recovery
Previous history of improvement with specific antidepressant therapy (drugs
   or electroconvulsive therapy)

Dysthymia

Compared with major depression, the symptoms of dysthymic patients are less severe but more chronic. In the past this disorder has been called *characterologic depression or depressive personality.* Dysthymic patients often seem to have been depressed their entire lives. Although they remain able to work and take care of themselves and their families, typically they don't enjoy life very much. They have some of the same symptoms found in major depression and melancholia, but these symptoms tend to be less severe and there are fewer of them.

Abbreviated Criteria for Dysthymia

Depressed mood most days for 2 or more years with at least two of
   Poor appetite or overeating
   Insomnia or excessive sleeping
   Low energy or fatigue
   Low self-esteem
   Poor concentration or trouble making decisions
   Feelings of hopelessness
No major depression, but never without symptoms longer than 2 months
   during the 2 years
No manic episode ever

Manic Episode

Patients with mania usually have a sudden onset of euphoric or irritable mood that is accompanied by overactivity and excessive speech. They are easily distractible, need less sleep than usual, and become involved in grandiose plans and schemes. As they become sicker, they lose insight, and judgment deteriorates. They say or do things they later regret: they may become sexually promiscuous, spend money they do not have, or make other decisions that later prove to have untoward consequences. Many begin to drink excessively. They feel abnormally strong or powerful, and may become deluded that they have special powers or have been set on earth for a special religious purpose. Most manic patients have episodes of depression, sometimes alternating regularly with the high phases; this pattern is called *bipolar disorder.* Even without treatment, most will eventually recover completely.

Abbreviated Criteria for Manic Episode

Distinct period of euphoria or irritability with at least three of

Grandiosity
Needs less sleep
Increased talkativeness
Racing thoughts or speech
Attention easily distracted
Heightened activity
Poor judgment (spends money, sexual indiscretions)
Severe enough to interfere with patient's life (job, friends, hospitalization)
There are no significant delusions or hallucinations without mania, and
the patient doesn't have a schizophrenia-like illness.

THE SCHIZOPHRENIAS

Although these disorders are usually spoken of as a singular disease, in reality
this category probably includes several different diseases.

Before the onset of their disease, these patients may seem perfectly normal. But as children many of them have been introverted, quiet social loners;
before the onset of the actual symptoms of schizophrenia, many would qualify
for a diagnosis of schizotypal or schizoid personality disorder.

The disease process itself usually begins early in life—late teens or early
twenties—and develops gradually over a period of many months. There is usually
an initial prodrome during which the individual may become interested in
philosophy, religion, or witchcraft; anxiety or perplexity may be the predominant
affect. Isolation may increase, and relatives or friends may note various behaviors
that are peculiar, although not exactly psychotic.

Gradually, hallucinations (most often auditory) become more insistent; delusions (especially persecutory) usually develop. As the patient becomes more
preoccupied with inner feelings and experiences, ability to function at work
or school falls off. It may be only at this stage that relatives notice a change
in the patient. Affect may become blunted, silly, or inconsequential. Flow of
speech is often loose. Patients can lose impulse control and, when markedly
agitated, sometimes become violent. Although orientation is usually retained,
typically insight is lost and judgment severely impaired. The disorder is chronic.
Treatment with neuroleptics can reduce or eliminate the most troublesome
symptoms of psychosis, but few patients completely recover to their premorbid levels of functioning.

Schizophrenia patients are usually given a subtype diagnosis. In *paranoid
schizophrenia* delusions and auditory hallucinations are the prominent symptoms;
onset is often when older (mid-thirties or later) than in the remaining subtypes.
In *catatonic schizophrenia* there are prominent disorders of motion: stupor, negativism, rigidity, excitement, or posturing. Delusions and hallucinations may be
present, but these are less prominent than in paranoid subtype. In *disorganized
schizophrenia* the principal symptoms are marked loosening of associations and
flat or inappropriate affect. Patients with *undifferentiated schizophrenia* are cur-

rently psychotic (have delusions, hallucinations, incoherent speech, or markedly disorganized behavior) but do not obviously fall into any of the previous three categories. Patients with *residual schizophrenia* are not currently psychotic, but have two or more of the residual symptoms listed in the D criteria.

Warning: Schizophrenia today has carefully delineated symptoms, so it shouldn't be overdiagnosed. But until a few years ago it was common to see patients with severe depression, mania, personality disorder, or organic psychoses misdiagnosed as having schizophrenia. Patients who for many years have carried the diagnosis of schizophrenia should be periodically reassessed for accuracy of diagnosis.

Abbreviated Criteria for Schizophrenia

The patient must have been ill continuously during a 6-month period that may include a prodrome and a residual phase.

Both A and B criteria must apply.

A. At least 1 week of any (1, 2, or 3) of the following groups of psychotic symptoms:
   1. Two or more of
      Delusions
      Prominent, lasting hallucinations
      Markedly loose associations
      Catatonic symptoms
      Affect that is blunted or grossly inappropriate
   2. Delusions that the patient's culture would consider bizarre *(such as being able to control the weather)*
   3. Auditory hallucinations
      Voice that makes remarks having no relation to depression or elation; or
      Voice that keeps up a running commentary on patient's thought or behavior; or
      Two or more voices talking with one another
B. Marked decrease in social functioning during the illness
C. Not due to schizoaffective, organic, manic, or autistic disorders
D. Prodrome and residual phases are defined by persistence of at least two of
   Social isolation or withdrawal
   Impaired functioning in job or school
   Bizarre behavior *(such as collecting used Styrofoam cups)*
   Decreased hygiene
   Blunted or inappropriate affect
   Abnormal speech patterns
   Magical thinking or odd beliefs that influence behavior *(such as sixth sense or clairvoyance)*
   Unusual perceptions *(such as recurrent illusions or halos)*
   Decreased initiative, interests or energy

DELUSIONAL DISORDER

These patients have delusions that are not bizarre, but do not qualify for other psychotic diagnoses, such as schizophrenia or organic psychosis. Once this illness strikes, it tends to be chronic. There is good preservation of mood and ability to communicate; when employed, these people remain able to work. They do have trouble in the social sphere, however, and it is often their families who instigate the referral for treatment. Several distinct types of delusional disorder have been described.

Erotomanic. This is characterized by the belief that someone (often someone famous or of higher social station) is in love with the patient. These people are sometimes in the news for following or otherwise harassing public figures.

Grandiose. These people believe that they have some special ability or insight; they may believe they have invented something of great value. As a result, they sometimes haunt the offices of various government agencies (patent office, police) in an effort to pursue their plans.

Persecutory. Most often, these individuals believe that a spouse is being unfaithful. They may pursue this idea by following the spouse or confronting the supposed lover.

Somatic. These patients often seek medical help for a belief that they have a foul body odor, parasites, or infestation of insects on or under the skin, or that some body part is misshapen.

Abbreviated Criteria for Delusional Disorder

Nonbizarre delusions lasting at least 1 month
If hallucinations are present, they are not prominent
Other than as relates to the delusion, behavior is not peculiar
Any mood disorder is brief in relation to the length of delusion
The patient has never met criterion A for schizophrenia
No organic cause for the delusion can be found

SUBSTANCE USE DISORDERS

The terminology keeps changing, but the basic disorders are the same: alcoholism and drug abuse. In the late 20th century there is an ever-widening variety of substances to abuse, but their use leads to a few common problems. These problems will be outlined in this section. For any of them, the diagnostician must specify the substance(s) responsible.

Abbreviated Criteria for Dependence

At least three of

Substance often used longer or in greater amounts than the patient intended

Persistent desire or attempts to control substance use

Much time spent getting, using, or recovering from substance

Intoxication or withdrawal (defined later in this section) often interferes with work, school, or home life, or patient uses substance of choice when it could be physically dangerous (e.g., driving)

Gives up or reduces important activities in favor of substance use
Uses despite knowledge that it causes or worsens significant problems
   (social, physical, psychological)
Shows tolerance to the substance (needs more to achieve same effect)
Has withdrawal symptoms characteristic of the specific substance
Uses substance to relieve or avoid withdrawal symptoms

Some of these symptoms have been present for a month or more.

Abbreviated Criteria for Intoxication

Recent use of a psychoactive substance
Maladaptive behavior due to central nervous system effects of the substance
A syndrome specific to the substance ingested:

Alcohol. At least one of
   Slurred speech
   Incoordination
   Unsteady gait
   Nystagmus
   Flushed face
Caffeine. At least five of
   Restlessness
   Nervousness
   Excitement
   Insomnia
   Flushed face
   Increased urination
   Gastrointestinal disturbance
   Muscle twitching
   Rambling speech
   Rapid or irregular heart beat
   Periods of inexhaustibility
   Agitation
Cocaine. Within 1 hour of using, at least two of
   Rapid heart beat
   Dilated pupils
   Elevated blood pressure
   Chills or sweating
   Nausea or vomiting
   Visual or tactile hallucinations
Inhalants. At least two of
   Dizziness
   Nystagmus
   Incoordination
   Slurred speech
   Unsteady gait
   Lethargy

Inhalants (cont.)
  Depressed reflexes
  Psychomotor retardation
  Tremor
  Muscle weakness
  Blurred vision or double vision
  Stupor or coma
  Euphoria
Marijuana. Within 2 hours of using, at least two of
  Red eyes
  Increased appetite
  Dry mouth
  Rapid heart rate
Opioids. Constricted pupils plus at least one of
  Drowsiness
  Slurred speech
  Impaired attention or memory
Phencyclidine (PCP). Within 1 hour of using, at least two of
  Nystagmus
  Increased blood pressure or heart rate
  Numbness or decreased pain sensation
  Difficulty walking
  Difficulty speaking
  Rigid muscles
  Seizures
  Excessively acute hearing
Sedatives, hypnotics, or anxiolytics. At least one of
  Slurred speech
  Incoordination
  Unsteady gait
  Impaired attention or memory
Stimulants. Within 1 hour of using, at least two of
  Rapid heart beat
  Dilated pupils
  Raised blood pressure
  Chills or sweating
  Nausea or vomiting

Abbreviated Criteria for Withdrawal

Marked reduction of intake after heavy use for several days or longer (alcohol, cocaine, or stimulants), or several weeks or more (opioids, sedatives/hypnotics/anxiolytics)
Specific to the substance of abuse
  Alcohol (uncomplicated). Coarse tremor and at least one of
    Nausea or vomiting
    Malaise or weakness
    Autonomic overactivity

Anxiety
Depressed or irritable mood
Hallucinations or illusions
Headache
Insomnia
Cocaine. Depression, anxiety, or irritability and, persisting for 24 hours, at least one of
   Fatigue
   Insomnia or excessive sleep
   Agitation
Nicotine. At least four of
   Craving for nicotine
   Irritability, frustration, or anger
   Anxiety
   Difficulty concentrating
   Restlessness
   Slowed heart rate
   Increased appetite or weight gain
Opioids. At least three of
   Craving for an opioid
   Nausea or vomiting
   Muscle aching
   Tearing or runny nose
   Dilated pupils, erection of hairs, or sweating
   Diarrhea
   Yawning
   Fever
   Insomnia
Sedative-hypnotic or anxiolytic. At least three of
   Nausea or vomiting
   Malaise or weakness
   Autonomic overactivity
   Anxiety or irritability
   Blood pressure falls when patient stands or sits up
   Coarse tremor
   Marked insomnia
   Grand mal seizures
Stimulants. Depression, anxiety, or irritability and, persisting for 24 hours, at least one of
   Fatigue
   Insomnia or excessive sleep
   Agitation

ORGANIC MENTAL CONDITIONS

Organic mental conditions are behavioral or psychological abnormalities that are associated with temporary or permanent brain dysfunctions. The cause can be an abnormality of brain structure, chemistry, or physiology; it is not always known. Organic mental conditions are recognized by four main types of cognitive impairment: intellectual functioning, judgment, memory, and orientation. Patients may also have abnormalities of mood and impulse control. Most such conditions can be broadly categorized as either a delirium or dementia.

Delirium

Delirium usually begins acutely. Patients become disoriented and easily distractible; they may have either increased or decreased motor activity. Their thought processes slow down; they have trouble solving problems and reasoning. Visual hallucinations may confuse them so that they cannot tell whether they are dreaming or awake. They may accept these hallucinations as reality, thereby causing anxiety or fear; sometimes they attempt to run away. All symptoms may worsen at night, a phenomenon called *sundowning*. Later recall for the foregoing symptoms may be spotty or nil.

The causes of delirium include endocrine disorder, infection, brain tumor, cessation of alcohol intake, drug toxicity, vitamin deficiency, fever, seizures, liver or kidney disease, poisons, and the effects of surgical operations. Often, multiple causes contribute to a single case. Delirium tends to begin acutely and to fluctuate in intensity. It is usually short-lived and resolves once the underlying condition has been relieved.

Abbreviated Criteria for Delirium

Wandering attention *and* trouble shifting attention to a new stimulus
Rambling, irrelevant, or incoherent speech
Two or more of
  Reduced level of consciousness
  Illusions, hallucinations, or misinterpretations
  Insomnia or daytime sleepiness
  Psychomotor activity that is increased or decreased
  Disorientation
  Impaired memory
Symptoms develop rapidly and fluctuate during the day
Evidence of specific organic cause *or* absence of nonorganic mental disorder that could account for the disturbance (such as schizophrenia causing hallucinations, staying up nights)

Dementia

The cardinal feature of dementia is loss of memory, beginning with recent memory for milder cases and, as the dementia worsens, involving more remote memories. Dementia patients show loss of ability to think and to remember that is severe enough to interfere with work and social life. Dementias may be transient, but more often they persist and progress, often to the point that the patient shows impaired judgment and abstract thinking. Severely demented patients may not recognize family; sometimes they get lost in their own homes.

The patient may confabulate (make up stories) to hide defects in memory. Failure of judgment and of impulse control can lead to loss of the social graces, as shown by making crude jokes or inattention to personal hygiene. Use of language is usually spared until late in the disease.

Onset is usually insidious, and the misperceptions (hallucinations or illusions) so common in delirium are often absent, especially early in the process. Usually an organic cause can be identified. A few causes (subdural hematoma, normal-pressure hydrocephalus, hypothyroidism) can be successfully treated, often leading to full recovery of the dementia symptoms. Causes include primary diseases of the central nervous system such as Alzheimer's disease, Huntington's disease, multiple sclerosis, and Parkinson's disease; infectious diseases such as neurosyphilis and AIDS; vitamin deficiencies; tumors; trauma; and a variety of diseases of liver, lung, the cardiovascular system, and endocrine disorders. Found mainly in older patients, the course is usually one of chronic deterioration.

Abbreviated Criteria for Dementia

Impaired short-term and long-term memory
One or more of
  Impaired abstract thinking (similarities, differences)
  Impaired judgment
  Other higher cortical disturbances such as aphasia
  Personality change
These impairments interfere with work or social life
Not due exclusively to delirium
Evidence of specific organic cause *or* no nonorganic mental disorder can
  account for the symptoms (e.g., depression causing apparent loss of
  memory and personality change)

Organic Amnestic Syndrome

The most common cause of this disorder is chronic alcohol use with resultant vitamin B_1 (thiamin) deficiency. Popularly known as Korsakoff's psychosis, these patients rather suddenly lose short-term memory, sometimes to the extent that they cannot even recall events that took place a few minutes earlier. Remote memory is usually less involved. Many patients confabulate information spontaneously or in response to prompting ("Did I see you in the bar last night?"). Recovery can occur, although chronicity is more the rule.

Abbreviated Criteria for Organic Amnestic Syndrome

Impaired short- and long-term memory
Not found exclusively with delirium
Evidence of specific organic cause

Organic Delusional Syndrome

The classical example of this disorder is the delusional state that sometimes accompanies chronic amphetamine use. The paranoid delusions may be indistinguishable from those of paranoid schizophrenia. Marijuana, hallucinogens, and temporal lobe epilepsy have also been implicated in the cause of this condition.

Abbreviated Criteria for Organic Delusional Syndrome

    Prominent delusions
    Evidence of specific organic cause
    Not found exclusively with delirium

Organic Hallucinosis

Alcoholic auditory hallucinosis, as it used to be called, is a prime example of the organic delusional syndrome. These patients complain of auditory hallucinations, especially when they are just withdrawing after a long drinking bout; the condition may last for a number of days. The hallucinogens can cause visual hallucinations that usually last only for a few hours.

Abbreviated Criteria for Organic Hallucinosis

    Prominent delusions that persist or recur
    Evidence of specific organic cause
    Not found exclusively with delirium

ANXIETY DISORDERS

Warning: Many mentally ill patients have anxiety symptoms as a part of their overall complaints. It is important not to let anxiety symptoms, which may be presenting complaints of many patients, obscure underlying diagnoses that may be more important for diagnosis and treatment. In this regard, be especially alert for the presence of depressive disease and substance abuse disorders.

Generalized Anxiety Disorder

These patients chronically seem unreasonably worried about multiple life circumstances. There is considerable disagreement as to the prevalence of this condition. Some authorities believe that it affects as many as 5% of the general population; others hold that it is often misdiagnosed when another, more specific anxiety disorder or some other Axis I or Axis II disorder is responsible for the patient's symptoms. When present, it usually starts in early adulthood; women are affected about twice as often as men. It may be encountered especially in the practices of internists and general practitioners.

Abbreviated Criteria for Generalized Anxiety Disorder

    Excessive, unrealistic worry about two or more life circumstances not related
        to the focus of any other Axis I mental disorder
    Occurs at times other than when patient has a mood disorder or psychosis

At least six of these symptoms are frequently present
  Tremor
  Muscle aching or tension
  Restlessness
  Fatigue
  Smothering sensation or shortness of breath
  Palpitations or rapid heartbeat
  Sweating
  Dry mouth
  Dizziness
  Abdominal symptoms such as diarrhea or nausea
  Chills or flushing
  Frequent urination
  Trouble swallowing or lump in throat
  Feels on edge
  Exaggerated startle response
  Trouble concentrating
  Insomnia
  Irritability

Panic Disorder

In this well-defined disorder, patients experience severe episodes of anxiety without identifiable cause. These occur frequently (weekly or more often) and usually last an hour or more. Panic disorder affects perhaps 2% of all adults; it may be somewhat more common in women than in men. It usually develops in young adults, although it can start at any age. Panic disorder has a strong genetic component. It is often associated with agoraphobia.

Abbreviated Criteria for Panic Disorder

  A month of repeated attacks (or the fear that one will be repeated) that
    are unexpected and not triggered by stage fright
  No organic cause can be established
  The patient reports at least four of these symptoms:
    Smothering sensation or shortness of breath
    Dizziness or faintness
    Palpitations or rapid heartbeat
    Tremor
    Sweating
    Choking
    Nausea or other gastrointestinal distress
    Depersonalization
    Numbness or tingling of extremities or around mouth
    Chills or flushes
    Chest pain
    Fear of dying
    Fear of losing control or losing mind

Agoraphobia

This term originally meant "fear of the marketplace," but it now comprises fears of being any place where escape might be difficult or help
might not be available. This results in the patient being unable to leave
home, or needing a companion to do so, or suffering some degree of
discomfort when away from home. Relatively uncommon (perhaps 1
in 200 adults), agoraphobia is more common in women. Often it begins early in life following a panic attack or a traumatic event. Most
patients with agoraphobia also have panic attacks.

Abbreviated Criteria for Agoraphobia

Fear of being in a situation from which the patient could not escape (or
where help might not be available) should symptoms develop, for examples, loss of bladder control, vomiting spells, dizziness, panic attacks
As a result of this fear, patient restricts travel, must have a companion when
traveling, or endures intense anxiety when traveling

Obsessive Compulsive Disorder

This well-studied disorder begins in the teens or twenties and often persists
lifelong. It is characterized by ideas or impulses that come unbidden into the
patient's awareness and is accompanied by anxiety or dread. These feelings are
experienced as foreign ("ego-alien"), silly, or irrational, and the patient tries to
resist having them. The main patterns include handwashing or cleaning and
compulsive checking to be sure that some action (such as turning off the stove)
has in fact been accomplished. Symptoms of depression are common.

Abbreviated Criteria for Obsessive Compulsive Disorder

The patient has distressing obsessions or compulsions (or both) that take
more than an hour per day or that significantly interfere with the pa-
tient's life
For obsessions, all four of
Recurrent thoughts or impulses are perceived by patient as intrusive and
senseless
The patient tries to resist or counteract these thoughts
They are seen as the product of the patient's own mind
The content of the thoughts is not related to any other major (Axis I)
disorder
For compulsions, all three of
Intentional, purposeful, repetitive actions made in ritualistic fashion or
as a response to obsessions
This behavior is meant to counteract some dreaded situation, but it is
not a reasonable resolution
The patient has insight into unreasonableness of this behavior

Anorexia Nervosa

These patients feel they are overweight when they are not. As a result, they severely limit food intake to the point of severe weight loss, malnutrition, and the cessation of normal menses. They may abuse diuretics and laxatives; sometimes they voluntarily vomit to maintain low weight. Severe cases can lead to death. This disorder is relatively common among young females (up to 1%); it is much less common among males.

Abbreviated Criteria for Anorexia Nervosa

>Persistent low body weight (15% under expectation for age and height)
>Fear of gaining weight or being fat
>Distortion of patient's perception of own body image
>If female, loss of menses for three or more consecutive cycles

Post-traumatic Stress Disorder

This modern term comprises what was formerly called *shellshock* in soldiers, as well as the reactions of civilians to any naturally occurring calamity such as earthquake, airplane crash, or rape. Three major features characterize this syndrome: (1) persistent reliving of the traumatic event through dreams or waking thoughts, (2) avoiding human relationships or reminders of the event, and (3) symptoms of hyperarousal. Development of symptoms may be delayed for weeks or years, and they often fluctuate over time; their severity is usually proportional to the intensity of the traumatic event. The condition is more likely to occur in children, the elderly, and those who are socially isolated.

Abbreviated Criteria for Post-traumatic Stress Disorder

An unusually traumatic event has resulted in the following symptoms for at least 1 month:

1. Repeated reliving of the experience in at least one of these ways:
   Intrusive recollections
   Distressing dreams
   A sudden feeling that the event is recurring
   Severe distress when reminded of event, as on anniversaries
2. Avoidance of trauma-related stimuli or numbing of general responsiveness as shown by at least three of
   Efforts to avoid thinking about the event
   Efforts to avoid situations that remind the patient of the event
   Inability to recall the event
   Loss of interest in activities
   Feeling isolated from other people
   Restriction in ability to love or feel strong emotions
   Patient feels life will be brief or unfulfilled (lack of marriage, job, children)

3. Two or more symptoms of hyperarousal
    Insomnia
    Irritability
    Poor concentration
    Hypervigilance
    Increased startle response
    Patient reacts physiologically when exposed to situations similar to or
      symbolic of trauma

SOMATIZATION DISORDER

Affecting perhaps 1% of adult women (rare in men), this disorder is characterized by multiple somatic complaints. Suspect it in any woman who presents
a complicated or vague history; responds poorly to treatment; is dramatic,
demanding, or seductive; has a family history of personality disorder; was abused
sexually as a child; abuses substances; or has depression with atypical features.
Many of these patients attempt suicide. This diagnosis is often missed, even
by mental health professionals.

Abbreviated Criteria for Somatization Disorder

By age 30, the chronic belief that one has many physical complaints
    At least 13 symptoms from the following list. To score as positive, a symp-
tom must (1) not be accounted for by organic lesion, (2) not occur only with
panic attack, *and* (3) have caused patient to take medicine, see a doctor, or change
life-style.

Gastrointestinal symptoms

1. *Vomiting (other than during pregnancy)*
2. Abdominal pain (other than when menstruating)
3. Nausea (other than motion sickness)
4. Bloating (gassy)
5. Diarrhea
6. Intolerance of (gets sick from) several different foods

Pain symptoms

7. *Pain in extremities*
8. Back pain
9. Joint pain
10. Pain during urination

Cardiopulmonary symptoms

11. Other pain (excluding headaches)
12. *Shortness of breath when not exerting oneself*
13. Palpitations
14. Chest pain
15. Dizziness

Conversion or pseudoneurological symptoms

16. *Amnesia*
17. *Difficulty swallowing*
18. Loss of voice
19. Deafness
20. Double vision
21. Blurred vision
22. Blindness
23. Fainting or loss of consciousness
24. Seizure or convulsion
25. Trouble walking
26. Paralysis or muscle weakness
27. Urinary retention or difficulty urinating

Sexual symptoms for most of life after opportunity for sexual activity begins

28. *Burning in sex organs or rectum (other than during intercourse)*
29. Sexual indifference
30. Pain during intercourse
31. Impotence

Female reproductive symptoms (patient judges them worse than in most women)

32. *Painful menstruation*
33. Irregular menstrual periods
34. Excessive menstrual bleeding
35. Vomiting throughout pregnancy

If all *italic* items are negative, you can assume that the patient does not have somatization disorder, and disregard the other items.

PERSONALITY DISORDERS

DSM-III-R lists some 11 personality disorders (more are waiting in the wings for inclusion), divided into three clusters. Of the 11, 5 have been reasonably well studied and therefore have greater validity than the rest. These five, which will be further described later, are italicized in the following outline:

Cluster A comprises patients who can be described as withdrawn, cold, suspicious, or irrational. Cluster A includes paranoid, *schizoid,* and *schizotypal* personality disorders.

In Cluster B are patients who tend to be dramatic, emotional, and attention-seeking; their moods are labile and often shallow. They often have intense in-terpersonal conflicts. Cluster B includes *antisocial, borderline,* histrionic, and nar-cissistic personality disorders.

Cluster C patients tend to be anxious and tense, often overcontrolled. This cluster includes avoidant, dependent, *obsessive-compulsive,* and passive-aggressive personality disorders.

Schizoid Personality Disorder

Beginning usually in childhood or teens, these patients relate poorly to others and show a restricted emotional range. Typically they are lifelong loners who feel little need to associate with other people. Thus, they appear unsociable, cold, and seclusive. They may succeed at jobs so solitary that others find them difficult to tolerate. These patients may daydream excessively, become attached to animals, and often do not marry. However, they do retain contact with reality. Although they themselves may develop schizophrenia, their relatives are not at increased risk for that disease.

Abbreviated Criteria for Schizoid Personality Disorder

Beginning by early adult life, an enduring indifference to social relationships and restricted emotional range as shown by at least four of

Rejects close relationships, including family
Prefers solitary activities
Doesn't experience strong emotions such as love, hate, or joy
Little sexual desire for others
Indifferent to praise and criticism
No more than one close friend or confidant, other than close relatives
Constricted range of affect

Schizotypal Personality Disorder

Because they have magical thinking, ideas of reference, illusions, or unusual mannerisms or dress, these patient can seem quite odd. Their relatives are at increased risk for schizophrenia, and they themselves may eventually become schizophrenic. Although they may get along poorly with others and sometimes decompensate under stress, many marry and work despite their odd behavior.

Abbreviated Criteria for Schizotypal Personality Disorder

Beginning by early adult life, poor interpersonal relations and peculiar appearance, behavior, and ideas as shown by five or more of

Ideas of reference (not delusional)
Marked anxiety in social situations
Behavior influenced by odd beliefs or magical thinking (e.g., superstitions)
Unusual perceptions (*"I felt like General Schwarzkopf was right there in the room with me"*)
Odd behavior or appearance (*e.g., talking to self*)
No more than one close friend or confidant, other than close relatives
Odd speech (vague, excessively abstract, impoverished)
Affect that is inappropriate to subject or constricted in range (*e.g., silly, aloof, unresponsive*)
Suspiciousness or persecutory ideas

Antisocial Personality Disorder

Although these patients often seem charming personally, from an early age (before 15) they cannot follow society's rules. This behavior affects nearly every life area. There may be substance abuse, fighting, lying, and criminal behavior of any conceivable sort: theft, violence, confidence schemes, and child and spouse abuse. These patients may glibly claim to have guilt feelings, but they do not appear to feel genuine remorse for their behavior. Although they may complain of multiple somatic problems and will occasionally make suicide attempts, the manipulative nature of all their interactions with others makes it difficult to decide whether their complaints are genuine.

It is important not to make this diagnosis if antisocial behavior occurs only in the context of substance abuse. Although these patients often have a childhood marked by incorrigibility, delinquency, and such school problems as truancy, fewer than half the children with such a background eventually develop the full adult syndrome. Therefore, this diagnosis should never be made before age 18.

Abbreviated Criteria for Antisocial Personality Disorder

Conduct disorder before age 15 as shown by history of three or more of

Frequent truancy
Runaway from parents overnight at least twice (once if returned)
Often started fights
Used a weapon more than once
Forced sex upon someone
Tortured animals
Physical cruelty to people
Deliberately destroyed property of others (except fire-setting)
Deliberately set fires
Often lied (except to avoid abuse)
Theft more than once
Robbery more than once

Since age 15, chronic antisocial behavior as shown by at least four of

Lack of sustained work effort as shown by any of
   Unemployed 6 months in 5 years
   Repeated absences from work not due to illness
   Quit jobs without realistic plans for other work
Repeated criminal behavior, whether arrested or not
Repeated physical fights or assaults
Repeatedly defaults on debts or financial obligations
Lack of planning as shown by either of
   Aimless wandering without a job
   No fixed abode for a month or more
Repeated lying, use of aliases, or conning others

Recklessness regarding safety of self or others
Irresponsible parenting, as shown by any of
   Patient's child is malnourished
   Child's illness is due to lack of adequate hygiene
   Failure to obtain medical care for seriously ill child
   Child must depend on others for food and shelter
   Child is left unattended
   Squanders money needed for household expenses
Lacks remorse for own injurious behavior

Borderline Personality Disorder

Borderline patients often appear to be in a crisis of mood, behavior, or interpersonal relationship. Often feeling empty and bored themselves, they attach
themselves strongly to others and then become intensely angry or hostile when
they believe that they are being ignored or mistreated by those upon whom
they feel dependent. They may impulsively try to harm or mutilate themselves.
Although borderline patients may experience brief psychotic episodes, these
episodes so quickly resolve that they are seldom confused with the endogenous
psychoses. Intense, rapid mood swings, impulsivity, and unstable interpersonal
relationships make it difficult for borderline patients to achieve their full potential socially, at work, or in school.

   Warning: Borderline personality disorder is a diagnosis frequently applied
to patients who have other disorders that are more important from the stand-
point of treatment. In the 1990s it may still be the most overdiagnosed condition in DSM-III-R.

Abbreviated Criteria for Borderline Personality Disorder

   Beginning by early adulthood, a pattern of instability as shown by at least
five of

   Unstable relationships that alternate between idealization and devaluation
   Self-damaging impulsiveness in at least two areas such as binge eating, reck-
      less driving, sex, or spending
   Marked, brief shifts of mood to anxiety, depression, or irritability
   Inappropriate, intense anger or lack of control of anger
   Recurrent self-mutilation or suicide thoughts or behavior
   Identity disturbance of two sorts: career choice or long-term goals, friends
      desired, self-image, sexual orientation, or values
   Chronic feelings of boredom or emptiness
   Efforts to avoid real or imagined abandonment

Obsessive Compulsive Personality Disorder

Lifelong, these patients tend to be rigid and perfectionistic, often to the point
that their resulting indecisiveness, preoccupation with detail, scrupulosity, and
insistence on doing things their way interfere with their effectiveness in work

or social situations. They may have trouble expressing affection; often, they seem quite depressed, and this depression may wax and wane, sometimes to the point that it becomes severe enough to drive them into treatment. Sometimes these people are stingy; they may be savers, refusing to throw away even worthless objects they no longer need.

Abbreviated Criteria for Obsessive Compulsive Personality Disorder

Beginning early, a pattern of rigidity and perfectionism as shown by five or more of

Perfectionism that interferes with a task
Preoccupation with details ("can't see the forest for the trees")
Insists that others do things the patient's way
Workaholism
Can't make decisions
Overly conscientious or scrupulous
Can't show affection
Stingy with time or money
Saves worthless items of no value

Appendix C:
Sample Interview

INTERVIEWER: *(Shakes hands with patient, a 59-year-old, white male who has just entered the room)* I want to thank you for agreeing to be interviewed on tape.

PATIENT: I'm glad to help you out.

INTERVIEWER: *(Motions toward chair)* A lot of the questions I'll be asking you've heard before. If there is anything you don't feel comfortable with, just say so and we'll go on to something else.

PATIENT: I will.

INTERVIEWER: Do you mind if I make a note or two?

PATIENT: Hey, we're being recorded!

The question about notes seems unnecessary, but old habits die hard!

INTERVIEWER: That's fine, then. First, could you tell me what sort of difficulty you've had that has brought you here.

PATIENT: Well, I've had depression for about—I guess about 3 months or more and then I got this suicidal feeling. I'd had it earlier and when it came back again, Dr. R_____ decided that I should come back into the hospital for further treatment. *(Pauses)*

INTERVIEWER: So you've had these problems before.

PATIENT: I've had these problems for about 39 years. *(Pauses)*

INTERVIEWER: Please tell me about them.

Two open-ended requests have been needed to tell the patient that more description is wanted. After this point, the patient spontaneously speaks at greater length.

PATIENT: Well, when I was 20, I was in a stressful situation where I was ordered to kill innocent women and children in Korea and I couldn't do this and that's the last thing I remembered for almost 8 months before I came around in a hospital. That's when I noticed the voices.

INTERVIEWER: What were they like?

At this point there are two areas of clinical interest that comprise three complaints. They are psychosis (hallucinations) and mood disorder (depression and suicide behavior). The interviewer chooses to follow up the one that is currently under discussion. but will later return to the area of depression.

PATIENT: First, they were very frightening because they were voices that were threatening to kill me. And it took me time and therapy to realize that possibly it was these women and children, in this village that we were ordered to destroy, saying that I should have tried to protect them. But it was an order which had come down from Army Intelligence. They said that there were Communist sympathizers in the village and they couldn't find out who they were, so the order was to destroy the village and kill everyone in it.

INTERVIEWER: So the voices that you hear are the voices of those women and children?

The interviewer asks a clarifying question. It is the first closed-ended question of the interview.

PATIENT: I think so. It's the best I've been able to work out through therapy. I had hypnosis and everything, too.

INTERVIEWER: Can you describe the voices any further?

The interviewer evidently feels that two areas of clinical interest are enough, and begins to explore the specifics of psychosis. Many interviewers would allow this patient more time for free speech.

PATIENT: They're generally quite clear. They're not garbled, and they feel like they're just in my head. They're not coming from outside.

INTERVIEWER: Does it seem to you that there are really people talking, or could it be your own thoughts?

PATIENT: It could be my own thoughts, feeling guilt about not trying to stop that massacre. But I couldn't have done much alone, anyway, I'm sure. I would have had my whole outfit turned on me if I'd have tried to do that.

INTERVIEWER: And do these voices talk to you in complete sentences?

PATIENT: Well, they say the same thing over again: "You're no good—I'm going to kill you." That's exactly what they say. It never changes.

INTERVIEWER: I see. Now, you said that you had been feeling guilty. Can you tell me about that?

Even though there are many areas of fact still unexplored, the interviewer makes a direct request for feelings.

PATIENT: Well, I did feel at first quite a bit of guilt. But, like many doctors have told me, there was nothing I could do. I would have probably either been killed by my own men or at least [been] put under court martial for disobeying a direct order in time of war.

INTERVIEWER: Did you feel depressed at that time, also?

Now, the second area of clinical interest.

PATIENT: Yes. But not serious depression, not until quite a few years later I started having depression.

INTERVIEWER: Tell me about that.

PATIENT: Well, it was probably about in 1963 that the depression started settling in. And at first it wasn't real deep depression, it was just sort of mild; I could function all right. But then at times I couldn't even talk about it. I got better under medication for a while. And I had shock treatments. They seemed to help me for a while, for a couple of years.

INTERVIEWER: When was it you had the shock treatments?

PATIENT: Well, I had the first ones while I was still in the isolation room, after I got back from Korea. They took me out for shock treatments after I wasn't responding to medication. I guess coming around where I was aware of what was going on around me.

INTERVIEWER: Was it the shock treatment that did bring you around at that time?

PATIENT: I think it had a lot to do with it because they had tried, they said, everything they could but they decided in the end that I'd have to have some shock treatments. And right then I was judged incompetent, so it was just a matter of the doctors signing the forms.

INTERVIEWER: Did you have shock treatments later than that, also?

The interviewer is trying to get a clear idea of the chronology of this patient's illness.

PATIENT: Yeah, I had them in a private sanitarium in Tennessee. I was there for about 4 months and I had shock treatments for about 3 of those months—both deep insulin and electric.

INTERVIEWER: And when would that have been?

PATIENT: That was about in the early 1960s.

INTERVIEWER: What symptoms were you having at that time?

PATIENT: Well, I was just in deep depression all the time. Couldn't get myself to eat properly or sleep properly, or even take care of myself properly. Neglected my personal hygiene, and they thought that the medication wasn't enough so they decided on the shock treatments.

INTERVIEWER: And did the shock treatments improve you then, also?

Further questions about depressive symptoms are left for later.

PATIENT: For a couple of years they did.

INTERVIEWER: Now—through all of this what was the relationship of the voices with the depression?

This interviewer often uses "Now," with a slight pause, to indicate the transition to a new topic.

PATIENT: Well, the voices went away, too, after the shock treatments. I under-stand that sometimes it does help even in certain schizophrenic cases. Is that correct?

INTERVIEWER: Yes, it can happen that way sometimes. Did the voices also go away for a couple of years?

The interviewer elects to respond briefly to this direct request for information, then move quickly on.

PATIENT: Maybe for 4 or 5 months, but they came back. But then I got an in-crease in my medication and I got over them again. So I haven't had them constantly.

INTERVIEWER: Now, have you had other problems besides the voices and depres-sion and suicidal ideas or attempts? Any other emotional difficulties?

Fishing for other problems.

PATIENT: Well, at one time I had this problem with the law. I was very self-destructive and I went out and opened all these checking accounts in St. Louis and I overdrew all of them purposely to get myself in trouble with the law. I thought I should be persecuted for my past behavior in Korea.

INTERVIEWER: You felt so guilty that you thought you should be punished? So you opened a lot of checking accounts and overdrew them on purpose?

Summary statement, to ensure that the interviewer has understood.

PATIENT: Yes. I felt that I should be arrested, and I was. Once I was sent to a reformatory in Wisconsin for about a year. But they had me in psychiatric care there, too.

INTERVIEWER: What year would that have been?

PATIENT: It must have been about '58.

INTERVIEWER: So, some years after you got out of Korea.

PATIENT: Right. But I constantly had this feeling of guilt for years. I don't have it now.

INTERVIEWER: I see.

PATIENT: But I did then, and I was trying to destroy myself in some way or perse-cute myself.

INTERVIEWER: Were you feeling very depressed at that time?

PATIENT: Not so depressed, as just hearing the voices. I think the fact that I was able to go and cash the checks in different bank branches made them think that I wasn't really in depression. They thought that someone would have recog-nized something wrong with me if I'd been in severe depression—my head hanging down, or slow speech, maybe—something.

INTERVIEWER: So they felt that you were doing this not because you were depressed but for some other reason. And the other reason was . . . .

PATIENT: Was that scene in Korea.

INTERVIEWER: I see. Did the authorities think that you just wanted money?

PATIENT: I don't think so, because I paid it all back. And then in New York—I was doing this in New York at a later time—they sent me to an institution for the criminally insane.

INTERVIEWER: And again was it because you wanted to be punished?

PATIENT: *(Nods)*

INTERVIEWER: You must have been feeling very guilty.

Interviewer shows empathy by predicting the patient's emotion under the circumstances.

PATIENT: Yes. I'm just trying to be honest with you, even the distasteful parts of this.

INTERVIEWER: I very much appreciate it. I can see that it's hard for you, but it's really important to try to get all of the information.

Interviewer builds rapport by acknowledging the difficulty the patient has tried to surmount.

PATIENT: I know it is.

INTERVIEWER: Right. Well, now, was there any other sort of legal problem?

PATIENT: No.

INTERVIEWER: Any other emotional problems of any kind?

PATIENT: No. Just the voices and the depression. And it would get to the point, as I said, that I couldn't eat properly, I couldn't sleep properly, I was skipping my medicine at times.

INTERVIEWER: Did the voices tell you to skip medicine?

PATIENT: No.

The interviewer never does find out why the patient skipped his medication. This is an error.

INTERVIEWER: Did the voices tell you to do anything else that you went ahead and did?

PATIENT: No. They just say the same thing over and over again—that I'm no good and they're going to kill me.

INTERVIEWER: Uh-huh. Now—let me ask you some questions about how you've been feeling just recently. Have the depressions been much worse?

PATIENT: Yeah, in the last 3 months it got worse.

INTERVIEWER: Has anything happened to make it worse?

PATIENT: Nothing other than being separated from my wife. I've felt bad about that—but we've been separated for a number of years now.

INTERVIEWER: So that's nothing new?

PATIENT: *(Shakes head)* We've gone back and we've tried to work things out. I think my gambling got in the way of that. I was involved too far in gambling in recent years.

INTERVIEWER: Ah! So gambling has been a problem between you and your wife. Tell me about the gambling.

Yet another new topic, 15 minutes into the interview.

PATIENT: At first it was all right. I could just go to a casino, play for 1 or 2 hours, and enjoy myself. And if I was winning I could walk away with the winnings. But then it got so that I just played until I lost everything, even if I had won a fair amount of money sometimes.

INTERVIEWER: How much would that be?

PATIENT: Maybe a couple of thousand dollars.

INTERVIEWER: And you'd stay until you lost it all?

PATIENT: Yeah.

INTERVIEWER: How long has the gambling gone on?

PATIENT: Well, real bad for about 6 years, I guess.

INTERVIEWER: But before then, you hadn't been a gambler.

A question asked in the negative: not good form.

PATIENT: I didn't even gamble until I was about 40.

INTERVIEWER: Uh-huh. What got you interested in it, do you think?

PATIENT: Well, we lived in California and I worked up at Lake Tahoe in a casino for part of the time. I did bookkeeping and accounting there. I should have known the pitfalls of gambling, but I didn't use my judgment right.

INTERVIEWER: Did you get a thrill out of gambling?

PATIENT: At first I did, but then later it was—I think it was just a self-destructive thing.

INTERVIEWER: Did the voices tell you anything about gambling?

PATIENT: No.

INTERVIEWER: How much do you think you've lost gambling, in total?

PATIENT: Oh, what I've actually lost wouldn't be much to a lot of people—maybe about $20,000—but to me that was a lot.

INTERVIEWER: Sounds like a lot of money to me. And that really made your wife mad. When did she leave you?

Interviewer identifies with patient's ideas of cost, to help solidify rapport, and at the same time turns the conversation in another direction.

PATIENT: Well, we separated and she stayed in Iowa. But originally we had been separated off and on for about 6 years. But the last couple of years it's been pretty permanent. I think that if I stopped gambling for a couple of years she'd take me back, because she hasn't tried to divorce me.

INTERVIEWER: How recently have you gambled?

PATIENT: Well, when I left the hospital this last time, and I went to—first I had these suicidal feelings and I had signed this paper that I wouldn't attempt suicide in the hospital, so I went to San Francisco and I couldn't buy a gun in a store because of the waiting period and because of the fact that I'm a mental patient. So I went over to Mission Street and found out from two fellows that I could get a used gun from someone, and bought that and went to Reno. At first I just went to my room. I didn't gamble at all at first. And I was thinking about shooting myself, but I never did. I started gambling, and then one morning I just took the gun and put it in a paper sack and dropped it in the trash, because I decided I wasn't going to commit suicide. But I lost everything I had, which was about $600.

INTERVIEWER: And that was when?

PATIENT: Just about, let's see, oh, about 4 weeks ago.

INTERVIEWER: Have you ever had any treatment for gambling?

PATIENT: I've gone to Gamblers Anonymous a few times, but not enough to help me, I guess.

INTERVIEWER: It hasn't been helpful, so far?

PATIENT: Well, I haven't given it up. I don't think I've given it enough opportunity to help me. I just went sporadically. I should have gone every day.

INTERVIEWER: That would be helpful, wouldn't it? Now—a moment ago you mentioned suicide. Could we talk about that a bit?

The transition is made reflecting back to the patient's own words.

PATIENT: I've made two attempts that they said I almost died from. One was an overdose of Thorazine. They found me in a public phone booth unconscious. I was in a coma for over a week.

INTERVIEWER: Over a week? Wow!

It took only four suitably inflected words to show the interviewer's recognition that the patient had said something that was both significant and affect-laden, and to encourage the patient to continue.

PATIENT: They thought I was going to die.

INTERVIEWER: Had you taken something other than Thorazine?

PATIENT: No, but I had taken—they figure from the bottle—maybe about 10,000 milligrams at one time.

INTERVIEWER: That's quite a lot. Do you remember when you took it?

PATIENT: I remember I was having crying spells and things like that.

INTERVIEWER: What was in your mind when you took it?

This and the next question are attempts to ascertain psychological seriousness of the attempt.

PATIENT: That I should be dead. That I didn't have any right to live.

INTERVIEWER: You felt that you deserved to die and you were really trying to kill yourself then?

PATIENT: *(Nods)*

INTERVIEWER: This was not just a matter of crying for help?

PATIENT: No. I went through some of those periods. It wasn't that. The other serious suicide was when I was in a hotel room one night and I bought these razor blades and I was crying uncontrollably. I cut up both arms pretty bad with razor blades. The maid found me the next morning.

INTERVIEWER: Was there a lot of blood?

The interviewer is looking for indications of medical seriousness.

PATIENT: Well, they said it wasn't as bad as it could have been. They might have found me dead but the arms had clotted some by morning.

INTERVIEWER: Do you recall how you felt when you were cutting your arms?

PATIENT: It's kind of confusing to me. I had just broken up with this girl and I was feeling that I had miserably failed again in my life, so I didn't think I deserved to live.

INTERVIEWER: How did you feel the next morning when you discovered that you hadn't succeeded?

PATIENT: I was depressed because I hadn't.

INTERVIEWER: Did you wish you were dead?

PATIENT: Yeah.

INTERVIEWER: And when you woke up after the overdose of Thorazine—how did you feel then?

PATIENT: For a while I wished I was dead. They had me on a locked ward under observation.

From this the interviewer can conclude that the patient had made two attempts that were at least psychologically serious.

INTERVIEWER: You must have been hospitalized a fair number of times.

PATIENT: Yes, quite a few times—about maybe 25 to 30 times.

INTERVIEWER: Uh-huh. And you've received a number of different kinds of treatments.

PATIENT: Right.

INTERVIEWER: Besides the shock treatment, what else has helped you?

PATIENT: Just good therapy. Talking out things in a group or individually with a doctor. I had a lot of individual treatment first and then I attended groups. These have helped over the years.

INTERVIEWER: So talking helps. What about medications?

PATIENT: Well, I've been on quite a few—Thorazine, Mellaril, and then of course I have been on Trilafon quite awhile; Sinequan and Elavil. Some others I don't remember, although my memory is generally pretty sharp.

INTERVIEWER: Have any of the medicines helped more than others?

PATIENT: Well, they had me on so much Thorazine at first I didn't function very well. But after they got me on lighter doses I began to take part in therapy more.

INTERVIEWER: How much Trilafon do you take now?

PATIENT: I think. . .16 milligrams twice a day.

INTERVIEWER: Did any medicine help your depression?

PATIENT: Well, the Sinequan and the Elavil were working pretty well until a few years ago, I guess. Then they found out the Elavil wasn't working as well as it should anymore, and that I'd have to change.

INTERVIEWER: Do you remember what the maximum dose of Elavil was?

This is to ascertain whether patient was prescribed an adequate dose, which he was.

PATIENT: Yeah. It was 300 milligrams a day.

INTERVIEWER: And were you taking Trilafon at that time also?

PATIENT: No. I don't think so.

INTERVIEWER: Have you ever taken a medicine called lithium?

PATIENT: No.

INTERVIEWER: Have you ever taken a medicine that meant that you had to be on a special diet—when you couldn't eat cheese and some other things?

Using a readily identified dietary precaution, the interviewer explores to see whether the patient has ever taken monoamine oxidase inhibitors, a type of antidepressant.

PATIENT: No.

INTERVIEWER: Now—let me ask you about when you feel depressed. Do you have trouble with your sleep then?

Interviewer wants to establish symptoms to subtype the depression. This and the next five questions look for vegetative symptoms of melancholia. These questions have been deferred for many minutes, while gambling and suicide were being explored.

PATIENT: The way it's working now is, I generally sleep too much.

INTERVIEWER: So you sleep excessively when you're depressed?

PATIENT: *(Nods)*

INTERVIEWER: Is that even if you're on medication or not on medication?

PATIENT: Well, when I'm on medication it's not quite as prevalent as it is when I'm off it.

INTERVIEWER: Have you had trouble with your appetite when you're depressed?

PATIENT: Yes. A lot of the time I don't feel like eating.

INTERVIEWER: Does your weight change?

PATIENT: I've lost, over the last 3 months, close to 20 pounds.

INTERVIEWER: Do you feel any better in the morning or in the evening, or does it make a difference?

PATIENT: I generally feel better in the evening. It takes a while for me to get going in the morning.

INTERVIEWER: Do you feel better when you're with people you like?

PATIENT: Oh, yes. Definitely. When I'm in the hospital I always try to make at least one close friend that I can talk with.

INTERVIEWER: You're a pretty friendly, sociable sort of person, are you?

PATIENT: Yes.

INTERVIEWER: Were you that way as a young man also?

This question searches for evidence that bears on premorbid personality.

PATIENT: More so. In fact, I was in the Boy Scouts and I became an Eagle Scout.

INTERVIEWER: Did you really!

This emphatic comment serves as recognition of an achievement and a stimulus for more disclosure of the patient's background.

PATIENT: Yeah. And I was a counselor in their camps one summer just before I went in the service.

INTERVIEWER: Eagle Scout is quite an accomplishment. You have to earn a lot of merit badges for that!

PATIENT: Yeah, I did. And I worked a job in high school after school and on Saturdays. I came from a poor family—my father was an alcoholic—so my mother had to divorce him because of his violence and, ah, the fact that he was sleeping with other women.

INTERVIEWER: So you had a lot of troubles when you were growing up. I want to ask you more about your background in a couple of minutes, but first I want to finish with some of the symptoms that you might have had. Did you ever have the opposite of being depressed? Feeling too good or too happy?

This rather long speech tells the patient that the material seems important to the interviewer, while delaying its exploration until the current line of investigation can be concluded. (The interviewer also appears to miss the point about the father's violence, and never inquires further about it.)

PATIENT: No.

INTERVIEWER: So manic episodes were never a problem for you.

PATIENT: No, sir, they've checked me out thoroughly a number of times.

INTERVIEWER: And speaking of symptoms, besides the voices, did you ever see things that other people couldn't see?

PATIENT: I used to see these women and children. Then the last time I was here I even thought my wife was dead for a few days.

INTERVIEWER: Did you really believe your wife was dead?

PATIENT: Yes.

INTERVIEWER: I mean you strongly believed that she was dead? If I had told you, "No, your wife isn't dead," you wouldn't have believed me?

The interviewer wants to make sure that the patient's belief was of delusional intensity, which it seems to be.

PATIENT: No, I had to get ahold of her again before I'd believe it.

INTERVIEWER: Then did you believe it?

PATIENT: Yeah.

INTERVIEWER: And this was the last time you were here?

PATIENT: Yes, sir.

INTERVIEWER: That was how long ago?

PATIENT: Well, that was a little over a month ago, I guess.

INTERVIEWER: Uh-huh. Have you had other false beliefs like that?

PATIENT: No. *(Sighs)* Except when I told you about writing these checks?

INTERVIEWER: Yes.

PATIENT: I really convinced myself that I had the money in the bank. I guess that's why they were so unhesitant about cashing them for me in different banks.

INTERVIEWER: You thought that you had the money?

PATIENT: But underneath it all was that drive to destroy myself.

INTERVIEWER: Uh-huh. Do you remember experiencing it as a drive to destroy yourself or, at the time, do you think it seemed more like "Wow, I'm a rich man. I've got lots of money!"

This question is not clear. Understandably, the patient does not respond with the information sought by the interviewer, who then must clarify.

PATIENT: No, because I didn't write—I mean it wasn't that big a sum of money. It was just enough to get in trouble over with.

INTERVIEWER: So at the time you thought that you were doing it to try to get yourself in trouble?

PATIENT: *(Nods)*

INTERVIEWER: Okay. Have there been any other things you believed at the time that turned out not to be so?

PATIENT: No, sir.

INTERVIEWER: Felt that people were spying on you?

PATIENT: Oh, I've felt that people were talking about me on jobs, and it got where I thought I was not being paid properly and I was doing other people's work for them. But 6 years ago the doctors told me that I should try to stop working because I just kept ending up in the hospital.

INTERVIEWER: I see.

PATIENT: So I did quit 6 years ago. I didn't have that great a job, really. I had gotten down to washing dishes by then.

INTERVIEWER: You started out as an accountant and you gradually moved down to washing dishes. How do you feel about that?

PATIENT: I just feel that I did the right thing. I tried to work. I wanted to pay my taxes like everybody else, be a part of society.

INTERVIEWER: You really have a good attitude about it. I think more people would do well if they had that kind of feeling.

By praising his attitude, the interviewer softens any underlying feelings of shame the patient might not be willing to express.

PATIENT: Well, it was hard for me to stop. But I realized the fact that it was all right. They had me put on some type of Social Security disability, too.

INTERVIEWER: I see. Have you been on Social Security disability ever since?

PATIENT: For about 6 years. They've never called me for an examination.

INTERVIEWER: How much do you get?

PATIENT: A little over $500 a month from Social Security, and I'm 100% service-connected.

INTERVIEWER: So you get that also?

PATIENT: My wife gets $700 a month now. She gets her checks separately since we've been separated.

INTERVIEWER: So how much does this leave you per month then, all things considered?

PATIENT: A little over $900 a month from the service-connected disability and about $510 from the Social Security disability.

INTERVIEWER: And so the total that you get. . . .

The interviewer lets the patient do the figuring, in part as a test of math ability.

PATIENT: A little over $1,400 for myself.

INTERVIEWER: And is that enough for you to get by on then?

PATIENT: Oh, it's more than enough. If I didn't gamble, I'd have money saved in the bank.

INTERVIEWER: I see. Now—sometimes when people have a gambling problem there's also a problem with alcohol or drugs.

By taking off from leads given by the patient, the interviewer obtains much information without seeming to overdirect the interview.

PATIENT: I never had a problem with it. The fact is that I didn't like it. So I hadn't drank for 25 years. Then about 3 months ago I did drink in Reno, and I got drunk on just a few drinks because of the medication I was on. And I tried to drive my car, and I was arrested for drunk driving, put in jail, and I had to pay a fine.

INTERVIEWER: Was that the only time that you drank? Just that one occasion?

PATIENT: Yeah.

INTERVIEWER: Have you done any drinking since then?

PATIENT: No, sir. And I never will.

INTERVIEWER: And have you ever had any other problems as a result of drinking?

PATIENT: *(Shakes his head at this and subsequent three questions)*

INTERVIEWER: Other legal problems? Or health problems? Or ever have any blackouts when you wake up in the morning and you cannot remember what happened the night before?

Note that the interviewer defines a term that the patient might not know.

PATIENT: No.

INTERVIEWER: Or lost friends? Or got into fights?

PATIENT: No. I never got into a fight in my life.

INTERVIEWER: Or set rules for yourself?

PATIENT: What sort of rules?

INTERVIEWER: Oh, like never drinking before 4 in the afternoon.

The interviewer had tried to use "shorthand" to ask the question about setting rules. An alcoholic patient probably would have understood. Fortunately, when the patient didn't understand, he asked for clarification.

PATIENT: *(Shakes head)* Well, as I said, I saw what my father went through and I didn't want to end up in the same position.

INTERVIEWER: What about experience with street drugs of any kind?

PATIENT: No. Never.

INTERVIEWER: Or ever take too much of the medicines that were prescribed for you by doctors?

PATIENT: No.

INTERVIEWER: Okay. Here's something else I thought of about the depression. Do you notice any pattern to the developing of the depressions? Anything that seems to cause the depression? Or any time of the year that depression seems to come on?

Interviewer is looking for stressors for depression and for seasonal mood disorder. Also, note that the transition is flagged with "Here's something else----"

PATIENT: *(shakes head at first two questions)* Well, sometimes the fall of the year bothers me because, quite a few years before I married my wife I was going with this girl and we were engaged. She was killed in an auto accident before we could be married.

INTERVIEWER: That must have been a very unhappy time, too.

PATIENT: Yes, it was.

INTERVIEWER: How old were you then?

PATIENT: I was about 23 or 24.

INTERVIEWER: So, this would have been after you got out of the service, then?

PATIENT: Right after I got out of the hospital.

INTERVIEWER: And the accident that she was in — were you with her at the time?

PATIENT: No. She was with a girlfriend of hers and they were driving home. I don't know if her girlfriend had been drinking, or what, but they ran into the back end of a platform truck, at quite a speed, I guess, and just sheared the top off the car.

INTERVIEWER: What effect did this have on you?

PATIENT: I ended up in the hospital.

INTERVIEWER: You got so upset you were hospitalized. What symptoms did you have?

PATIENT: I did have severe depression then. That one time I did.

INTERVIEWER: And how were you treated?

PATIENT: They gave me some subinsulin treatments. Is that what they're called?

INTERVIEWER: Subcoma insulin treatments. Yes.

This corrects the mistake without impeding the flow of information.

PATIENT: Yeah. I guess they mainly tried to relax me.

INTERVIEWER: Did they help you any?

PATIENT: I got relaxed again after quite a few treatments and in talking to the doctors. I talked to her parents and they were very sympathetic.

INTERVIEWER: After that, how long was it before you got married to your wife?

PATIENT: I married my wife in 1963.

INTERVIEWER: So that was about 10 years later.

PATIENT: *(Nods)*

INTERVIEWER: And did you date other women during that time?

PATIENT: Nothing serious. Just a movie or dancing or casual dinner.

INTERVIEWER: What about your sexual functioning during all of that time?

No introductory comments, no embarrassment; the interviewer just jumps into the subject of sex, and the patient follows right along.

PATIENT: I haven't had any sex drive for about 15 years. Some doctors say it may be all the heavy medications I've taken over a period of time.

INTERVIEWER: What about when you were a younger man?

PATIENT: I was fairly normal then.

INTERVIEWER: Did you have any problems?

PATIENT: I never had sex when I was a young man. I mean, when I was in Boy Scouts and stuff. I never got involved in it until after I was out of the service.

INTERVIEWER: Uh-huh. And did you ever have any problems with sex—getting an erection or maintaining one?

PATIENT: Oh, I had a little trouble toward the end, but that was mainly I was losing my sex drive, I guess.

INTERVIEWER: I understand. What about children?

PATIENT: My wife had four from her first marriage. She was unable to have any when I married her. I deliberately married a woman who couldn't have any because the doctors had told me that it would be better not to have children. They didn't think my nervous system could handle that.

INTERVIEWER: Now—let's jump back in time for a bit. I'd like to find out about when you were growing up and your childhood.

A sympathetic acknowledgment of this significant statement would have been appropriate here. The interviewer does mark an abrupt transition.

PATIENT: Well, as I said, even despite my father being an alcoholic, he had responsible jobs. He was a supervisor of mechanics in a car dealership in St. Louis.

INTERVIEWER: Is that where you were born?

PATIENT: Yes. St. Louis.

INTERVIEWER: And were you the oldest child?

PATIENT: No. I was right in the middle. I had two older sisters and two younger; I didn't have any brothers.

INTERVIEWER: So you were the only boy. How was that?

PATIENT: It wasn't bad. My second-to-the-oldest sister was a tomboy, so we played football and baseball together.

INTERVIEWER: Did your mom work outside the home?

PATIENT: Yeah. She had to, to provide a living once my dad became an alcoholic because he just drank it all up.

INTERVIEWER: What kind of work did she do?

PATIENT: At first she did housework, and then the only wealthy relatives I had told her that they would put her through school so she could get a better job. So she became an RN, after going to school for 4 years, working a job on the side. She was a very strong woman.

INTERVIEWER: She must have been. Did she have any time for you?

PATIENT: Yes, she made sure that she took us to church and Sunday School. She always tried to get off for school activities.

INTERVIEWER: So she gave you pretty good parenting?

PATIENT: Yes, she did.

INTERVIEWER: What religion were you?

PATIENT: Baptist. Conservative.

INTERVIEWER: Are you still?

PATIENT: No, I smoke now and I've been gambling, so I'm not a very good conservative Baptist.

INTERVIEWER: Do you go to church at all?

PATIENT: At home I've been going to an American Baptist church.

INTERVIEWER: How about your health when you were a kid?

PATIENT: It was good.

INTERVIEWER: You didn't have to be taken to doctors much? Or have any operations? Or injuries?

PATIENT: (Shakes head at each question)

INTERVIEWER: As an adult?

PATIENT: I just had this hernia operation while I was still in Germany.

INTERVIEWER: And did you have any other operations ever in your adult life?

PATIENT: (Shakes head no)

INTERVIEWER: Any other medical problems now?

PATIENT: No.

INTERVIEWER: Any allergies?

PATIENT: Just morphine. That's the only thing.

INTERVIEWER: Morphine?

PATIENT: Yeah. I got that in Korea when I got hit once. I had to have morphine until they got the shrapnel out.

INTERVIEWER: You were hit by an exploding grenade or something?

PATIENT: Yes.

INTERVIEWER: Were you knocked unconscious?

PATIENT: No.

INTERVIEWER: You were quite young when you went into the military?

Having obtained the pertinent medical history, the interviewer begins a fairly lengthy inquiry into the personal and social history.

PATIENT: Seventeen. I graduated a year early because I skipped a year in school.

INTERVIEWER: So you were smart in school.

PATIENT: Yeah. I had a 138 IQ, they said, when they tested me for college.

INTERVIEWER: Really! So you must have done quite well in school.

PATIENT: Yes. Math was my best subject. After the Army I got an AA from the University of Missouri.

INTERVIEWER: Great! And you were in the Army for how many years?

PATIENT: 1948 to '51.

INTERVIEWER: And you got out then as a result of the. . . .

PATIENT: Breakdown. I had re-upped. I went just over 3 years, because I had re-upped again for Korea.

INTERVIEWER: What rank did you make?

PATIENT: Just a corporal. I didn't want anything higher than that. I didn't want the responsibility of people's lives.

INTERVIEWER: Did you ever have any kind of problems in the military?

PATIENT: No.

INTERVIEWER: Disciplinary problems or. . . .

PATIENT: No.

INTERVIEWER: Nothing like that. Now—do you live by yourself?

PATIENT: Yes.

INTERVIEWER: In an apartment or what?

PATIENT: No, it was a retirement hotel, but I left there recently. When I lost all my money, I was supposed to go get another place to live, but I ended up in the mission a few nights as I had to have a place to sleep.

INTERVIEWER: Now, you said that you'd worked as an accountant. What's the longest job that you had?

PATIENT: Almost 8 years. I worked up at the lake.

INTERVIEWER: Did you like that pretty well?

PATIENT: There was a lot of stress, but it was well paying.

INTERVIEWER: What about any leisure activities, interests, hobbies, that sort of thing?

PATIENT: I don't have any, anymore. I used to play chess in college.

INTERVIEWER: But you haven't had any interests like that for some time?

PATIENT: No.

INTERVIEWER: Do you like to watch TV or read?

PATIENT: I don't read too much. I watch a little TV, but I don't go to the movies very often because most movies today I wouldn't pay to see. I watch older movies on TV at night.

INTERVIEWER: When you watch a movie on TV, can you keep your mind on it pretty well?

PATIENT: Yes.

INTERVIEWER: Your concentration's pretty good?

PATIENT: Yes, sir.

INTERVIEWER: Do you mind if I test your concentration and memory?

The interviewer manages a smooth transition into the mental status exam.

PATIENT: No.

INTERVIEWER: Let me ask if you remember what the date is today.

Of course, orientation isn't a function of memory, but it does assist in the transition.

PATIENT: It's February 22, 1991.

INTERVIEWER: And the day of the week?

PATIENT: Friday.

INTERVIEWER: Uh-huh. And what is this building called?

PATIENT: *(Correctly identifies the facility and city where it is located)*

INTERVIEWER: Okay. And you've been here for how long now?

PATIENT: I think I came in on the 8th, if I'm not mistaken. So I've been here about 2 weeks.

INTERVIEWER: Let me ask you if you can remember who the president of the country is.

PATIENT: George Bush.

INTERVIEWER: And who was president before him?

PATIENT: Ronald Reagan.

INTERVIEWER: And before him?

PATIENT: Ah — *(hesitates)* — Gerald Ford, I think.

INTERVIEWER: And do you remember before Mr. Ford?

PATIENT: No.

INTERVIEWER: Okay, that's fine. Who's the vice president now?

Even though the previous answer is incomplete, the interviewer apparently senses that the patient needs some encouragement.

PATIENT: I was trying to think of his name and I don't remember. I know Dan something or another.

INTERVIEWER: That's fine. Do you know the governor?

PATIENT: Wilson.

INTERVIEWER: Very good. Now I'd like to ask you to remember three things—a name, a color, and a street address. The name is John Smith, the color is green, and the address is 4550 Scott. Can you repeat those for me now?

PATIENT: John Scott—

INTERVIEWER: *(Interrupting)* John Smith.

The real purpose is to test short-term memory. To do that, the patient must first have the test items straight in his head.

PATIENT: John Smith, and the color is green, 4550—I've forgotten the street already.

INTERVIEWER: Scott.

PATIENT: Scott. That's where I got the Scott from.

INTERVIEWER: Okay, good. Can you subtract seven from one hundred for me, please?

PATIENT: *(Quickly)* 93, 86, 79, 72, 65, 58, 51, 44, 37—

INTERVIEWER: *(Interrupting)* That's terrific! Somebody's asked you to do this recently before, I'll bet.

PATIENT: I've been asked it a lot of times.

INTERVIEWER: You've got it down perfectly.

PATIENT: Math is my favorite subject. Even with the voices I can—you probably know this—it's forced concentration, but I can concentrate on things, even despite the voices.

INTERVIEWER: And, all the time we've been talking the voices. . . .

PATIENT: The voices have been threatening to kill me.

INTERVIEWER: I think it's remarkable that you've been able to concentrate as well as you have. Let me ask you one or two other questions. In what way are an apple and an orange similar?

PATIENT: They're both fruits.

INTERVIEWER: And what is the difference between a child and a dwarf?

PATIENT: Their height. I mean, one is an adult and the other is a child.

INTERVIEWER: Okay. Now, do you recall the three things I asked you to remember?

PATIENT: John Smith, green, 4550 Scott.

INTERVIEWER: Perfect. That's the best anybody's done it for me for weeks. Let me go back and pick up on one other thing that I forgot. You mentioned that your father had an alcohol problem. Did anybody else in the family?

PATIENT: Not that I remember.

INTERVIEWER: No drug or alcohol problems?

PATIENT: *(Shakes head)*

INTERVIEWER: Anybody else, including grandparents, uncles, aunts, cousins, nieces, nephews?

PATIENT: My one niece does. She's an alcoholic.

Note that this piece of information would have been missed if interviewer hadn't asked about specific relatives.

INTERVIEWER: And how old is she?

PATIENT: I guess she's about—she must be about 30, I would guess.

INTERVIEWER: Anyone else in your family who's had any kind of emotional problems, nervous breakdowns, psychosis, schizophrenia, manias, depressions, suicides, suicide attempts, drinking problems, drug problems, criminality? Gambling problems? Addictions of any sort? Compulsions or obsessions?

"Gambling problems" isn't one of the questions this interviewer normally includes in the family history. This material is added because of the patient's own history.

PATIENT: *(Shakes his head at each question)* Not that I know of.

INTERVIEWER: Have *you* had any other compulsive behavior or obsessional thinking? You know, things that you do over and over again even though you know you shouldn't or wished that you could stop?

Many patients don't know the meaning of obsession and compulsion; routinely giving a definition of this (and other difficult terms) often prevents misunderstandings.

PATIENT: There was just this writing out checks and the gambling.

INTERVIEWER: Just those two things?

PATIENT: And I don't even have a checking account now. I never opened one after that.

INTERVIEWER: What about anxieties? Do you have much in the way of anxiety?

PATIENT: I feel uptight a lot of times.

INTERVIEWER: Do you ever get really panicky?

PATIENT: No, that's very unusual.

INTERVIEWER: You don't get feelings like, very fearful that something awful is going to happen to you so that your heart beats fast and you sweat and you can't breathe or feel like you're going to smother?

PATIENT: No, sir.

INTERVIEWER: Anything that you're afraid of? Heights, being closed in, animals, or flying, or anything of that sort?

PATIENT: No.

INTERVIEWER: All right. Let me just summarize what you've told me so far, to see if I've left anything out. You've had a problem with voices for many years, and on and off you've also had depression. There have been some suicide attempts that have at times been associated with your distress over gambling. What little drinking you've done was just recently, but it hasn't been a chronic problem. I wonder if there's anything else that I haven't covered that you think might be of interest or might be of importance in describing your difficulties.

This brief summary checks that the interviewer has uncovered the major themes of this patient's illness.

PATIENT: No, sir. I'm getting rather tired now.

INTERVIEWER: Okay. It's probably time to go back to the ward. I wanted to ask you some more about the gambling, and about the stress you suffered in Korea. But we can cover those issues tomorrow. Let me ask you one other thing now, and that is, are you feeling suicidal now?

PATIENT: No, I'm not suicidal right now.

INTERVIEWER: And how long has it been since you were suicidal?

PATIENT: It's been about 11 or 12 days.

INTERVIEWER: So you're much better since you've been in the hospital?

PATIENT: I'll be all right.

The interviewer has made sure that the patient is well enough to return to the ward unsupervised.

INTERVIEWER: Well, thank you very much for speaking with me.

PATIENT: Thank you.

Appendix D:
Sample Written Report

This is a write-up of the patient interview detailed in Appendix C.

Identifying data: This is the third admission to this facility and approximately the 30th psychiatric hospitalization for a 59-year-old white man who is married but currently separated from his wife.

Chief complaint: "I've had depression for about 3 months or more, and then I got this suicidal feeling."

Informants: Patient's previous chart and patient, who is considered to be quite reliable.

History of the present illness: This patient was well until about the age of 20 when, he states, while serving in the Army in Korea, he was ordered to kill innocent women and children. He blacked out and began to have auditory hallucinations, which have continued for nearly 40 years. These voices are generally quite clear, not garbled, and are generally located inside his own head. Speaking in complete sentences they say, "You're no good—I'm going to kill you." He believes that these are the voices of the women and children he was ordered to kill, but sometimes thinks they could be the result of his own thoughts. Since Korea he has been ill more or less continuously, requiring neuroleptic medication during most of his adult life. Adequate doses usually cause the voices to remit, as they also did after he had electroconvulsive therapy in the early 1960s.

His second problem is that for years he has been intermittently depressed. His first serious depression occurred when he was about 23. It was precipitated by the death of his girlfriend in an auto accident. He was hospitalized and treated with insulin therapy. The next episode, in 1963, he thinks was due to guilt over the Korea massacre. It was mild at first and improved with medication, but in the early 1960s he had electroconvulsive therapy, which for about 2 years produced a complete remission of the depression. He has lost up to 20 pounds over a 3-month period. Other symptoms have included loss of appetite, hypersomnia, neglect of personal hygiene, marked guilt feelings, and suicidal ideas. He typically feels better in the evening than in the morning. He has continued to have auditory hallucinations even when he is free of depression.

He has made suicide attempts on two occasions. The first time, during his initial episode of illness, was with an overdose of 10,000 mg of Thorazine that put him into a coma for a week. This was also a psychologically serious attempt: He felt that he should be dead and that he had no right to live. His second suicide attempt occurred some years later when he cut his arms with a razor blade after he had checked into a hotel. At that time he had just broken up with his girlfriend and felt that he had "miserably failed again in my life." He was found the next morning by the maid, but did not sustain serious loss of blood. He later regretted that he did not complete suicide at that time.

The patient says that he has taken a variety of medications including Thorazine, Mellaril, Sinequan, and Elavil. Elavil at a maximum daily dose of 300 mg helped him until a few years ago, when it lost its effect and he stopped taking it. He has never taken lithium or monoamine oxidase inhibitors. He currently takes Trilafon 32 mg per day.

Although there has been no recent precipitant, he says that the depression has been considerably worse over the past 3 months. After his most recent hospitalization, he again developed depression and sustained a weight loss of 20 pounds. He purchased a gun with the intent of using it on himself. Instead he went to Reno, began to gamble, and eventually disposed of the gun. On admission he said that he planned to kill himself by jumping in front of cars on the freeway. He has increasingly heard voices telling him that he will be killed; he has once again suffered decreased appetite and loss of sleep. He feels that he cannot care adequately for himself and was unable to leave his apartment for several days prior to this hospitalization. He was admitted on the request of the physician who has been following him in outpatient clinic.

Personal and social history: The patient was born in St. Louis, the third of five siblings. He was the only boy in the family, but had a close relationship with an older sister, who was a tomboy. His father, an alcoholic, was a supervisor of mechanics in a car dealership in St. Louis. After the father began to chase women and drink heavily, the patient's parents were divorced. His mother worked outside the home, first cleaning houses and then as an RN, after going back to school for several years. Because his mother made sure that the children went to school and to church, the patient feels that he received good parenting overall.

He was reared as a conservative Baptist. As a young man he was an Eagle Scout and worked as a camp counselor one summer before he entered the Army. He was considered smart in school and skipped a year, graduating from high school at age 17. His tested IQ was 138. Math was his favorite subject.

He entered the Army immediately and served for 3 years. He had no difficulties in the military, although he never progressed past the rank of corporal because "I didn't want the responsibility of people's lives." He had just reenlisted when he had the breakdown that initiated his long series of hospitalizations.

After his military service, he graduated from college with an AA degree in accounting. Subsequently he worked as an accountant in gambling casinos in Reno, but during the last few years of his working life he gradually descended to washing dishes. Six years ago doctors told him to stop working "because I just kept ending up in the hospital," and recently he has been living on Social

Security Disability and his VA pension. He currently receives about $1,400 a month, which he says is adequate for his needs.

He was married in 1963 and has been separated for about the last 2 years. Although for 15 years he has been essentially impotent, he had no difficulties with sex previously. He and his wife had no children of their own, although he has four stepchildren. Until recently he was living in an apartment hotel, but for several nights prior to his current hospitalization he has been homeless, sleeping at a mission.

His wife left him because of his gambling, which began about 20 years ago and has been especially heavy during the past 6 years. He has lost a total of perhaps $20,000, and he states that he believes she would come back to him if he got his gambling under control. He has made desultory attempts at finding treatment, and has gone to Gamblers Anonymous a few times.

He has also had past legal difficulties because of intentionally overdrawing his checking account. He claims that he did this on several occasions so that he would be punished (for the guilt he felt over Korea). In 1958 he actually spent a year in a Wisconsin reformatory, where he also received psychiatric care for the auditory hallucinations. Subsequently, he served time in an institution for the criminally insane in New York. At least on some of these occasions, he has believed that he actually had enough money in the bank to cover his bad checks. It is unclear whether this belief was of delusional intensity.

The only time he has had significant trouble with alcohol was about 3 months ago when in Reno, when he was arrested for driving while intoxicated. It was the first time he had touched alcohol in 25 years. He was jailed and fined. He denies previous trouble with alcohol, and denies ever using street drugs or abusing prescription medications. He does smoke cigarettes.

He describes himself as a friendly, sociable person who even today tries to make at least one friend each time he is hospitalized. He played chess some in college, but does not now have a wide range of interests. He reads little, watches some TV; he feels he can concentrate on old movies.

Past medical history: He was hit by an exploding grenade when he was in Korea. He also had a hernia operation when he was in the Army in Germany. He denies any other major health problems. He is allergic to morphine.

Family history: Other than alcoholism in his father and a niece, family history is negative for mental illness.

Mental status exam: The patient appeared a little younger than his stated age of 59. He was a casually dressed white man who sat relaxed in his chair during the interview. There were no abnormal mannerisms, and he maintained good eye contact throughout the interview. His affect was about medium, showed normal lability, and was appropriate to the content of his thought. His flow of speech was completely normal. He specifically showed no loosening of associations or abnormalities of rate or rhythm of speech. He admitted to having auditory hallucinations as noted above. He currently has no delusions but has had them recently, believing when he was admitted that his wife had been killed. He has no history of obsessions, phobias, or anxiety attacks.

He was fully oriented for day, date, month, and year, and knew how long he had been in the hospital. He correctly named Bush as the current president, and Reagan and Ford before him. He believed that the vice president was "Dan something" and he named the current governor of California. He quickly and accurately subtracted serial sevens to 37, repeated a name, color, and street address after 5 minutes. He was easily able to abstract a similarity between an apple and an orange, and to state the difference between a child and a dwarf. His insight appeared to be good in that he recognized that he had a mental illness, and his judgment was good in that he agreed to remain in the hospital.

Impression

Axis I: Psychiatrically ill, undiagnosed
  1. Psychosis
     Probable chronic schizophrenia, paranoid type
     Rule out schizoaffective disorder
  2. Depression
     Probably major depression secondary to psychosis
     Consider major depression with psychosis
  3. Pathological gambling
Axis II: No personality diagnosis made
Axis III: No current physical disorder
Axis IV: Moderate (3); Ongoing marital separation
Axis V: Global assessment of functioning
  35 current
  65 past year

FORMULATION

Summary

This 59-year-old, separated white man, 100% service-connected for psychosis, was admitted for his third hospitalization for depression and suicidal ideas. He has a 20-year history of chronic psychosis, which has never completely responded to any treatment, upon which has been superimposed depression that has occasionally warranted electroconvulsive therapy. In recent years he has also had the problem of compulsive gambling. The current hospitalization was prompted by another bout of depression with suicidal ideation when he felt that he could not care for himself.

Differential

Schizophrenia. Supported by 20-year history of chronic delusions and clear auditory hallucinations that do not respond completely to medication; they persist even when he is not depressed.

Major depression. Supported by multiple vegetative symptoms (loss of appetite, weight loss, hypersomnia, guilt feelings, and suicidal ideas). It has previously responded to medication and to electroconvulsive therapy.

Schizoaffective disorder. Supported by presence of both mood disorder and psychotic features (hallucinations). There have been episodes during which there were hallucinations without prominent mood symptoms.

Pathological gambling. Probably meets criteria for this disorder, but the interview did not pursue them in sufficient depth.

Posttraumatic stress disorder. Possible, but insufficient information to rule in or out.

Best Diagnosis

The most likely diagnosis is chronic schizophrenia, paranoid type, with occasional secondary bouts of major depression. There has been a recent history of pathological gambling.

Contributing Factors

There is no family history to suggest a biological basis for any of his possible mental disorders. The severe trauma the patient suffered in Korea may have precipitated his psychosis; other traumas, such as death of girlfriend years ago and separation from his wife, may act as a stimulus for continuing symptoms. Gambling could be in part a defense against feelings of depression.

Further Information Needed

Previous charts from earliest hospitalizations could help to confirm symptoms and course of illness. Interview with patient's wife would give information about more recent symptoms. In a later interview, more details will be obtained about pathological gambling and possible posttraumatic stress disorder.

Treatment Plan

Trilafon 16 mg twice a day
May want to change to a higher potency neuroleptic such as fluphenazine
Trial on lithium to address recurrent depression and as a possible augmentation of neuroleptic treatment of chronic psychosis
Consider trial on fluoxetine for depression
Daily group therapy
Individual psychotherapy twice a week, to form relationship with clinician
Encourage to attend Gamblers Anonymous
Veterans Center referral to address issues of posttraumatic stress

Prognosis

Although schizophrenia seems the most likely diagnosis, if the trial on lithium proves successful, there could be a marked improvement in this man's overall course. If pathological gambling cannot be controlled, condition may worsen considerably.

Appendix E:
Assessing Your Interview

All patients, and therefore all interviews, are different. Instructors also vary in the emphasis they place on the several aspects of the initial interview. However, there are many aspects that most clinicians agree are crucial for the typical interview. These aspects include factual material as well as items that contribute to the process of obtaining information. They are listed in this appendix, where a rough numerical value is assigned to each.

You can score your own interview from a tape recording, or have a colleague do it for you while you are interviewing. The overall score and subsection scores should help you plan where to expend additional effort. The scoring system used has been adapted and extended from articles by Maguire and associates (Appendix F).

For each section below, score 0 if the rated behavior or item of data was not observed or covered at all. Score the maximum number of points if the item was covered completely (as judged from the patient's case notes in chart), or for desired behavior that was consistently present. Give proportional credit for partial answers or behaviors.

The maximum score is 200 points. For a beginner, any score above 140 is acceptable, although advanced interviewers should average above 180.

Mental status data are not included in this self-assessment, which was designed to evaluate only the historical and interactive portions of the initial interview.

1. *Initiating the interview* (10 points)

Interviewer	No	Yes
a. Greets the patient	0	1
b. Shakes hands	0	1
c. Mentions patient's name	0	1
d. Mentions own name	0	1
e. Explains status (training?)	0	1
f. Indicates where to sit	0	1
g. Explains purpose of interview	0	1
h. Mentions time available	0	1
i. Mentions note-taking	0	1
j. Asks whether patient is comfortable	0	1

2. *History of present illness* (58 points)

Interviewer asks about	No								Yes
a. Main complaint(s)	0	1	2	3	4	5	6	7	8
b. Onset of problems	0	1		2		3			4
c. Stressors	0	1		2		3			4
d. Key events in course of illness	0	1		2		3			4
e. Current medication									
1. Name or description	0			1					2
2. Dose	0			1					2
3. Wanted effects obtained	0			1					2
4. Side effects noted	0			1					2
5. Duration of effect	0			1					2
f. History of previous episodes									
1. Type	0	1		2		3			4
2. Similarity to present episode	0	1		2		3			4
3. Previous treatment	0	1		2		3			4
4. Outcome of treatment	0	1		2		3			4
g. Effects of illness on work	0	1		2		3			4
h. Effects of illness on family	0	1		2		3			4
i. Patient's feelings about problems	0	1		2		3			4

3. *Past medical history* (10 points)

Interviewer asks about	No		Yes
a. Relevant data on physical illness	0	1	2
b. Allergies to medications	0	1	2
c. Operations	0	1	2
d. Previous hospitalizations	0	1	2
e. Relevant review of systems	0	1	2

4. *Personal and social history* (20 points)

Interviewer asks about	No		Yes
a. Details of family of origin	0	1	2
b Education	0	1	2
c. Marital history	0	1	2
d. Military history	0	1	2
e. Work history	0	1	2
f. Sexual preference and adjustment	0	1	2
g. Legal problems	0	1	2
h. Current living situation	0	1	2
i. Leisure activities	0	1	2
j. Source of support	0	1	2

5. *Family history of mental disorder* (6 points)

Interviewer asks about	No		Yes
a. Symptoms to make diagnosis	0	1	2
b. Response to treatment	0	1	2
c. All first-degree relatives	0	1	2

6. *Screening questions* (26 points)

Interviewer screens for	No		Yes
a. Depression	0	1	2
b. Panic attacks	0	1	2
c. Phobias	0	1	2
d. Obsessions and compulsions	0	1	2
e. Mania	0	1	2

6. *Screening questions* (cont.)

f. Psychosis	0	1	2
g. Childhood abuse	0	1	2
h. Alcohol/drug abuse	0	2	4
i. Suicidal ideas/attempts	0	2	4
j. History of violence	0	2	4

7. *Establishing rapport* (18 points)

Interviewer	No				Yes
a. Smiles, nods at appropriate times	0	1	2	3	4
b. Uses language patient understands	0	1	2	3	4
c. Responds with feeling, empathy	0	1	2	3	4
d. Maintains eye contact	0		1		2
e. Maintains appropriate distance	0		1		2
f. Appears self-assured and relaxed	0		1		2

8. *Use of interview techniques* (44 points)

Interviewer	Poor				Good
a. Explores verbal leads to new material	0	1	2	3	4
b. Controls flow of interview while allowing patient scope for response	0	1	2	3	4
c. Clarifies uncertainties to obtain complete information	0	1	2	3	4
d. Makes smooth transitions; if abrupt, they are pointed out	0	1	2	3	4
e. Avoids use of jargon	0	1	2	3	4
f. Asks brief, single questions	0	1	2	3	4
g. Does not repeat questions already asked	0	1	2	3	4
h. Uses open, nondirective questions	0	1	2	3	4
i. Facilitates patient's replies verbally and nonverbally	0	1	2	3	4
j. Encourages precise answers (dates, numbers where appropriate)	0	1	2	3	4
k. Seeks out and sensitively handles emotionally loaded material	0	1	2	3	4

9. *Ending the interview* (8 points)

Interviewer	No		Yes
a. Warns that interview is nearly over	0	1	2
b. Gives brief, accurate summary	0	1	2
c. Solicits questions from patient	0	1	2
d. Makes a concluding statement of appreciation, interest	0	1	2

Appendix F: Bibliography and Recommended Readings

BOOKS

American Psychiatric Association. (1987). *Diagnostic and statistical manual of mental disorders* (3rd ed., rev.). Washington, DC: Author. [The renowned and well-regarded DSM-III-R, indispensable for a thorough understanding of current diagnostic thinking.]

Cannell, C. F., & Kahn, R. L. (1968). Interviewing. In G. Lindzey & E. Aronson (Eds.), *The handbook of social psychology* (2nd ed., pp. 526–595). Reading, MA: Addison-Wesley.

Cormier, W. H., & Cormier, L. S. (1985). *Interviewing strategies for helpers* (2nd ed.). Monterey, CA: Brooks/Cole. [Massive, detailed textbook for all mental health professionals, but especially slanted towards psychologists and social workers. Material on different types of therapy, as well as interviewing strategies.]

Gill, M., Newman, R., & Redlich, F. C. (1954). *The initial interview in psychiatric practice.* New York: International Universities Press. [Classic description of interviewing style that focuses on patient's needs and capabilities.]

Leon, R. L. (1989). *Psychiatric interviewing: A primer* (2nd ed.). New York: Elsevier. [This volume covers much of the same material as *The First Interview.* The author explicitly favors a nondirective approach to gathering information.]

MacKinnon, R. A., & Yudofsky, S. C. (1986). *The psychiatric evaluation in clinical practice.* Philadelphia: Lippincott. [Only the first third of this book concerns clinical interviewing. The balance is given over to clinical laboratory testing, personality tests and rating scales. The section on psychodynamic case formulation provides some information not readily available elsewhere.]

Othmer, E., & Othmer, S. C. (1989). *The clinical interview using DSM-III-R.* Washington, DC: American Psychiatric Press. [Encyclopedic in its coverage, this book adheres strictly to the DSM-III-R format.]

Shea, S. C. (1988). *Psychiatric interviewing: The art of understanding.* Philadelphia: W. B. Saunders. [Long-winded and occasionally pretentious, it nevertheless introduces a great deal of relevant material.]

Simms, A. (1988). *Symptoms in the mind.* London: Baillière Tindall. [A British text that contains more in the way of current mental health terminology and definitions than any other I have seen.]

Sullivan, H. S. (1954). *The psychiatric interview.* New York: Norton. [An early, classical description of how to do an initial interview.]

ARTICLES

Note: Articles are listed chronologically within author groups, rather than alphabetically by author, for purposes of the comments.

Sandifer, M. G., Hordern, A., & Green, L. M. (1970). The psychiatric interview: The impact of the first three minutes. *American Journal of Psychiatry, 126,* 968–973. [Half of all observations made by interviewers in this study were made within the first 3 minutes of an experimental interview. These data can sometimes have a decisive impact on diagnosis.]

Rutter, M., & Cox, A. (1981). Psychiatric interviewing techniques: I. Methods and measures. *British Journal of Psychiatry, 138,* 273–282. [The introductory article in this series. The series of seven articles by these authors is a landmark in the study of interview technique. These studies are based on interviews with mothers of child psychiatry patients and compare four interviewing styles that have been recommended by experts. Although the research they report has not been replicated, the findings are so logical, the methodology so impeccable, that they strike the reader as received truth. These articles provide much of the basis for this manual.]

Cox, A., Hopkinson, K., & Rutter, M. (1981). Psychiatric interviewing techniques: II. Naturalistic study: Eliciting factual material. *British Journal of Psychiatry, 138,* 283–291. [This article demonstrates that "a directive style with specific probes and requests for detailed descriptions" produced facts of better quality than did an approach that was more freestyle. Informants talked more when interviewers talked less and used more open-ended questions. Double questions led to confusion, but multiple-choice questions sometimes were helpful.]

Hopkinson, K., Cox, A., & Rutter, M. (1981). Psychiatric interviewing techniques: III. Naturalistic study: Eliciting feelings. *British Journal of Psychiatry, 138,* 406–415. [Several techniques facilitate expression of emotion. These include "a low level of interview talk with few interruptions, a high rate of open rather than closed questions, direct requests for feelings, interpretations and expressions of sympathy."]

Rutter, M., Cox, A., Egert, S., Holbrook, D., & Everitt, B. (1981). Psychiatric interviewing techniques: IV. Experimental study: Four contrasting styles. *British Journal of Psychiatry, 138,* 456–465. [The authors taught two interviewers to use any of four interviewing styles: (1) "sounding board" used minimal activity; (2) "active psychotherapy" tried to explore feelings and elicit emotional linkages and meanings; (3) "structured" used active cross-questioning; (4) "systematic exploratory" combined high use of both fact- and feeling-oriented techniques.]

Cox, A., Rutter, M., & Holbrook, D. (1981). Psychiatric interviewing techniques: V. Experimental study: Eliciting factual material. *British Journal of Psychiatry, 139*, 29–37. [This paper reports data on the study described just above. The authors conclude that "it is desirable to begin clinical diagnostic interviews with a lengthy period with little in the way of detailed probing and in which informants are allowed to express their concerns in their own way." Systematic questioning is essential to elicit good-quality facts. "Better data were obtained when interviewers were sensitive and alert to factual cues and chose their probes with care."]

Cox, A., Holbrook, D., & Rutter, M. (1981). Psychiatric interviewing techniques: VI. Experimental study: Eliciting feelings. *British Journal of Psychiatry, 139*, 144–152. [A variety of interview styles can be used to elicit feelings from patients. Gathering good factual information is entirely compatible with eliciting feelings.]

Cox, A., Rutter, M., & Holbrook, D. (1988). Psychiatric interviewing techniques: A second experimental study: Eliciting feelings. *British Journal of Psychiatry, 152*, 64–72. [Expression of emotions was maximized when interviewers used "active" techniques such as interpretation, reflection of feelings, and expression of sympathy. This was especially true if the informant's "spontaneous rate of expression was relatively low."]

Maguire, G. P., & Rutter, D. R. (1976). History-taking for medical students. 1: Deficiencies in performance. *Lancet, ii*, 556–560. [Senior medical students showed significant deficiencies in taking histories. These include avoidance of personal issues, use of jargon, lack of precision, failure to pick up on cues, needless repetition, poor clarification, failures of control, inadequate facilitation, and inappropriate question style (leading or complicated questions).]

Platt, F. W., & McMath, J. C. (1979). Clinical hypocompetence: The interview. *Annals of Internal Medicine, 91*, 898–902. [House officers in internal medicine also have problems with initial interviews. These include poor rapport, inadequate data base, failure to formulate hypotheses, excessive control of interview (patient complains of not being listened to), and acceptance of patients' reports of lab data or interpretations of what another health care giver has said, rather than the primary data of symptoms. Examples are given.]

Maguire, P., Roe, P., Goldberg, D., Jones, S., Hyde, C., & O'Dowd, T. (1978). The value of feedback in teaching interviewing skills to medical students. *Psychological Medicine, 8*, 695–704. [In a randomized trial, feedback (video, audio, or ratings of practice interviews) led to greater ability to obtain relevant, accurate facts. Only the video and audio groups also showed improved technique.]

Maguire, P., Fairbairn, S., & Fletcher, C. (1986). Consultation skills of young doctors. I: Benefits of feedback training in interviewing as students persist. *British Medical Journal, 292*, 1573–1576. [Young physicians who had either been given feedback training by video or allotted to conventional teaching in interview skills were followed up 5 years later. Both groups had improved since graduation, but "those given feedback training had main-

tained their superiority in the skills associated with accurate diagnosis."
The authors conclude that feedback training should be given to all
students.]

OTHER ARTICLES USED IN THE PREPARATION OF THIS BOOK

Othmer, E., & DeSouza, C. (1985). A screening test for somatization disorder
(hysteria). *American Journal of Psychiatry, 142,* 1146–1149.
Kendler, K. S., Silberg, J. L., Neale, M. C., Kessler, R. C., Heath, A. C., & Eaves,
L. J. (1991). The family history method: Whose psychiatric history is measured? *American Journal of Psychiatry, 148,* 1501–1504.
Pollock, D. C., Shanley, D. F., & Byrne, P. N. (1985). Psychiatric interviewing and
clinical skills. *Canadian Journal of Psychiatry, 30,* 64–68.
Rosenthal, M. J. (1989). Towards selective and improved performance of the men-
tal status examination. *Acta Psychiatrica Scandinavica, 80,* 207–215.

Index